RENEGADES OF THE EMPIRE

RENEGADES
OF THE
EMPIRE

How Three Software Warriors Started
a Revolution Behind the Walls of
Fortress Microsoft

MICHAEL DRUMMOND

CROWN PUBLISHERS
NEW YORK

Published by Crown Publishers, 201 East 50th Street, New York, New York 10022. Member of the Crown Publishing Group.

Random House, Inc. New York, Toronto, London, Sydney, Auckland
www.randomhouse.com

CROWN is a trademark and the Crown colophon is a registered trademark of Random House, Inc.

Printed in the United States of America

Design by Leonard Henderson

Library of Congress Cataloging-in-Publication Data

Drummond, Michael, 1964–
    Renegades of the empire : how three software warriors started a revolution behind the walls of fortress Microsoft / Michael Drummond
        p.   cm.
    1. St. John, Alex, 1967–   . 2. Eisler, Craig, 1965–   . 3. Engstrom, Eric, 1965–   .
    4. Businessmen–United States—Biography.   5. Computer software industry–United States.
    I. Microsoft Corporation.   II. Title.
    HD9696.63.U62D78   1999
    338.7′610053′092273—dc21
        [B]   99-34657
                                                                            CIP

ISBN 0-609-60416-3

10 9 8 7 6 5 4 3 2 1

First Edition

For the ones who make me whole—Alison, Harper Rose, and Eli

CONTENTS

CONTENTS

ACKNOWLEDGMENTS

A fter dinner and drinks one night, former Microsoft evangelist Alistair Banks and I were going to board his boat and speed across Lake Washington in an amphibious assault on the beachfront home of Eric Engstrom, one of the main characters in this book. Banks wanted to confront Engstrom about some of the versions of events chronicled in these pages. Storming a man's property in the middle of the night, by water no less, seemed risky. But Banks is English, and the Brits possess a fine tradition of naval engagement. Unfortunately for history, Banks's boat had engine troubles, and we never launched our attack. Life is like that. Sometimes our experiences are forever shaped, our destinations inexorably altered by something as simple as, say, a faulty spark plug. Likewise, the genesis of this book came about by a seemingly unconnected series of incidents that led me from my native San Diego, to the Pacific Northwest, to Dayton, Ohio, and then back to the Northwest—home of Microsoft, the petri dish that germinated the characters, events, and substance of the following narrative. Without further ado, let me get down to thanking those who either influenced me and/or made this work possible.

Marilyn "Mother Goose" Johnson was my spiritual mentor and I her surrogate son for more than a decade. She taught me that the cosmos is much more than the sum of its parts. She left this world before this book went to print, but her invisible loving hand guided me through the course of the project.

All things have an origin—this book is no exception. If I had to pick a date of conception, I'd pin it on that day in June 1992 when I was fired from a harmless little daily in a San Diego suburb. Let the record show that I was terminated for reporting the truth. And the truth, as they say, shall set you free. I thank the former mayor and my former publisher for inadvertently catapulting me 1,500 miles north, where I eventually fell into the orbit of Dell Burner, my editor at the *Daily News* in Longview, Washington. Among other things, Dell taught me that a great story should have the added benefit of being true.

Later, a chance encounter at a journalism conference in Nashville, Tennessee, put me in contact with John Erickson, a Pulitzer prize–winning editor at the *Dayton Daily News*. He recruited me and he and his family made me and my family feel welcome in a foreign land. Had it not been for Erickson's faith in me, I never would have had the opportunity to meet one Paul Scholz, a warm-hearted and skilled tech-head who asked if I would be interested in writing a book about a then-classified project at Microsoft. It was he who plopped the 400-pound lemon at my doorstep, as it were. All I had to do was juice it. Make no mistake, without Scholz's initial entreaties with the Micro-soft Beastie Boys, this story probably never would have been told—at least in this format and certainly not by me.

And so it is that they make my thank-you list. They sat and some-times suffered through hours of interviews when they could have been doing something else with their time.

My friends Chris and Sally Norred made my many forays to Seattle considerably less expensive and certainly more hospitable by open-ing their home to me. They offered comfort and companionship, insisting on nothing in return. I wish them and their new baby, Louie, happiness.

Likewise, I'm deeply indebted to my mom, Betty Kenworthy, who allowed me and my family to use her beautiful home as a staging area during the writing of this book. She has been supportive in so many ways—far beyond the call of motherhood. Special thanks go to my grandparents, Marjorie and Larry Fitzpatrick, for their many prayers, and Teresa Torres, the household's matron saint.

Along the way I had plenty of behind-the-scenes support, some from people I never met face-to-face. These were the online voices, people represented as lines of text. They include Diana Gruber and Mike Kelleghan. Thanks for making sense of the strange world of computer gaming.

My agent, James Levine, helped salvage my initial proposal and has been a tireless advocate, promptly responding to my need for gratuitous positive feedback no matter where he happened to be in the world. Bruce Buehner, who's known me for decades and yet still regards me as his best friend (and he mine), also receives a nod for moral support.

My first editor at Crown, the charming Ayesha Pande, played an important early supporting role. And clean-up editor Bob Mecoy delivered on his promise to give this book, as he put it, legs.

Last, and by no means least, a loving tribute goes to my wife, Alison Jacques, who supported me through the lean and very mean times during the creation of this book. We walked into the dark valley of credit-card debt, crashed vehicles, family tragedy and other assorted horrors over the past eighteen months, and emerged, largely intact, on the other side. Alison also was my insightful first line editor, making sure my copy was readable before I sent it to editors in New York.

My daughter, Harper Rose, gets her own thank-you for inventing the name of this book's first chapter. Her younger brother, Eli, and uncle Rick also earn a thanks—just because.

PREFACE

LET THERE BE BILL

edmond residents weren't prepared for the invasion of 1986, when Bill Gates and Microsoft stormed Seattle's oldest suburb, plowing aside horse farms, covering clear-cuts, and uprooting strawberry fields that, alas, were not forever. Ranch houses gave way to mega-subdivisions and yuppie warehouses—upscale apartment and condominium complexes with names such as Cambrian and Carrillon Heights and Sonoma Villero.

Within fourteen years, Gates's initial occupying force of one thousand programmers, product managers, and public-relations people swelled to about twenty thousand. A legion of Microsoft millionaires clogged the city's narrow streets and aging freeways with dark European cars and the latest sport utility vehicles. And they gladly paid cash for homes that had more than doubled in price in little more than a decade. Microsoft wasn't the region's only highflier. Other high-tech companies mushroomed in the giant's shadow, propelling the Pacific Northwest economy into the stratosphere. Quite a turnaround from the bleak 1970s, when recession and unemployment had triggered a massive exodus and spawned the famous Seattle billboard, "The Last Person to Leave, Please Turn Out the Lights."

During its growth spurt in the 1990s, Microsoft exploded from a six-building cluster on aptly named One Microsoft Way to a fifty-unit business-park scattered over some three hundred acres of hilly sub-urban woodland. The construction uncovered secret "booze tun-nels," legacies of liquor-smuggling Prohibition days, and at the same time provided the infrastructure for what would become America's wealthiest corporation. Microsoft would be forced to deploy the second-largest fleet of shuttles in the state to transport workers around the far-flung campus, where ribbons of asphalt run past the company's groomed soccer fields.

As the various high-tech companies spawned, the locals joked that the white construction cranes that stabbed the Redmond skyline should have been designated the city's official bird. Some of Microsoft's moves weren't so amusing. So rapid was its expansion that the company often started construction without the requisite build-ing permits.

Conforming to local ordinances sometimes was an afterthought, reflecting the contempt for political authority that would later haunt the company. It also reflected Microsoft's boldness—some would say hubris—which started with Gates and bled through the organism he had conceived with longtime friend Paul Allen. During the company's first two decades, a take-no-prisoners corporate mentality had allowed Microsoft to ignite a computer revolution, displace giant rivals such as IBM, and emerge as the world's mightiest software company.

To build his empire, Gates recruited the most able warriors. He used to say that he would rather hire a physicist over a programmer to write code, because anybody who could master theoretical physics would find coding somewhat trivial. Of course, Microsoft didn't limit its hiring to Ph.D.'s and Harvard grads. The company employed a high-IQ cross-section of society, including bikers, boozers, former politicians, blue-haired punk rockers, and even a few transsexuals. Who cared if she was really a he, as long as he/she could code? Contrary to industry myth, Microsoft didn't necessarily hire clones of Gates (although there were plenty on the corporate campus) so much as recruit those who shared some of Gates's more notable traits—arrogance, aggressiveness, and high intelligence.

One of the keys to Microsoft's success was its ability to retain these techno-soldiers. Certainly lucrative stock options helped keep talent. But the truly brilliant also needed professional motivation, and as any combat veteran knows, nothing motivates quite like fear.

Gates is infamous for ridiculing someone's idea as "stupid," or worse, "random," just to see how he or she defends a position. This hostile managerial technique invariably spread through the chain of command and created a culture of conflict. Much has been written about Microsoft's cutthroat business tactics, such as requiring clients to use Microsoft technology to the exclusion of others, or allegations that it courts partnerships with smaller firms only to jilt them after getting a peek at their software. Yet it is inside the walls of Microsoft where some of the most brutal fighting in the high-tech industry occurs. Microsoft nurtures a Darwinian order where resources are often plundered and hoarded for power, wealth, and prestige. A manager who leaves on vacation might return to find his turf raided by a rival and his project put under a different command or canceled altogether because it was seen as a threat. Some might call this cruel. Nature calls this survival of the fittest.

Against this backdrop of phenomenal business success and internecine warfare, three of Microsoft's most controversial, but heretofore largely unknown, warriors met and conspired to create groundbreaking software. Like the company itself, which constructed buildings without permission, these renegades built their software first and asked questions later. The Beastie Boys, as they were known, ran over and around the backs of supervisors. They upstaged rivals at industry trade shows with technical demonstrations linked to themes of horror, orgies, and alien abduction. Their crowning achievement was DirectX, which allowed Windows to run computer games and revolutionized an industry. But when the expected riches and glory failed to materialize, the three targeted a new type of technology for the Internet—Gates's holy battleground.

RENEGADES OF THE EMPIRE

1

ALEX IN WONDERLAND

His five-year romp through Bill Gates's Camelot was over. Microsoft security would be walking in any moment to clean out his desk and scan his computer's hard drive. No sensitive materials could leave the building. Alex St. John could almost hear the bootsteps. He knew what to do. He grabbed a handful of Hershey's kisses from a friend's office and dumped them on his desk with a note—"Help yourself!"

St. John, one of Microsoft's fabled "evangelists," was fired that day. He and two colleagues had built DirectX, revolutionary computer-game technology that had turned Windows-based PCs into the world's most popular game platform. The three were now building controversial Web technology, a "browser on steroids" code-named Project Chrome.

While he had helped feed hundreds of millions of dollars into Gates's software Empire, the fact remained that St. John was a rogue soldier who didn't understand how to follow orders and had never paid much attention to the chain of command. Management had any number of reasons to terminate him. Once, after Gates had just inked a major deal with three Sega executives, St. John had piled the visitors into his customized, purple Humvee and torn across the company's manicured lawns—in front of several horrified senior Microsoft officers.

Like the man who buys a pit bull for its ferocity only to have the animal attack him later, Microsoft had it coming.

Before the Empire called, St. John was happily self-employed as a computer consultant on the other side of the country. Then his name began pinging on the radar screens of Microsoft talent scouts. St. John had cultivated a reputation in the industry as an innovative and charismatic programmer—an articulate nerd who could charm even better than he could code. True, he had snapped at previous bosses over what he thought were impractical business decisions. But Microsoft wanted an evangelist, a breed that's sometimes hard to handle.

The Empire began calling in fall 1992. St. John was working at home when an independent recruiter phoned to ask him, if he could work for any company, which would it be? St. John was reluctant to answer because he wasn't interested in working for a boss again and doubted any company could pay him as much as he was making on his own. The headhunter stroked St. John's voluminous ego, reminding him of his talents and how those talents could pay handsomely.

St. John was a Macintosh programmer, impressed with Apple Computer Corp.'s elegant operating system, a system he thought superior to the early Windows kluges Microsoft was pushing at the time. He conceded that he would once have considered working for Apple, "but they're dead," he told the recruiter. When pressed, St. John said he might be interested in Adobe Systems Inc. and, maybe, Microsoft Corp. Maybe.

After some cajoling, the recruiter set up an interview for St. John with a local Adobe representative. The session went well, and the Adobe rep said he'd refer St. John to the company's California headquarters. But Adobe never called back and St. John didn't make any follow-up inquiries. Just about the time he had put Adobe out of his mind, Microsoft called. St. John says he kept stalling, but Microsoft kept calling and he finally agreed to meet a company rep in Boston.

"They said they were looking at me for a number of positions," he recalls. "This was very surreal. They never explained what it was exactly they wanted me to do."

St. John had been a fan of Microsoft since Bill Gates outmaneuvered IBM in the operating-system realm and usurped Big Blue's monopoly. Think of a computer as a sports stadium. The operating system is the playing field or platform on which all the programs run. All computers need an OS or platform to run word processors, spreadsheets, databases, whatever. Without operating systems, computers are empty stadiums without playing fields. IBM had underestimated Gates and allowed him the rights to license DOS, the Disk Operating System that would become a standard on the first generation of personal computers before Windows.

St. John grew more nervous the closer he drew to the interview, scheduled to take place at a downtown Boston hotel.

"I didn't realize what my résumé must have looked like to them. I was very naive," St. John says. "I never thought in my wildest dreams I could be working for a company like that."

He met with Lee Cole, a Microsoft recruiter. The interview lasted all of ten minutes. Cole didn't seem interested in his work history and was unfazed when he told her he had no formal education. Yet she was aggressive, in-your-face, and wanted to know why St. John wanted to work for Microsoft.

"I don't want to work for Microsoft," he recalls saying.

Then she asked the crucial question: "What do you like about Microsoft?"

"Bill kicks ass," St. John said. "I like kicking ass. I enjoy the feeling of killing competitors and dominating markets."

Good answer. Cole suggested that St. John fly out to Microsoft headquarters in Redmond, Washington, for a Friday interview and a weekend stay, all expenses paid. Just a visit, really. No pressure. He walked out of the interview more curious than ever.

After discussing it with his wife, Kelley, St. John flew to the Northwest in mid-December 1992 to see what the storied campus was all about. By the early nineties, Gates was already legendary. He was the visionary Harvard dropout who had spawned the personal computer revolution and whose company was destined to become one of the most revered and feared in history.

The morning after St. John arrived, a grueling, eleven-hour round of interviews began. This was not the "no pressure" weekend stay he had been promised. Interviewer after interviewer grilled him—one even leveled questions while cleaning his fingernails with a menacing bowie knife. An interviewer wondered how St. John would design a better remote control. Another asked, if St. John had ten red balls and ten white balls, how would he distribute them between two boxes, so that a blind man reaching into one of the boxes had the best chance of grabbing a red ball? And, yes, one even wanted to know why manhole covers are round, a question that has become part of the Microsoft cliché.

Manhole covers are round so they won't fall through. The question is designed to test for thought process, not necessarily for a correct answer—although in this instance, a correct answer is almost a must. Microsoft is also big on asking applicants how they would improve the design of gadgets be they bicycles or remote controls. Microsoft wants applicants to demonstrate their problem-solving skills on the fly, not how well they have memorized pat answers. In that same vein, the company also scours résumés for any hint of padding.

"If you put the word *expert* on your résumé, that was like painting a target on your back," says one former Microsoft executive. "You say expert, you better be one."

And an interview at Microsoft is not a brief sit-down with a supervisor and maybe the human resources director. Applicants for key positions face a platoon of interviewers, which include managers and would-be peers. Like cops peering through one-way glass, interviewers talk about the candidate behind a wall of E-mail.

While St. John gave answers, previous interrogators would E-mail the guy now doing the questioning.

"Ask him what interrupt would he hook from DOS if he wanted to get a real-time clock."

"See if he knows the difference between an Adobe type-1 font and a TrueType font," another asked.

St. John was put through the IQ meat grinder.

Later, he would turn the tables on his masters at Microsoft. He would become a management nightmare, tolerated only because of his Svengali-like ability to sway software developers to the Microsoft cause and his capacity to generate piles of money. But he also excelled at blowing mountains of company cash on wild marketing stunts. In the end, St. John's reckless behavior and disregard for authority exhausted the company's capacity for tolerance. By the time his reign of creativity and terror at Microsoft ended, when his six-foot frame had ballooned to well over three hundred pounds and he had grown a Unabomber beard, some at Microsoft were convinced he was raised by wolves.

Not quite.

He was raised in the Alaskan wilderness, in tiny villages where his parents had gone to teach under a grant from the Ford Foundation. Bush teachers, he calls them. As St. John tells it, their assignment to the Last Frontier was part exile for protesting the Vietnam War while teaching at Berkeley and part atonement for ancestral white sins. St. John was told that in the eighteenth century Russian fur traders used to maroon Aleut natives on barren islands to hunt seals. After a while the traders would return with enough food and supplies to hold the Aleuts over until the next season. A kinder cultural plundering occurred when the United States purchased Alaska from Russia in the nineteenth century. Missionaries reached the frontier to show the natives about the loving ways of Christ. Later, educators arrived to teach indigenous people about vowels, consonants, and things like the Pythagorean theorem.

St. John's parents were among those educators. Born February 3, 1967, in Berkeley, California, he was the eldest of four children. Despite the Alaskan isolation, his was not a tight family.

"In many ways I was an only child," he says.

His father has doctorate degrees in physics and linguistics, speaks seven languages, and at one time enjoyed experimenting with explosives. He once built an acetylene cannon to fire rubber chickens across the yard.

"He was sort of a mad scientist," St. John says.

His mother was an elementary and high school teacher. Some of St. John's earliest memories are of flying to remote villages, where his parents would teach Athabascan Indians to read and write, or sailing to islands to teach Aleuts how to solve math problems. St. John was home schooled. He never knew what it was like to run with a pack. His sense of isolation was amplified by living in a land that surrenders to six months of winter darkness.

During summer months beginning when he was eleven, his parents would leave him at the University of Alaska in Fairbanks.

"My family's idea of day care was leaving me at the library at the university all day, while dad worked on one of his Ph.D. theses," he says.

It was here St. John discovered the school's Honeywell computer system, and he started playing computer games. Hangman. Some chess. Mostly Star Trek. A couple of benevolent nerds would sometimes take time to explain the complexities of computers to him. St. John's digital seduction had begun. Little did he realize that computer games would one day launch him into the front ranks of the world's largest software maker, where he would make a fortune, gain prestige, win adulation, and lose a family.

When he was thirteen, his parents bought him a Commodore VIC-20 personal computer. If thirteen-year-old boys are capable of epiphanies, this was his. While some of his peers were playing war or snickering at the forbidden pages of *Playboy*, St. John was teaching himself the early programming language BASIC (Beginner's All-purpose Symbolic Instruction Code) and writing his first program. Fearful that he might not be smart enough to survive in the real world, he typed in four thousand vocabulary words and created a computerized flash-card system.

"I was a geek from then on," he says. "I wanted to be the geek lord."

He continued his home schooling. In his spare time he studied math and physics books. Yet by the time he was seventeen he had grown distant from his parents. His mom was busy with his two-year-old brother. His dad was often busy studying or drinking. St. John applied for the University of Alaska's School of Electrical Engineering, but he had no transcripts and no general equivalency degree. The school rejected his application.

"I was always very insecure that I couldn't measure up, that I had missed so much by not attending high school," he recalls. "The university's reaction was that I must be terribly uneducated. This was what was first reflected at me and I was incredibly paranoid."

He had to wade through an alphabet soup of entrance exams—SAT, ACT, GED—before the university would even consider his application. His insecurity and obsessive desire to measure up to others his age drove him to study as many as twenty hours a day. Even as a teen, he developed the work ethos that would one day make him attractive to Microsoft recruiters.

"I was so obsessed with doing well on those tests that I nearly killed myself to ensure I would do well on them," he says.

Indeed, St. John earned a perfect 1600 on his SAT and did nearly as well on his ACT. The university admitted him, but required him to take prerequisites before allowing him into the School of Electrical Engineering. He signed up for the advanced classes anyway, again demonstrating the sort of moxie that would be a blessing and a curse at Microsoft. He did well and showed the results to a guidance counselor, who promptly waived the prerequisites.

Still, St. John remained insecure, perhaps a legacy of his time isolated from peers during his formative years. The question burned: "Am I smart enough?" It was this person, an unaware genius, who walked into a soup kitchen in Fairbanks one day and met the woman he would love, marry, and abandon. He claims he walked in to volunteer. Kelley Farrell, the woman who became Kelley St. John, has a different take.

"I think he was there to get something to eat," she says from her home in Bangor, Maine.

Kelley was doing Methodist missionary work as a volunteer at the soup kitchen. She is a foot shorter than he and is six years his senior. Her life was devoted to humanity, not machines. She didn't know anything about computers. Theirs was a case of opposites attracting. They married within a year of meeting.

"Terribly eccentric and dangerous" were her first impressions of him.

Kelley says she fell for Alex because of his disregard for social mores. When they arrived at the chapel to get married, the church was locked. St. John and his best man broke in by taking the door off its hinges before the minister showed up. Later, when introduced to Kelley's grandmother, the elderly woman told St. John he was fat.

"He said, 'Well, you have a big nose,' " Kelley recalls. "He was unconcerned about what people thought of him. I was totally concerned about what people thought of me. He always looked mischievous, like he was always up to something. And usually he was. It took me a while to realize this."

St. John excelled in his studies, breezing through classes while his peers struggled. In two years he had completed two-thirds of his undergraduate work. He would have graduated, but Kelley's mission at the soup kitchen was over and she wanted to return to her native Maine. St. John quit the University of Alaska and looked forward to applying to the Massachusetts Institute of Technology.

Yet when they arrived on the East Coast, St. John discovered they didn't have the money nor did he fit the student-loan profile to gain entrance into MIT.

"That was incredibly frustrating for me," St. John says.

His dream of attending MIT dashed, he enrolled at the University of Maine outside of Bangor. The disappointment only mounted. The University of Alaska was renowned for its math and science departments. Students there tended to be older, more serious—a phenomenon St. John ascribes to the remoteness of the campus. He found University of Maine lectures to be remedial and his peers to be immature drunkards. During this time, St. John demonstrated the type of unpredictable behavior that would be his hallmark at Microsoft. He and Kelley were in Portland, Maine, where he was catching a bus to see his parents in Boston. Kelley drove back to her apartment in

Bangor and found, to her shock, St. John waiting at the door. He never got on the bus.

"This was a man who didn't have two pennies to rub together and he took a cab all the way back to Bangor, which is like two hours," Kelley recalls.

The bus was too crowded with smokers, St. John says.

Shortly afterward, Kelley crashed their only car. Unable to afford another, St. John quit the University of Maine to search for work in the Boston area. He quickly got a job at Hell Graphics Systems, a German company, and the St. Johns moved to Woburn, Massachusetts.

By now he had learned fourteen computer languages, and Hell put him to work helping the company's resident PostScript expert. PostScript is Adobe's technology that allows a printer to spit out text and graphics exactly as they appear on a computer screen. His assigned mentor asked him to study PostScript, expecting it would take the young upstart a few months—after all, it had taken him two years. St. John returned the next day professing to know the technology. His supervisor, shrugging him off as an arrogant kid, told him he was stumped by a PostScript problem. St. John looked over his mentor's shoulder and suggested what he thought was an obvious fix. It worked. Soon, St. John was solving his mentor's problems regularly.

"It was all very surreal," he recalls. "After two years he was still struggling. He had all this power and authority based on this ignorance of PostScript he had amassed. I discovered I knew PostScript better than this guy. And he was supposed to know it better than anyone in the company."

St. John realized that his fears of inadequacy were mere phantoms. He calls it the epiphany from Hell.

He went on to design PostScript products that simplified printing tasks. St. John's acumen, intelligence, and innovation did not go unnoticed. Nor did his personality quirks. He sometimes goose-stepped around the office to mock his German coworkers.

In the late 1980s, Linotype bought Hell and the company wanted to relocate product development and St. John to Kiel, Germany. But by now he was having run-ins with his German masters over business and technology decisions. He declined the promotion with an unambiguous "Fuck no!"

He quit. Any hopes Kelley had of spending more time with her husband ended when he was offered and took a job at Harlequin Ltd., based in Cambridge, England. He relocated to Harlequin headquarters, leaving his wife in Maine. She would come for "conjugal visits," as he puts it. But the distance between them, before measured in time, was now also measured by some four thousand nautical miles.

She continued work as a camp counselor while he ascended in the computer industry. He went supernova at Harlequin. The company was run, in his words, by research "jerk-offs" primarily interested in developing artificial intelligence programs. But as it turned out, one of the company's engineers had written his graduate thesis about a PostScript interpreter, and Harlequin hired St. John to help develop this scholarly work into a marketable PostScript product. St. John says he discovered that the British are "brilliant and have no idea how to make products for consumers." Nonetheless, at the age of twenty-one, he and a chap by the name of Jeremy Kenyon built the Harlequin PostScript Interpreter or RIP. The technology turned the publishing industry on its ear because it was two to three times faster than anything Adobe had for low-end PCs. St. John also helped Harlequin develop what's called throughput technology that freed up networked Macintosh computers during printing. Before, the Mac would freeze until a printing job was finished, creating delays of minutes or hours, depending on the size of the document and how many other Macs had work queued to the printer. St. John's product was a hot seller and gave competitor Adobe Systems fits. St. John's name started showing up in trade journals and on the target lists of computer-industry headhunters.

During her second conjugal visit, Kelley realized she was pregnant. She made a couple of round-trip forays, including one late in her pregnancy. But she returned to Maine to have the baby.

"I had to fly back," she says. "I didn't want to have the baby in England. I wanted to be with my family. I knew if I had the baby in England, I would have it alone. Alex was working long hours."

Rhomni St. John was born May 4, 1992, the first of two girls the couple would have. Shortly after his daughter was born, Harlequin opened a field office in Salem, New Hampshire. St. John returned to the States and to his family.

Soon after, Harlequin decided it wanted to start making hardware accelerators because Adobe had announced plans to make them. An accelerator, as its name implies, speeds computer performance. St. John fought with his Anglo bosses over that strategy, arguing it was best to focus on its moneymaker—PostScript interpreters, the software that takes what's on-screen and tells a printer to put it on paper. It had been St. John's idea to base the American office in Salem, where taxes were cheaper and traffic less a nightmare than in Boston. But shortly after the move, company executives in England thought it would be thrilling to have their field office located in Cambridge, a twin to the Harlequin headquarters in Cambridge, England. This was the beginning of the "ego wars" as Kelley calls them.

"I was not going to move to Boston, where my taxes would be eleven percent higher without additional compensation, for such a delusional idea," St. John says.

After two years at Harlequin, he quit. He was just twenty-five. Kelley wanted to find work as a camp director, but was having problems landing a job. Camps were skittish about hiring a young mother, whose first priorities would be to her baby, not camp business. Meanwhile, St. John worked as a freelance computer consultant and was on pace to make a quarter of a million dollars a year.

St. John enjoyed the freedom of being his own boss. He was interviewed by and wrote pieces for computer trade publications such as *Seybold* and *Color Publishing* magazines.

"The press adulation was fun," he says.

But as intoxicating as seeing his name in print was, nothing would compare to the rush of being courted by the mightiest software company on the planet.

During that first day in Redmond, St. John recalls a mix of exhilaration and intimidation. Microsoft's inquisitors challenged him more than anyone else ever had. "What interrupt would you hook to get an 18.2 millisecond clock tick on the PC?" "How could you chain the hook so as not to disrupt the whole system?" He was unsure how he was doing and thought he stumbled when asked if he was a "people person."

"No, I think most people are idiots," St. John replied.

He didn't really know for what position he was interviewing. Some told him for the Visual Basic team, but most said he might make a good evangelist. Now there was a curious term.

Evangelist teams were created under the rubric of Developer Relations Group, the brainchild of Steve Ballmer, Gates's Harvard buddy who had become second-in-command at Microsoft. Ballmer's idea, borrowed from Apple, was to marshal a force of brilliant engineers with aggressive personalities. Nerds with charisma. Microsoft would deploy these strike teams into the field, ostensibly to encourage software developers to use Microsoft products. Neither customer support nor marketers, per se, they were evangelists and showmen with technical expertise and a hypnotist's gift for persuasion. Their job was to meet face-to-face with developers and information-technology buyers at corporations in an effort to control "mindshare," to get customers to develop software for Windows or, at the very least, get them to frame their thinking in terms of Microsoft.

Michael Winser—a tall, skinny, blond-haired Microsoft evangelist who loved Ultimate Frisbee games and wore Day-Glo suits—was a good example of the breed. St. John recounts how Winser could convince software developers that he knew what he was talking about, even on those rare occasions when he didn't have a clue. If faced with a question he couldn't bluff his way through or otherwise dismiss, he'd whip out a notebook and scribble lines of gibberish to make it look as if he were taking meaningful notes. The subtext of this gesture was "I'll get back to you." In reality it was a diversion.

At one time, Microsoft evangelists were also usually chartered with disrupting competitors by showing up at their conferences, securing positions on and then tangling standards committees, and trying to influence the media.

In short, evangelists did whatever it took to win—to advance Microsoft's interests.

St. John was told the job entailed travel "and you tell people how cool Microsoft technology is." But it wasn't until he had lunch that first day with former master Microsoft evangelist Ken Fowles that the meaning of the job description became more clear.

"We're the group at Microsoft whose job is to fuck Microsoft's competitors," St. John recalls Fowles saying. "He was very frank."

Fowles spoke to St. John in war metaphor, a language both men understood well. One mission of Developer Relations Group evangelists was to bolster smaller allies. By supporting smaller competitors, Microsoft could help fragment market share and weaken the position of principal rivals, such as Apple, Borland International, and Oracle Corp. Fowles told St. John how Developer Relations Group evangelists did more than encourage other companies to use Microsoft technology. Evangelists were also in the business of mind control.

"You'd insert your hand into their brains and adjust them," St. John says. "You'd put the world in terms of Microsoft for them. To make that a thought for them on a daily basis. If they loved you or hated you, that didn't matter, so long as they were thinking about you."

St. John saw Fowles as a kindred soul. Fowles feels the same way.

"I knew I wanted to hire him within the first minutes of talking to him," Fowles recalls. "I've come across interesting and obnoxious people at Microsoft, but nobody like Alex."

Fowles is a study in contrasts—a cerebral wild man. He's an accomplished violinist who played in the Seattle Symphony at the age of twelve and earned a music scholarship to the University of Washington when he was sixteen. Fowles sees over the horizon when it comes to computing. He was the one arguing that Windows should have had the capability to understand different languages such as Spanish and German, rather than shipping thirty different versions of the operating system in thirty different languages. Only later did Microsoft seize on that idea. He also rides a Harley-Davidson and would roar it through Microsoft's underground parking lots to see how many car alarms he could trigger. He wears his hair in a long black ponytail and has been known to guzzle vodka from a bottle when camped on road trips to Sturgis, South Dakota, site of the annual Harley riders gathering.

Fowles told St. John that Microsoft didn't hire evangelists, it made them. Like members of the Special Forces, evangelists were elite.

So began St. John's indoctrination. Yet he was comfortable, if not professionally challenged, in Maine. He was able to spend time with his wife and baby daughter. Life wasn't all that bad. But Microsoft wanted him. On Saturday, Doug Henrich, second-in-command of Developer Relations Group, invited St. John to breakfast. Henrich told St. John that everyone with whom he'd interviewed the day before had recommended hiring him. He offered St. John a salary of $58,000 and 2,880 stock options. St. John didn't fully appreciate the offer—while the salary was relatively paltry, the stock options would be worth millions in a few years.

The breakfast was cordial, but noncommittal. St. John felt flattered, but didn't tip his hand. He was impressed with the caliber of smarts at Microsoft and the campus itself, which he thought of as the prestigious center of the computer industry. On the East Coast, everything felt old. Even many of his computer colleagues there had gray hair. In Redmond, the glass-and-brick buildings looked new, set against stands of Douglas fir, hemlock, and spruce. Everyone seemed to be his age. People walked the halls in bare feet! The amenities of the sylvan campus weren't bad either—free drinks, quality food, most every office had a view. After breakfast, St. John told Henrich he'd think about the offer and returned to his hotel room. Meanwhile, Henrich called Fowles and told him to turn up the heat—Microsoft wanted St. John.

Ten minutes later Fowles called St. John and invited him to Microsoft's Christmas party. Gates had rented out the Seattle Center and was flying in thousands of employees from all over the globe. The party was for employees only, but Fowles told St. John he'd arrange something. St. John accepted the invitation, and that night Fowles arrived in his black Jaguar with his wife and son.

Slipping St. John in legitimately was a problem, even for a man in Fowles's position. St. John was not an employee. So Fowles forged a badge for St. John to wear during the party. Fowles had photocopied his own and used colored felt pens to fill in detail. In line at the Seattle Center, Fowles flashed the guard his badge and those for his family, turned as if he were retrieving a badge from St. John, only to flash his own badge again. The sleight of hand worked. The guard unwittingly scanned the same badge twice and St. John was smuggled in.

Once inside, Fowles set St. John free to take it all in. This party far eclipsed the rubber-chicken and ice-sculpture affairs of most office bashes. Microsoft employees checked their coats and children at the door. Each parent got a beeper and each kid got a corresponding wrist tag. The kids were escorted off to a separate party so the adults could enjoy the main event. Civilized bacchanalia filled the entire Seattle Center, a giant hall usually dedicated to boat shows and conventions. A two-story castle of helium balloons floated a few feet off the ground. Halls were partitioned into various theme rooms. There was the Roaring '20s speakeasy room. Another room had a Halloween theme, with ghouls walking around to the song "The Monster Mash." There were jazz halls, western halls, and carnival halls. A merry-go-round twirled. Sword swallowers slipped blades down their throats. Clowns walked around yukking it up among men in tuxedos and women in evening gowns. This being a Microsoft party, many showed up in jeans and T-shirts. Food flowed from tables. Wine, beer, and cocktails poured freely. Alex had entered Wonderland.

Fowles had said earlier that St. John would have to change his life's purpose to see what Microsoft evangelism was all about. He would have to be willing to completely retool any plans he had made about his future. It was an intriguing challenge. But the Christmas soiree was what seduced St. John. He knew he wanted to be part of a company that could party like this. He returned home to tell Kelley all that he had seen. She agreed to move, provided they return to Maine in two years.

"I had to see what was on the other side," St. John says. "I was evangelized."

2

THE UNHOLY TROIKA

Some of the most innovative technologies ever to emerge from Microsoft were born inside a weight room amid the grunts of men and clank of iron.

Inside the Pro Club near the company's Redmond campus, three of Gates's evangelists would gather to build bulk, argue technology, and battle for physical and intellectual supremacy. The newly recruited Alex St. John, just twenty-five years old, would team with a young Canadian code monkey named Craig Eisler and a resourceful backwoods genius named Eric Engstrom—forming an alliance that would change the entire computer-gaming industry. Each came from a different corner of the Northern Hemisphere, brought together by chance or fate or whatever serendipitous force it is that sometimes pulls those of notoriety into mutual orbit. The trio would soon create technology that made it possible for computer games to run on Windows 95, a seminal technological feat that had the added benefit of frustrating rival Apple Computer Corp.

They built their technology without initial approval from their superiors and rammed it through with ruthless determination and indifference to internal political decorum. They captured new market terrain and generated untold millions of dollars for Gates's company. But their victory earned them a long line of enemies inside

Microsoft. The three had expected fame and recognition in the form of generous stock-option bonuses and meteoric career advancement. When much of that failed to immediately materialize, the trio conspired to seize new ground again—this time on the Internet, Bill Gates's most important battlefield.

The three called their new mission Project Chrome, an attempt to bring motion-picture-quality 3-D graphics and high-fidelity sound to the World Wide Web. Think of the movie *Toy Story* meeting the Web and you had an idea of Chrome's potential. And as far as their careers at Microsoft were concerned, they hoped it would succeed where their gaming technology had come up short.

Chrome would do for the Web what color did for television— improve the user experience, generate mass interest, and give reasons for consumers to spend more money on faster computers. Chrome would make it easy for almost anyone to build 3-D Web pages, heretofore a technically demanding task that relatively few people knew how to do. Creating 3-D graphics like the ones used in computer games requires a Poindexter's math skills. Complex calculations must be solved to achieve the illusion of light shading and depth. Most Web pages used two-dimensional graphics that were simple drawings or photographs of real-world objects. But a 3-D object, when put inside a Web page, could be moved, scaled, and animated in dynamic ways not possible with 2-D images. Instead of just showing a car, say, a 3-D Web page could allow users to climb inside the car and check out the roomy interior.

Moreover, Chrome would send this richer content to people's personal computers in a fraction of the time of it took conventional static Web pages to load. And it would do so using existing dial-up phone connections with standard-speed modems, the devices that connect PCs to the Internet. The world would not have to wait for the television and giant telecommunications companies to roll out expensive broadband cable modem service or high-speed digital subscriber lines to households. Best of all from Microsoft's perspective, Chrome, as initially conceived, would not be free. Unlike the company's Internet Explorer browser—the software that allows computer users to view pages on the Web—this new "browser on steroids" would come as an option to Windows 98 and Windows NT 5.0.

Finally, Gates would have a Web browser he didn't have to give away. That is, if the U.S. government's antitrust hounds or even enemies inside Microsoft itself didn't torpedo Chrome first.

Less than a year after he started with Microsoft, St. John had ballooned to more than 340 pounds. His wife, Kelley, was pregnant with their second daughter. By mid-1993 he was working fourteen-hour days at his office or on the road, evangelizing Microsoft's printing technology—technology he knew to be inferior to Apple's. Familial neglect and playing pitchman for what he called a "pitiful" line of printing technology compelled St. John to swallow a lot of stress, an easy thing to do at Microsoft, where free sodas and vending machines are around almost every corner and the cafeterias cater a gamut of fast-food and semifine cuisine.

St. John had been a dedicated weight lifter when he lived on the East Coast, and rather than spend less time at the office and more time with his family, the avowed workaholic decided he needed to get back to the gym. He had lost a spotter when he and his family moved from Maine, and he tried desperately to find a lifting partner at Microsoft.

"But I was in the land of scrawny nerds," he says.

His luck changed when he met Craig Eisler, a short, stocky Canadian who had done some competitive power-lifting while a high school student in Thunder Bay, Ontario. In June 1993, Eisler was hired as an evangelist, an unlikely fit for a twenty-eight-year-old man who many felt was more at home behind a computer keyboard than in front of people. But Eisler, a stellar student, had been a coding demon since he sold his first computer game built on a borrowed Commodore PET at age sixteen. Pudgy as a youth and forced to proselytize door-to-door with his mother, a devout Jehovah's Witness, Eisler hadn't had an easy time growing up.

"I was the kid that everyone liked to beat up," he says.

That was one reason he took up power-lifting while a student at Fort William Collegiate Institute. He also mastered the power of computing. He earned his credentials as a maverick genius while at the University of Waterloo, near Toronto, a school renowned for its mathematics and computer science departments. Once, while working for the Bank of Montreal under the university's co-op program, he hacked his way into the bank's master list of customer passwords. Billions of dollars were suddenly at his young fingertips. Of course, he didn't disappear with the money. Nonetheless, the experience was an epiphany of sorts as he came to realize technology's awesome potential. He later learned the corollary lesson about technology's inherent fragility when he inadvertently triggered a nationwide computer crash. When he and others at the bank failed to run a routine security program after he'd made changes, the result was like pushing over a row of digital dominoes. One by one computer terminals went black.

"No teller anywhere had a computer working for an hour," he recalls. "All of Canada was out for a little while. At the time it was like the coolest thing I'd ever done."

But one of Eisler's greatest achievements—and the one that captured the interest of Microsoft—was developing the first 32-bit extender for Windows 3.0 while a programmer at Watcom International Corp., later to become Sybase Inc., his first job out of college.

Windows 3.0, a vast improvement on the original version of Windows released in 1985, was a 16-bit operating system. The term *16-bit* refers to how much code the software and hardware can process at any one time. The largest contiguous chunk of memory the older operating systems would allow an application to use was 64 kilobytes, expressed as 64K. To write an application that used more than 64K, developers had to manually accommodate for this limitation via 32-bit extenders. Many companies had written 32-bit extenders for DOS, the Windows predecessor. But Windows was much more difficult to extend. Still, Eisler did what some at Microsoft had told him was impossible—he was the first to write software that extended Windows 3.0 to accommodate 32-bit programs.

"Microsoft didn't want someone upstaging them," recalls Fred Crigger, one of the original founders of the old Watcom. "They don't like people doing that."

But Eisler, an incredibly fast code writer, had a way of doing things that couldn't—or shouldn't—be done.

"His output was prodigious," recalls Greg Bentz, who joined Watcom after Eisler. "Sometimes it wasn't the most elegant code, but the volume was amazing. The technical competence was amazing—and the ego grew with that."

Indeed, Eisler believes that intelligence in the universe is exceedingly rare and that he is smarter than those around him. He's not afraid of saying so and doesn't suffer fools lightly. Crigger recalls that Watcom management cringed when Eisler handled calls from customers.

"He was like two people," says Crigger. "Nice and helpful with customers, but he'd curse their stupidity after they hung up."

Eisler's gruff attitude earned him rebukes from managers, who suggested he learn to work better with others, all the while boosting his pay. In response to one admonishment, Eisler customized his PC desktop with the large-typeface words "Happy Thoughts!" dripping blood.

Some at Watcom were astonished when Eisler said he was leaving to become an evangelist at Microsoft, a job that entailed smiling a lot and pressing the flesh. They shouldn't have been surprised. Microsoft was where the money was.

"Part of his motivation to leave for Microsoft was for financial gain," says Bentz. "He had materialistic goals. Still, it was like, 'You're going to be an evangelist? The way you are with people?' "

Moreover, by hiring Eisler, Microsoft prevented him from innovating for someone else, a hiring rationale that has become one of the keys to the company's success.

St. John knew the minute he saw Eisler that he had done some weight lifting. In fact, although Eisler stood but five foot six inches, he was pound for pound much stronger than St. John. Although Eisler "had the personality of a surly troll," St. John says he cajoled him into coming to the Pro Club with him. The first few sessions went predictably badly. Each had his own ways and theories on the proper mechanics of lifting heavy objects.

"The first few times we didn't get along," St. John says. "He was completely anal from my point of view and we argued constantly. But he was in just as much need of a lifting partner as I was, and over time it developed into a friendship."

As close as Eisler and St. John were becoming, there was still something—or rather someone—missing. That someone was Eric Engstrom.

Engstrom, a self-taught programmer and corn-fed boy from the wilds of Oroville in eastern Washington, had also been a Microsoft evangelist. Engstrom's evangelical wanderings had thrown him into contact with Eisler at Watcom. The two shared a mutual loathing of people in general—Engstrom was once heard telling one unfortunate soul, "Understand, I have as much in common with you as you have with the cows you eat." And yet you couldn't paint Engstrom simply as an arrogant misanthrope. He savored conversation with the right company. And his Viking laugh and use of the phrase "That's a real hoot" bespoke an undeniable homespun charm.

As a boy growing up in tiny Oroville, Engstrom was constantly tinkering with electronic gadgets. The kitchen table was so cluttered with radio gear and other electro-flotsam that his parents would serve guests meals on TV trays.

Like many four-year-old boys in 1969, Engstrom was captivated by Neil Armstrong's Apollo 11 lunar landing and the classic "one small step for man" moon walk. Swain Porter, a childhood friend who would later work with Engstrom at Microsoft, recalls their sandbox days:

"The other kids would be playing and he would be by himself counting backwards from a hundred, get to zero, and yell, 'Blastoff!' He already was thinking of going to the moon."

That captivation became an obsession. Engstrom was determined to travel into space. When he was eleven, he and a friend built a Netronics Elf computer from a kit—by all accounts the first home computer in Oroville—which Engstrom planned to mount inside his homemade robot. The robot, of course, would help guide Engstrom's spaceship.

"At about twelve years of age it became clear to me I had to really start working on this project if it were really to succeed," Engstrom says. "I was a very serious young man. I still intend to finish that one of these days."

Even when Engstrom ascended to the upper ranks at Microsoft, the steel carcass of his robot still rested in a scattered heap in the foyer of his million-dollar waterfront home in Kirkland, Washington.

Engstrom had written his own business software as a teen and even started his own company, Concentric Software Design, which built accounting packages for apple growers in eastern Washington. He folded the company and tried attending Washington State University, which proved to be a mind-numbing experience. He quit school and sought fortune as a contract software programmer, embellishing his résumé and successfully bluffing his way through job interviews. But when one company he worked for went belly-up, he grew dejected and returned to live with his parents.

Joy and George Engstrom conceived Eric when they were middle-aged—she was in her forties, he in his fifties. The upside was that as a youth, Eric spent a lot of time bonding with his father, who by then had largely retired from running the GRJ Western and Variety Store in downtown Oroville. The downside was that by the time Engstrom turned thirty-one, old age had claimed his mother's life and had stolen his father's short-term memory.

Engstrom was twenty-three and operating the Little Oasis car wash when an old friend from Oroville, Stan Gazaway, called from Seattle. Gazaway had been doing some consulting work for Microsoft, knew that Engstrom was spinning his wheels in Oroville, and implored him to come to the Emerald City.

"I spent hours on the phone, convincing him he could get this job at Microsoft," Gazaway recalls. "I told him, 'You're smarter than ninety percent of the people I've met here.' "

The position was a contract job for the company's product-support services, answering questions via phone and mail about programs written in C and Fortran, a computer language about which Engstrom knew little.

Engstrom showed up for his first interview at the Empire in full Oroville regalia.

"I bought the best plaid shirt I could find and brand-new jeans," he says. "Washed them up just spiffy. I looked like a complete and utter idiot, in retrospect. But an idiot in clean and newly purchased clothing."

Because the job was for a contract position, the interview was relatively easy—not one of the intellectual brain grinders that have become part of Microsoft lore. Engstrom got the job and started the next day. Fortunately, most Fortran programmers needing assistance were used to dealing with punch cards, the antiquated way of feeding information into a computer. Those programmers' proclivity was to submit questions via mail, giving Engstrom a little extra time to formulate answers.

Within his first week on the job, Engstrom eyed Ann McCurdy, an intern at Microsoft, and asked her out. She demurred. But two days before his monthlong contract at the company was to end, she relented and agreed to go out with him. They would romance for more than three years and set a wedding date.

At the end of his contract, Engstrom found himself courted by two companies—Microsoft and nearby Data I-O. Microsoft offered Engstrom $2,000 less a year than Data I-O, but threw in 1,600 stock options and an annual 15 percent salary bonus. Companies issue stock options as up-front signing and performance inducements on the theory that if you own shares of the company, chances are you'll do a better job. Stock options are issued at the existing market price. The options have a date when you're allowed to buy the stock at the optioned price. When you exercise or cash in on those options years later, the exercise price is usually lower than the current share price, meaning you usually get the stock at a substantial discount and step into some serious money.

Engstrom, for all his computer savvy, failed to grasp this concept. "Stock options," he muses. "I said to myself that's one of those things they pull on people in plaid shirts. They give stock options to trick people out of the real money."

Engstrom took the job with Data I-O, a decision he only half-jokingly says cost him about $20 million.

He bounced around to a couple of companies and finally quit when one of his employers was about to be swallowed by Cupertino, California-based software maker Symantec Corp. Engstrom, now twenty-six, found himself unemployed when Microsoft came calling again in the fall of 1991.

Ann McCurdy, Engstrom's fiancée, was now working full-time at Microsoft. Bob Taniguchi, one of Microsoft's original evangelists, asked her if Engstrom would be offended if he offered him a job. She didn't reveal that her husband-to-be was out of work, but indicated that he might be open to an offer.

"Microsoft needs coders with strong people skills," Taniguchi told Engstrom, who thought the pitch ironic.

What Engstrom did have was strong rhetorical skills. Never one to shrink from an argument, Engstrom once successfully debated with a hobbyist astronomer that Venus, not Polaris, was indeed the North Star. A good evangelist need not be burdened with facts. He aced his second interview at Microsoft and got the job as technical-tools evangelist in the company's Developer Relations Group.

But the honeymoon didn't last long. Engstrom was six months into his job as a technical evangelist at the still-rising software company when, three days before he was to be married, his fiancée unceremoniously dumped him for another Microsoft employee. The jilt crushed him.

"I didn't do much of anything for two years," Engstrom says.

Every day for months Engstrom arrived at Microsoft and did what few at the company ever got away with—sat in a chair and stared at the ceiling. After his marriage plans collapsed, Engstrom would shuffle into work and spend hours gazing from his office at the window across campus, the one with the words "Just Married!" happily spray-painted on the pane.

As miserable as he was, Engstrom still enjoyed getting together with Eisler. Engstrom had met him after the Canadian developed the 32-bit Windows extender at Watcom and the two nurtured a friendship initially out of self-interest. Eisler looked to Engstrom as an entrée into Microsoft. Engstrom, on the other hand, claimed the Canadian as one of his evangelical success stories, despite the fact Eisler was working on the Windows extender before Engstrom had started paying visits to Watcom.

"He was the tools evangelist and needed to get results for the [Windows] platform," Eisler says. "I was the only independent software developer that would do anything for him."

During this time, Eisler only half-jokingly said he wanted Engstrom's job.

"I told him he could have it," says Engstrom. "And I was serious."

Eisler soon had Engstrom's evangelist position.

An emotionally devastated Engstrom went to hide inside the company's newly created Advanced Consumer Technology division. ACT was formed under the direction of chief technology officer Nathan Myhrvold, the *über* genius who once worked for astrophysicist Stephen Hawking. The unit was a subset of Myhrvold's Advanced Technology group, the pure-research domain to explore natural-speech recognition, pen-based computing, and other technologies. Despite its title as a "consumer technology" group, however, it produced few consumer products relative to its multimillion-dollar budget. For Engstrom, a hands-on guy who demands fast results—he even clips his own hair with a Wahl-brand shaver—the lab-coat atmosphere of Advanced Consumer Technology didn't fit, reinforcing his misery.

Engstrom was on the verge of walking away from Microsoft altogether when Eisler and St. John came to the rescue in their own inimitable way. They teased the depressed Engstrom that he was soft and needed to do something about his flabby biceps. The harassment worked and Engstrom started coming to the morning workout sessions. St. John had known Engstrom when he was an evangelist, but until now the two were just casual acquaintances. The daily gym regimen would, at least initially, be good for Engstrom both physically and mentally. Not only would it be a place to vent some steam, it would offer an opportunity for Engstrom to bond with other like animals—Eisler and St. John.

And an unholy troika was born.

3

FLIGHT OF THE EVANGELISTS

By 1991, Bill Gates was battling a multifront war. Competitors were accusing Microsoft of stealing ideas. The government was probing whether Microsoft was violating antitrust laws. And mighty IBM vowed revenge after Gates officially pulled out of a joint project to build an alternative operating system to DOS.

Gates needed warriors to sell the world on Windows and to dispel the notion that Microsoft was evil. And so Microsoft embarked on a recruiting frenzy in 1991, a year in which the number of evangelists grew from fewer than a dozen to more than forty. Eisler, Engstrom, and St. John eventually were among the chosen.

The evangelical hiring rush owed its origins to an ill-fated deal Microsoft and IBM had struck in 1986 to jointly develop OS/2, the ersatz heir apparent to DOS. It was a confusing time in personal computing's brief history. Apple had introduced its revolutionary Macintosh in 1984. Microsoft had rolled out its first version of Windows late in 1985 and then turned around and started boosting OS/2 in 1986. Amid uncertainty over which operating system would displace DOS, many software developers hesitated to embrace either Windows or OS/2.

Microsoft had told *ComputerWorld* magazine in 1989, "We look forward to a time when major applications [for OS/2] begin to ship, and people will say, 'Aha, now I understand [the benefits of OS/2].' "

The plan originally announced was for the consumer version of Windows to give way to OS/2 at some point. A more sophisticated network version of the operating system—Windows NT—was being created to service corporate users. But the release of Windows 3.0 in the spring of 1990 changed Microsoft's tune. Sales of the Windows upgrade unexpectedly shot through the roof, largely because the operating system used a mouse, had a point-and-click graphical user interface like the Macintosh, and could run DOS programs. More than 2 million copies of Windows 3.0 were sold within the first two months of its release. Microsoft soon found it didn't need a partner to build a successor to DOS, and despite previous pledges to IBM about OS/2, it could not turn its back on consumer demand. At the urging of Senior Vice President Paul Maritz, Gates decided to walk away from the joint project.

While the decision to abort OS/2 was tantamount to declaring war on IBM, it also triggered internal combat between those working on Windows and those toiling on Windows NT, the operating system initially targeting the corporate high end. Eventually, Microsoft planned to phase out Windows—bloated, inefficient, and unstable software that ran on top of DOS—in favor of OS/2 and Windows NT. But the accidental success of Windows forced Microsoft to support this poorly designed operating system, a move that altered internal political dynamics in profound and enduring ways. Now two major groups inside Microsoft were fighting for control of resources, stock options, and head count. This internecine conflict put Windows NT Senior Vice President Jim Allchin on a violent collision course with Brad Silverberg, the VP in charge of Windows and a man who would have a profound influence on Eisler and Engstrom. This megabattle would shape countless internal power struggles throughout the company and greatly influence a series of jarring reorganizations in the mid-1990s.

By snubbing IBM, Gates earned the admiration and scorn of many in the industry. He was the young executive who had delivered a left hook to the pompous chin of Big Blue. It was one reason why St. John admired him and, in a way, figured into his decision to join the company. Likewise, Engstrom also looked up to his boss as the guy who "liked to kick ass." Yet the ass-kicking mentality that left IBM alone with OS/2 also left many in the computer industry furious.

Some software developers, at the urging of Microsoft, had invested money and valuable time into developing software programs for OS/2, only to have Microsoft pull its support for the fledgling platform. In the face of this outrage, Microsoft recruited evangelists, who were deployed to clean up the mess and move the masses to Windows.

"Microsoft's original group of evangelists spent all their time pumping independent software vendors for OS/2," recalls Fowles, the Harley-riding evangelist who hired St. John. "All the sudden it was their job to tell ISVs [independent software vendors] not to build for OS/2. You can imagine how pissed these companies were. Talk about some tough meetings."

Neither programmers nor salesmen, evangelists nonetheless possessed the powers of both. They didn't push product as much as capture "mindshare." Microsoft evangelists were prized for their powers of persuasion, their ability to think quickly on their feet, and their firm grasp of technology. Technical evangelists were Bill Gates's frontline storm troopers, who marched the Microsoft flag into offices of rival and friendly software companies to champion the Redmond cause. This was a job to be conducted with military zeal. In fact, E-mails announcing training sessions sometimes contained the subject headings "Evangelism is WAR!" and promised attendees that they would come away with a sense of "godlike empowerment" and "relentless aggression."

Apple invented evangelism in 1984 to boost the sales of its then-new Macintosh computers. The Mac was launched with a $15-million marketing campaign that kicked off with one of the most memorable television ads in history. The ad showed rows and rows of catatonic workers dressed in prison-camp gray staring at a Big Brother figure on a large screen droning on about the marvels of the computer. Then a glistening, toned woman in red shorts ran up an aisle and hurled a sledgehammer, smashing the screen. Everything went black. A message appeared: "On January 24, Apple

Computer will introduce Macintosh. And you'll see why 1984 won't be like 1984." It was Apple's not-so-veiled smite at the IBM "clone" computers that had come to dominate the PC market. (And continue to do so.) IBM introduced the first personal computer in 1981, but Microsoft retained licensing rights to the operating system—the single biggest factor that led to Microsoft's astronomical success. The Redmond company licensed DOS to other computer makers, which emulated and improved upon IBM machines. The Computer Age was launched.

Apple's Macintosh, however, used its own sleek hardware and proprietary operating system—a "computer for the rest of us," as cofounder Steve Jobs said. But the Mac needed more than just memorable TV ads. It needed third-party developers to write software for the Mac, which was harder to program for than its predecessor, the Apple IIe. Without software, there would be no reason for consumers to buy the Mac, dooming the sleek machine to a slow death. Apple's chief evangelist, Guy Kawasaki, and lieutenants Mike Boich and Alain Rossmann, paid cold-call visits to independent software developers, Macs in hand, to sell companies on Apple technology. It's what Kawasaki called hitting the beach. After storming ashore, Apple's strategy "was to occupy the territory and make things more efficient," Kawasaki told *InfoWorld* magazine in 1985. "Apple lives or dies depending on its third-party relations."

Kawasaki, Boich, and Rossmann were responsible for encouraging the ISVs to bring more than six hundred Macintosh programs to market.

Apple invented evangelism. Microsoft improved upon it.

Steve Ballmer, Microsoft's head cheerleader and second-in-command, introduced evangelism to Gates's Empire in 1987, three years after Apple launched its evangelist team. But evangelism at Microsoft really took off under the direction of Cameron Myhrvold, brother of Nathan Myhrvold, Microsoft's celebrated chief technology officer. Cameron germinated the company's evangelist team under the auspices of the Developer Relations Group. If one Kawasaki could help bring hundreds of programs to the Mac, just think what a team of Kawasakis could do for Windows, the successor to DOS, which already enjoyed dominant market share. Microsoft's original six evangelists were Alistair Banks, Kevin Egan, Viktor Gabner, Doug Henrich, Bob Taniguchi, and Adam Waalkes, a corps of charismatic coders deployed to convince software developers and the technical staffs of companies big and small to use Microsoft technology and write programs for Windows.

"They would read negative press about Microsoft and converge on whoever was quoted and pound on them to see Microsoft's point of view," says Fowles, who has since left Microsoft to start his own business.

St. John, who would become one of Microsoft's most notorious evangelists, recalls that Cameron taught that evangelism was not just to advance the Microsoft cause, but also to torpedo the competition.

"He told us, 'Your job is to fuck up a competitor,' " St. John says. "A competitor will never willingly adopt your technology. It's like cocaine. They're not going to willingly get addicted. You have to push cocaine on them."

One of Microsoft's evangelist tricks, according to St. John, was to nurture smaller companies around the ankles of a larger, established competitor. This would dilute market share and make it easier for Microsoft to move in. He cites Borland International, the database company.

"You find all of Borland's nearest competitors and wanna-bes and you help them with joint press releases, marketing dollars, support for using Microsoft technologies," St. John explains. "Borland now has five or six real competitors. Now, all the sudden they have a problem."

Like their Apple counterparts, Microsoft evangelists were authorized to travel virtually anywhere in the world at a moment's notice to knock on doors, gain audience with partners and competitors alike, and sell the Microsoft story. But in the early nineties, Microsoft's story was a tough sell. In addition to the OS/2 fiasco, the Federal Trade Commission had launched an investigation into allegations that Microsoft had abused its operating system monopoly by charging original equipment manufacturers (OEMs) lump-sum licensing fees. The practice effectively forced OEMs to pay for Microsoft's operating systems whether or not they installed them in new computers. In a market where price often determined the consumer's buying decision, this discouraged manufacturers from installing any non-Microsoft operating system, such as OS/2.

The government also was probing allegations that Microsoft courted potential software partners only to peek at their codes and steal ideas. For all the stormy accusations, however, the FTC stopped short of taking punitive action after it deadlocked 2–2 in 1993. A Justice Department inquiry ensued, resulting in a consent decree's being signed in 1995, ironically by U.S. district court judge Thomas Penfield Jackson, the same judge who would preside over a new massive antitrust case against Microsoft three years later. The 1995 decree forced Microsoft to charge computer makers a per-processor fee, instead of the lump-sum fee.

Cameron Myhrvold told *PCWeek* in 1991 that the decision to expand the evangelist group had nothing to do with the FTC investigation. "We really want to push Windows to market dominance," he was quoted. "That's really what has dictated it."

Moreover, Myhrvold had a potentially bigger problem on his hands. Many independent software vendors, known as ISVs, saw Microsoft as a competitor with an unfair advantage. Not only did the company make the operating system, it made programs that would run on the operating system. They accused Microsoft's operating-systems and applications teams of collaborating to enable Microsoft's programs to run better on Windows, at the same time sabotaging competing software. Microsoft deployed evangelists to appease independent software vendors and convince them that there was a "Chinese wall" between the company's applications and operating-systems groups. ("Chinese wall" may have been a poor metaphor. History records that unhappy Chinese troops garrisoned at the frontier on the Great Wall of China would often let Mongol armies through the gates to raid the homeland.)

Myhrvold and the company understood that, like Apple, it needed independent software developers to write applications for Windows, for operating systems without programs are like railroad tracks without trains. Microsoft is huge, but it's not big enough to make every program on the planet. Myhrvold told *PCWeek* that it was Developer Relations Group's job to be "the champions of ISVs at Microsoft. I see it as my job to see there's a level playing field."

In other words, Microsoft would help competitors compete against Microsoft.

"We used to fly the pirate flag," says Steve Banfield, a former Microsoft evangelist. "We saw ourselves as one of the true champions of what developers wanted, the rest of the company be damned."

Despite Myhrvold's spin, many independent software vendors didn't see the field as very level, and they had what they considered evidence to support that fear. Andrew Schulman, a programmer from Cambridge, Massachusetts, had written books about hidden coding inside DOS and Windows. These pieces of coding—application programming interfaces known as APIs or "calls"—tell the operating system how to respond to programs. When a user clicks an icon to launch a word-processing application, for example, an API makes the call to the operating system to get things going. If competing software companies don't know about certain APIs in the operating system, then their programs may not run as well. Microsoft later admitted that its Excel spreadsheet and Word applications used undocumented APIs in Windows, but that these undocumented APIs were more or less temporary. There was no guarantee they would be compatible with future iterations of the operating system, and if other companies used them, Microsoft argued, it could render their software useless on future versions of Windows or DOS.

Given all this controversy, it's easy to see why Microsoft was looking for an extraordinary breed for its stable of evangelists. And warriors such as St. John, Eisler, and Engstrom were nothing if not extraordinary. Yet Eisler soon discovered what Engstrom already knew: short of cleaning the campus urinals, a software tools evangelist was one of the most unenviable jobs ever created at Microsoft. Eisler says software companies accused him and other Microsoft evangelists of with-holding information about Windows coding. Taking pages from Schulman's books, *Undocumented Windows* and *Undocumented DOS,* the independent software vendors told Eisler they believed he was keep-ing secrets about certain coding tricks inside Windows so Microsoft's own word-processing, spreadsheet, database, and other programs would work better than software made by the competition. Some threatened to complain about Eisler to Brad Silverberg, Microsoft's senior vice president of Applications and Client Group.

"They were constantly wanting more information," recalls Eisler. "The big companies especially, like Borland and Symantec, were hard on me."

Eisler felt like the enemy, an evangelist wearing Satan's robe. Eisler's account does not show he was part of some orchestrated scheme to have Microsoft software work better on Windows or DOS than the competition's software. In fact, he says even he had trouble getting information from inside Microsoft, a reflection of the long-standing schism between the company's marketing staff and its legions of programmers, who live secure in the knowledge that they're higher on the intellectual food chain.

"Our developers didn't want to be bothered," Eisler recalls. "Not 'cause they didn't want to give up the information; it was they had better things to do. I was just some random marketing guy as far as they were concerned."

St. John says it was often a chore to get Microsoft programmers to heed the pleas of evangelists, who were out in the field listening to the desires of software makers. His fantasy was to have Microsoft pro-grammers work jointly with targeted software vendors, so that when a project was finished, the targets would be fully and organically evangelized.

"Instead we'd get handed some foolish crap someone at research and development or whomever had been cooking up in isolation for several years and get told that we had to make people use it," St. John says.

At the same time Microsoft needed developers to make software for Windows and convince them—in the face of contrary information—that there were no hidden APIs, the company also wanted consumers and businesses to buy its word processors, databases, spreadsheets, etc. This, too, was a tough sell. Even Microsoft officials in the early 1990s privately conceded what many in the computer industry were saying: Microsoft applications weren't all that good.

"I can't think of a single product in 1990 that the company had that was the best," says Fowles. "I could almost say that today.

"Microsoft was not the leader in anything [other than operating systems]," he adds. "Office didn't exist. We were not the leader in word processing, not even in spreadsheets. Multimedia was just a joke. All down the line. Even Intel had better software than us."

Indeed, three analysts—Piper Jaffray & Hopwood, Dataquest, and Ragen MacKenzie—estimated that based on 1990 shipments for personal computers, WordPerfect, Lotus Development (now part of IBM), and Ashton-Tate owned the majority market share for word-processing, spreadsheets, and database software applications respectively. Microsoft was either a distant second, or in the case of databases and desktop publishing, not even on the lists. Microsoft evangelists, armed with an almost limitless arsenal of cash, charged into these and other markets. Within a few short years, Microsoft's word-processing, spreadsheets, and computer-network operating systems emerged as market leaders.

It was in this charged atmosphere of government investigation, industry hostility, and brutal competition that Eisler, Engstrom, and St. John entered Fortress Microsoft and the unholy troika fused. Their mutual love/hate relationship with evangelism acted to bond them. Had they not been evangelists, they would never have met and perhaps computing history would have played out differently.

The Pro Club proved to be a valuable incubator, where the three nurtured a growing friendship, relieved stress, and began conceiving ways to build their own technology, rather than proselytize software built by others at the company. The workout arguments became more intense. The three hotly debated current issues and sometimes broke the monotony of lifting heavy objects with seemingly nonsensical intellectual drills—"evangelism exercises in persuasion," mental tests to see how credible they could make the most absurd argument sound.

"Quick, Craig, defend the proposition that black is the same color as white!" went one typical challenge.

"What is white?" Eisler would respond. "A bunch of photons at random frequencies—the fewer you have, the less white you have until your eye can't see them anymore and you perceive black. They're on the same continuum. Black is just a subset of white."

Still another: Suppose you need to solve a calculus problem and you lived in a universe with rats. That's all you get is rats. What do you do?

"You could teach a rat to push a button on food cues," St. John says. "That's a transistor. With a rat transistor you can build a computer. So, we may have found a way to have a rat solve calculus."

St. John likened Microsoft to a giant rat computer: "All Bill can do is hire the smartest rats he can. That's his only hope."

Eisler, Engstrom, and St. John were smart rats. Now that the three had found one another, what would they put their ambitious minds to? That question would be answered as Microsoft geared up to launch Windows 95, the most hyped software in history.

4

INTERNAL WARFARE

St. John opened his E-mail one morning in 1993 and discovered that one of America's richest men was furious at him. St. John had had the temerity to tell *InfoWorld* magazine that Microsoft's PostScript printer drivers for Windows 3.1 were "not up to snuff" and acknowledged that the company was doing its best to catch up with Apple. A driver is a small chunk of code that tells the computer what sort of device or hardware is being used. PostScript drivers would tell the printer what kind of font or graphic the computer had been instructed to produce.

Gates had been led to believe Microsoft's technology was superior and wanted to know where St. John was getting his "false" information and why he was spewing it in public.

Gates upbraided St. John for revealing that Microsoft's printing architecture was weak and demanded to know why St. John wasn't using the company's PR apparatus, noting that "There's a reason we pay those people."

St. John was devastated by the rebuke. He shuffled around the Redmond campus for about an hour, certain that his days at Microsoft were numbered. He had been hired to evangelize Microsoft's printing technology, not trash it. Yet the more he thought about the incident, the angrier he became. His boss had handed him the phone and told him to talk to the *InfoWorld* writer. Didn't everyone know

Microsoft's printing technology lagged behind Apple's? Even Doug Henrich, Microsoft's group manager for Developer Relations, was quoted in the same article saying basically the same thing. What good would it have done to lie? St. John's dread of perhaps losing his job morphed to rage.

He stomped back to his office and shot off his own irate E-mail to Gates, saying, "How do you expect me to have any credibility with this community by denying that we have problems?"

Gates quickly responded, saying that Microsoft's printing technology was "ten times" better than Apple's.

St. John, stunned by the ignorance of Gates's position, volleyed, giving detailed reasons why Apple's support for PostScript technology surpassed Microsoft's. The Mac was more reliable and faster. The Mac generated PostScript images in binary format, in the ones and zeros that computers talk in, allowing it to process more information faster. Windows shoved PostScript code out in raw ASCII text, making print jobs, particularly ones with graphics, slow to a relative crawl. St. John reminded Gates that as a printing-architecture expert, Alex's opinion on this subject was golden. Gates grasped St. John's technical explanation. Now he wanted answers from his senior advisers.

St. John's first internal political skirmish at Microsoft skipped right over the midlevel managers and put him at odds with some of the company's real heavyweights. The company's upper hierarchy pounced with its full weight.

Brad Silverberg, then senior vice president in charge of Windows, personally wrote St. John, telling him to stop whining to Gates. Silverberg, perhaps loyal to a fault, believed what his people were saying: that Microsoft's print drivers were completely acceptable and that St. John had no clue.

St. John pushed back, telling Silverberg exactly what he had explained to Gates. Silverberg had heard enough. St. John either refused to read the political subtext or was too naive to get the message that more feedback on this issue was unwelcome. Silverberg had been getting his information from Dennis Adler, then group program manager of the Windows 95 design team. St. John's position

clashed with Adler's, forcing Adler to orchestrate an "end around" to salvage his credibility, St. John says.

Adler sprayed E-mail to Silverberg and other senior executives, saying that he was way in front of the issue and had already negotiated a partnership with Adobe to redo the flawed PostScript drivers. Adobe had talked to St. John about such a partnership months before, because the company wanted its type fonts to work better on Windows. According to St. John, Adler and others had spurned the offer at the time, only to backtrack and take Adobe up on the deal only after Gates learned that his company's PostScript drivers were inferior.

"I thought I saw mirrors moving on the walls," St. John says. "Microsoft didn't like Adobe at all and the two were warring over font technology. Adler did a great job of covering his own ass."

With the Adobe deal hastily sealed, St. John's position was muted. While he may have lost that political battle, St. John nonetheless gained credibility and a reputation as an ass-kicker. Others in the company realized that this evangelist was not going to be silenced easily. Moreover, in this and subsequent battles his opinions were usually correct, which only enhanced his credibility. Microsoft is a company that admires those who can argue well. Although St. John had angered higher-ups, he had also gained their respect.

"Microsoft tends to believe in people who believe in themselves," St. John says. "The people who stuck by their guns were the ones who shaped the company's direction. This was true all the way to Bill, who would aggressively challenge people on everything and only respected people who answered fast and concisely."

St. John tells the story of a man who was pontificating on some subject with Gates.

"Bill leaned forward and said, 'Really. That's not what my people say about it.'

"This made the guy all flustered and start to hedge his statements. Bill lets him hang for a while, then smiles and says, 'Actually I'm just kidding. I wanted to see if you really knew what you were talking about."

St. John had emerged from his initial entanglement stronger and became bolder, brasher, and more obnoxious in face-to-face meetings with his Microsoft colleagues. He delighted in dismantling the credibility of others who had positioned themselves as experts without the expertise to back up their statements.

Shortly after the confrontation with Gates, St. John was invited to sit in on a meeting of Windows NT program managers who were discussing that platform's printing support.

"The NT PostScript driver was broken and primitive," St. John recalls. "But they were absolutely convinced that they were making the best printer driver ever."

St. John began to challenge David Snipp, the manager making the presentation, peppering him with questions about data compression, translation, and other technical matters. About eight other developers and managers in the room watched as Snipp and St. John traded shots.

"Do you even know what you're talking about?" St. John finally demanded, and pulled out a 1985 book on PostScript technology. Snipp fought back and told St. John that, yes, he had read the book. Windows NT printing architecture was based on it.

St. John reached into his bag and pulled out a revised edition of the book and heaved it across the table at Snipp.

"Here," St. John said as the book whizzed by Snipp. "I suggest you read this version. You're reading from a book that's six years old!"

Snipp resigned a few weeks later. St. John was asked to help interview candidates for the vacancy.

By 1994, St. John's exploits had caught the attention of Rick Segal, who was looking for an evangelist to champion the company's multimedia capabilities. Trouble was, multimedia capabilities at Microsoft was an oxymoron. Sound, graphics, animation, and video did not work well on any version of Windows to date. Microsoft was making incremental progress, but needed a bold marketer to retell the company's multimedia story to the computer world. In St. John, Segal found the evangelist he needed. Unwittingly, his decision would set in motion a series of events that would change the course of the computer-gaming industry.

Segal was a former Aetna Insurance Company programmer who,

like many combative engineers, had come to Microsoft to conquer new technological terrain. Segal arrived at Microsoft in 1991 as an eagerly courted evangelist assigned to advance Windows in the new struggle against OS/2. Segal tired of that battle when it became clear Microsoft had won, and he turned his sights to become the company's director of multimedia evangelism in Developer Relations Group.

For years Microsoft had been chasing Apple's lead in multimedia, specifically QuickTime, the software that allows users to play, record, and edit small movies on a computer. By 1994, Segal and a handful of others at the Redmond company were embarrassed by Microsoft's multimedia development. The advent of CD-ROMs, which could contain an entire encyclopedia complete with audio, movie clips, and animation, and the maturation of computers and software had made multimedia de rigueur. Microsoft's Windows 95—scheduled for release in the summer of 1994 but arriving more than a year later— would look embarrassingly anachronistic if it handled multimedia as poorly as its predecessors. Despite this clear business imperative, Microsoft was slow in moving to fix this glaring deficiency, which contributed in part to the delayed launch of history's most anticipated software.

"Everybody was arguing over what to do," Segal recalls. He says that Microsoft "didn't have its heart into developing multimedia tools," in part because the company's senior executives didn't believe that's where the gold was buried.

Microsoft launched its first version of Windows in 1985, and although it boasted the point-and-click graphical user interface similar to Apple's Macintosh, it wasn't built for multimedia. A graphical user interface, or GUI (pronounced "gooey"), is the name given to the area of a computer screen where you interact or interface with your computer. Instead of arcane text commands, a GUI uses little clickable pictures called icons or pull-down menus to launch programs or open files. Windows was designed for business software and worked well as long as it was dealing with text or lines for bar graphs.

But when it came to rendering sound, video, animation, and the like, it was an abomination. Unlike DOS, which allowed direct access to a computer's video cards, sound cards, and other hardware, Windows got in the way and slowed things down. The overlaying structure of Windows simply prevented fast playback of multimedia. And what good is a slow, jerky shoot-'em-up game?

The result: Few developers in the industry were writing games and multimedia applications for Windows. With scant multimedia software coming to market, a sort of self-fulfilling defeatism gripped Microsoft's multimedia developers. In many ways Microsoft's multimedia strategy was like time locked inside a black hole—it didn't really move forward or stand still. It simply didn't exist.

Microsoft's treasures were operating systems and business applications, not multimedia. Given such low priority, the company's primary multimedia development team was left to the rudderless direction of formal naval officer Paul Osborne. His stern, slightly distant demeanor reminded some of *Star Trek: The Next Generation*'s Captain Jean-Luc Picard. Unlike the fictional captain, however, Osborne was almost universally looked upon as ineffectual and incompetent.

"He was one of the few guys I ever met at Microsoft who was in 'rest and vest mode,'" Segal says, using the derisive term for clock sitters who are more interested in watching their stock options mature than making leading-edge technology. "You just can't do that at Microsoft," Segal adds. "People figure out you're not doing any work."

After surveying the company's multimedia situation, Segal thought he had a way to kill off Apple, the acknowledged multimedia leader and innovator. He paid no less than three visits to Bill Gates, requesting more money, more personnel, and more authority to grab animation and graphics technologies from the company's consumer side. Segal also oversaw development of Surround Video, which turned photos into navigable 3-D scenes. Segal's stated goal in pitching these requests to Gates was to attack QuickTime and bury Apple.

Gates eagerly agreed. Apple's superior QuickTime technology gave the software titan fits. History records that while QuickTime survived and triumphed over Microsoft's Video for Windows, Apple itself almost perished. Although Apple proved to be its own worst enemy in the late 1980s and early 1990s, Segal and others at Microsoft had done their level best to bring the Cupertino company to its knees.

"We were hell-bent to kill those guys at Apple," Segal says.

He notes that by the late nineties—with the Justice Department on the prowl—the last thing Microsoft wanted to be caught doing was strangling a vanquished foe. "But I didn't have that constraint back then," Segal adds.

By marshaling resources and promoting selected products, Segal helped Microsoft's multimedia efforts gain a little momentum. Indeed, Segal's attempt to corral the company's various multimedia initiatives marked the first time Microsoft had tried to unify its approach to multimedia on the desktop. The company would hype the new multimedia technologies and would tell the world they would be among the key features in the upcoming Windows 95 operating system, code-named Chicago. Yet even as Microsoft's multimedia strategy began to coalesce in 1994, Segal and others realized the company was leaving untapped a $5-billion gold mine—computer games.

Before the launch of Windows 95, almost all games for the PC were written for the old DOS operating system because games ran too slowly on Windows 3.1. Because games were—and are—among the main reasons consumers bought computers, it made sense to ensure Windows 95 could run the hottest-selling games. Moreover, it also made sense to Segal that Microsoft should be the one to develop game technology for the new operating system.

He told Gates and others that if a company such as id Software, makers of the popular titles Quake and Doom, could find a way to make games work well on Windows and establish its own standard multimedia engine, Microsoft would have to make its operating system conform to someone else's specifications. Segal knew what buttons to push. Any threat to Windows received the full attention of Gates and his executives.

"All I had to do to get games support from senior management was say we're going to lose our [application programming interface] franchise," Segal says. "They threw money at us."

Yet even as Segal persuaded senior management to get behind a unified multimedia strategy, that message was often diffused along the way. Segal would eventually deliver on his promise to give Windows multimedia capability, but he never succeeded in consolidating all of the company's multimedia efforts, some of which were under development in the Windows NT group and others inside the Windows 95 camp. Segal and others say "random" managers and executives would take it upon themselves to build multimedia projects, often never finishing them, never targeting a market, or never deploying them effectively. Among the various initiatives were Talisman, a proposed and much talked about 3-D hardware chip from Microsoft's Advanced Consumer Technology group; Raptor, the misguided input or joystick-device application programming interface from the company's consumer division; and OpenGL, an API that enabled personal computers to run animated 3-D multimedia graphics, a technology some on the Windows NT group were tinkering with.

These and other multimedia projects competed for the same pool of resources inside Microsoft, meaning some of the more promising technologies may not have received the fortification they deserved. Moreover, the uncoordinated projects often doubled the workload of evangelists, who sometimes maneuvered to keep independent software vendors—key Microsoft customers—away from some of Microsoft's more unappetizing entrées.

"There would be random pockets of people with authority fabricating multimedia foolishness, and telling Bill that they had his solution to QuickTime for him," St. John says. "I had already been in DRG long enough to have seen what happened when Microsoft pushed a technology on developers and then didn't follow through. The development community became immune to evangelism, DRG got hung with cleaning up the mess long after the internal group had disbanded, while the perpetrators moved on to other exciting projects."

Clearly, Segal faced not only technical challenges, but serious internal political challenges in trying to create a team to get Windows to run games better than DOS could.

While Windows 3.1 was awful at running games, DOS also had its problems. To make games fast and visually realistic enough to run on DOS, developers had to invest large chunks of time and money writing device drivers that would control all the different combinations of video, graphics, and sound cards in the marketplace. Games that worked well on one brand of PC and one type of hardware often didn't work well on another. Users sometimes had to spend hours configuring their games just so their computers could run them. Technical support was a nightmare. High-end UNIX machines—big mainframe computers used by many of the world's large corporations—had solved this problem with a system called Open Graphics Language or OpenGL, a 3-D graphics language developed by Silicon Graphics Inc. While programmers at Microsoft and elsewhere were working on bringing OpenGL game support down to desktop computers, nobody had yet succeeded.

There were no standards. Personal-computer game development was in a kind of anarchy.

Moving games off DOS and onto Windows could standardize games for the PC, hook more developers on Microsoft's newer operating system, and in turn, hook more consumers. The problem, however, was Microsoft still had little multimedia credibility and little in the way of Windows game titles to demo.

"The game guys wouldn't talk to us," recalls Segal. "Why would they? Write games for Windows 3.1? Not in your wildest dreams. Never going to happen."

Even Microsoft acknowledged in a handbook that "game graphics under Windows made slug racing look exciting."

Segal soon discovered Chris Hecker, who was working on WinG (pronounced "win-gee"), a way to potentially boost game performance on Windows 3.1. Hecker was coding his creation at Microsoft's Advanced Consumer Technology research division, the same place Eric Engstrom was hiding after his fiancée had dumped him. Segal may potentially have found an answer to game performance on Windows, but he also found that Hecker had a robust disrespect for authority.

"He absolutely, positively didn't care what anybody in the company, up to and including Bill Gates, thought about him," Segal says. "He was writing this mail, 'I don't give a shit what anybody says, this is my fucking code and I'll ship [WinG] when I say we'll ship.' [Applications and Systems Group Vice President Paul] Maritz sends me back mail saying, 'Who is this guy? Send him to charm school.'

"Hecker was just perceived as a total asshole," Segal adds. "He just happened to be a brilliant one."

Given Microsoft's track record in multimedia, WinG would not be an easy sell. Segal realized he needed one of Microsoft's best warrior evangelists to battle for the hearts and minds of game programmers, known in the computer industry for their irreverence, independence, and hostility toward the Redmond company. On Segal's short list were St. John and Craig Eisler, both of whom competed fiercely for the job. In the end, it was an easy choice—the best beast for this assignment was "the Saint."

In one unkind regard, Segal's timing could not have been better. St. John's wife retreated to Maine with their two children shortly after Alex's twenty-seventh birthday in February and later filed for divorce. St. John was no longer a family man. He was a company man.

Kelley St. John had grown literally ill from living with St. John, who by that time had become consumed with money and his job.

"On Saturdays he was home," Kelley recalls. "He'd sit in a chair and the kids would be playing on the floor and he'd say, 'Can't they go somewhere else?' "

Before, he had never given much thought to money or possessions. Now that he was making big money and was exposed to conspicuous consumption, he coveted them. Eisler and Engstrom once laughed at the puniness of his television. The next day, St. John clipped the set's electrical cord, pronounced the TV "broken," and bought the biggest model on the market.

The severing moment of the marriage, however, occurred when St. John bought a house in Redmond three weeks after the birth of his second daughter, Amelia, in November 1993. He was tired of living below noisy neighbors and wanted to try to make Kelley happier. So he insisted on buying the house. That he and Kelley had agreed they would be moving back to Maine within two years didn't enter into the equation. To compound the tension, St. John had invited his estranged family over for Christmas. When his relatives arrived, he barely saw them because he was working so much. Kelley had been abandoned with two babies and a new house full of in-laws over the holidays.

St. John claims he didn't see the breakup coming. He was so stunned, he refused to speak with his estranged wife for six months after she and the kids left. It was during this time that Segal acquired his new evangelist—a wounded animal who now weighed more than 340 pounds. St. John, who had once trimmed his beard, now let it grow to an auburn thicket. His regimen at the weight room with Eisler and Engstrom was surpassed by his visits to the ubiquitous vending machines at Microsoft, as well as the company's well-provisioned cafeterias.

Rather than a polished salesman, such as Brad Chase, Microsoft's slick marketing vice president, St. John "looked like a bomb going off," Segal says, something gamers, at least, found appealing.

Gamers may have liked him, but Hecker, the WinG programmer, didn't. Hecker dismissed St. John as a marketing wonk; St. John, ironically enough, thought Hecker was recklessly arrogant. The two once argued over a particular way games ran on DOS using a process known as page flipping. Many DOS-based games used a computer's video card memory and cycled through screen shots frame by frame to give the effect of animation, much like a child's flip book. St. John says Hecker didn't believe that technique was used for quality games such as Doom. St. John told Hecker that Microsoft's own game group had pried into the assembly code of Doom and determined that it, indeed, used page flipping. St. John also warned Hecker not to tell anybody about Microsoft's exploratory surgery. Although it wasn't technically illegal to look under the hood of someone's software, the company didn't want anyone knowing about its bit of reverse engineering. Such a revelation could bring embarrassment and legal scrutiny.

St. John says Hecker promptly called John Carmack, the founder of id and creator of Doom, and told him Microsoft had bored into the game. Carmack confirmed that, yes, page flipping was used in Doom.

Although Hecker was proved wrong, he boasted to St. John about the call, further souring relations between the two.

"Jesus, why did you do this when I thought we had an understanding?" St. John recalls. "It's really a sensitive issue. That's not something you want getting out."

Despite his personality battles, Hecker made headway on WinG. In April 1994, at the Computer Game Developers Conference in Silicon Valley, he fired up a prototype of Doom on Windows 3.1. Soon after, Microsoft made available beta or test versions of WinG on a developer's forum through the Internet service CompuServe. It marked the first time Microsoft had released software specifically targeting game developers.

WinG wasn't the prettiest piece of coding, Segal says. "But the fact remained [Hecker] was able to take a piece of shit called Windows and make games work on it. He strapped a jet engine on a Beechcraft and got the thing in the air."

Engstrom says WinG created the "biggest debacle in the computer industry." Yes, Hecker fused a jet engine with a Beechcraft. But he got exactly the results one would expect.

"The wings came off first, followed by the rest of the plane," Engstrom says.

Meanwhile, Eisler, whose mantra is "I don't play to lose," was stewing that he had lost out on the games-evangelist job to St. John.

Eisler would soon be pacified. After a cursory survey of game developers, St. John prepared a list of items he believed he needed to assemble a credible games-development team, which included a request for several programmers. St. John also wanted to help Eisler get inside the company's multimedia group, and this presented a perfect opportunity. However, group director Paul Osborne balked and rejected much of St. John's wish list. St. John says Osborne disliked him because "I was constantly in his office demanding things." Unable to get what he wanted through the front door, St. John ran around the back. He asked Segal to talk to Osborne, but insisted he not mention that St. John and Eisler were friends. Segal obliged and suggested Osborne would need someone to take over for Hecker "because Hecker was certifiable and was probably going to quit anyway." Segal strongly recommended Eisler.

Osborne agreed to hire Eisler, which helped him come to terms with the loss to St. John. Besides, Eisler reasoned, he didn't want to be an evangelist anyway. The Canadian computer whiz preferred coding to paying visits to hostile companies.

Osborne assigned Eisler to work with Hecker. Accounts vary as to what happened between the two, who worked together for eight weeks in Microsoft's Building 9, a replica of the X-shaped edifice next to Gates's lair. Eisler maintains he was the "damper" for Hecker, the one who "stayed up all night running tests" and helped move WinG along.

"I sat on the process," Eisler says. "Chris was really young and full of himself. A little arrogant. It was great working with Chris. A little annoying, but I loved it."

St. John recalls that rather than sitting on the process, Eisler had to "sit on Hecker's chest" to get him to finish the WinG code.

Segal, meanwhile, says he had to make sure that "Craig wouldn't kill Hecker. Hecker wouldn't report to Craig. Hecker just didn't like anybody—he was a real piece of work."

Yet the two hypercompetitive nerds shared much in common. Once, over a catered dinner at Microsoft, the two debated whose recent surgery was more vile. Eisler argued that his still-healing wound troubled him more, going into rich detail about how the scab would stick to the inside of his undergarments. Hecker countered with lurid details about a polyp removal and painful catheter procedure, arguing that his experience was far more heinous. St. John, who recalls the dinner all too well, says the conversation killed everyone's appetite.

Hecker declined to be interviewed for this book, but he did offer some insight on his relationship with Eisler by way of an E-mail to the author:

"Have you ever been in one of those situations where explaining what actually happened would take so long that it wouldn't be worth it, even though you know several people will probably try to make you look stupid if you don't? That's me with your book. I'm really sorry (and I'll probably be more sorry after it comes out), but I just don't have the time or inclination to dredge up this stuff."

St. John was in his element with the gaming community. His own disregard for Microsoft authority figures was equaled only by the game developers' antipathy for the big Redmond company. Microsoft once held a trade-press meeting at the campus to demonstrate WinG. Segal put St. John in charge of the presentation, but didn't want to know what St. John was going to do, "so I could claim ignorance and run cover for him when the shit hit the fan."

St. John emerged onstage at the Microsoft theater and told the trade-press writers, "Yep, I know what you guys think about Windows."

He booted up a computer. The blue start-up screen with clouds and Windows 3.1 logo came to life on a large display. A graphic of a shotgun barrel rose from the bottom of the screen. With the audience looking down its sights, the gun blasted five holes in the logo. The press erupted with laughter and approving applause.

Brad Chase, Microsoft's senior marketing vice president, turned crimson and told Segal, "You gotta fire this guy." Chase was so enraged he considered going onstage and putting an end to St. John's show. Segal set Chase straight:

"I looked Chase right in the face and said, 'You don't have a clue.

He just gained all the credibility in the world from these press guys. They think you're a slime bag; they think he's a hero. I don't think you getting up there will help.'"

St. John wasn't finished. He demonstrated WinG.

"I know this is a hack," St. John said, using the derogatory term for patchy software coding. "But the people who use this crappy hack are going to make some damn money."

St. John was seduced by the ensuing adulation. Like a techno David Letterman, he later developed an act that included lampooning Microsoft. The more approval he received at subsequent presentations and trade shows, the bolder he became. His shtick of mocking Microsoft bureaucracy, his disrespect for senior executives—Gates excluded—and his disregard for political correctness played well, for the most part, with game developers even as it made him enemies at the company.

"He called people like Chase morons and [game developers] loved it," Segal says. "Executives at the company couldn't get over it. They thought he was doing damage. But the gamers loved it. They thought they had someone who had their interest at heart. To this day, I don't think Eisler or Engstrom could have pulled it off."

In 1994, Microsoft announced it would install WinG in Windows 95. The company spent millions of dollars promoting WinG, giving out free software development kits at trade shows and conferences and even hiring Brent Spiner, who played the android Data in *Star Trek: The Next Generation,* to make special promotional appearances. So aggressive was St. John in plugging Microsoft's new gaming technology that after one computer game conference, an IBM marketer sent Segal a white flag with a note stating, "I surrender."

WinG, the trade journals announced, was going to be huge.

"Many games developers see DOS's games domination ending thanks to WinG," wrote *Byte* magazine in November 1994.

"Games utilizing Microsoft Corp.'s WinG specifications could help boost retail sales and stem returns for Windows games starting this fall," read a lead in the August issue of *Computer Retail Week.*

That same month, *Computer Gaming World* magazine said Windows 95, blessed with WinG, "may bring the computer gaming world one step closer to the 'plug-and-play' dream. Certainly, anything that will dispel the nightmares of installation and hardware configuration for DOS and Windows gamers will be welcomed with open arms."

Little did the world know that Eisler, Engstrom, and St. John would kill WinG in midflight, replace the technology with their own, and trigger a battle inside Microsoft over what was the best approach for games for Windows—a war that eventually spilled into the game community at large and would throughout the nineties.

While it was true WinG could run Doom on Windows 3.1, St. John and Eisler saw flaws in the technology and thought they could improve on it. WinG was fast only with certain types of graphics and did nothing to boost performance control with joysticks, sound cards, and multiuser play. Yet Hecker had convinced others at Microsoft that WinG could enable all games to work on Windows.

"It didn't," St. John says. "It was a neat hat trick that fell over when you actually tried to make a real game run. WinG just made for a good demo, and people who didn't know any better at Microsoft thought it was enough."

Eisler and St. John didn't know exactly how, but they were convinced they could do better. Moreover, they understood the company was marshaling all its forces to produce Windows 95, the most heavily hyped software the world had ever known. Their careers would take off if they could hitch their boosters to that money rocket.

In August 1994, Eisler and St. John worked up a survey, and in the spirit of evangelism, St. John took it to some thirty top game developers and asked the crucial question: "What could Microsoft build that would compel you to write games for Windows?" The two compiled the results and wrote a white paper titled "Taking Fun Seriously," which outlined what steps Microsoft needed to take to make Windows 95 a successful game platform.

But before they embarked on what would be a jihad over the company's game technology, Eisler knew they needed a program manager, someone to write specifications for the technology, oversee production, and ensure the nascent development team had enough resources and personnel. Just as important, the role also demanded some "blocking" duties, to keep Osborne occupied so Eisler could code without management distractions. Eisler and St. John decided to liberate Engstrom from his self-exile at Microsoft's Advanced Consumer Technology.

The two urged their weight-lifting buddy to interview for a position in the multimedia group, but not to mention anything about their friendship, a contrivance they believed would go unnoticed, would help Engstrom's chances, and would in the end help advance all their careers. Almost two years had elapsed since Engstrom got jilted, and the memory still caused him to weep, friends say. He had been thinking about quitting Microsoft. But the chance to do something new was alluring and would prove cathartic.

Engstrom didn't know anything about games. In fact, he hated them—the shoot-'em-up games made him nauseous; the so-called strategy games bored him. None of that mattered. St. John told him that nobody with whom he'd interview, especially Osborne, knew anything about multimedia or computer games. Nonetheless, Engstrom read the preface of a 3-D graphics book to prepare himself.

"The typical Eric thing to do is to read just enough to have some vocabulary," Engstrom says.

Engstrom also reviewed some game screen shots so he could mention them during the interviews. He breezed through the technical interviews, in large part because the interviewers knew he had been a technical evangelist, and at least in the early nineties, you didn't get to be a Microsoft evangelist unless you knew your stuff. The ease of those interviews, however, would almost be his undoing.

Engstrom then faced Heidi Breslauer, a multimedia program manager at the time whose perceived lack of technical and leadership skills earned her the derisive nickname Brussels Sprouts. She asked Engstrom how his technical interviews had gone.

"They weren't all that technical," Engstrom casually told her.

Breslauer interpreted this to mean that Engstrom had not been grilled hard enough, presumably because he wasn't technically fit. She left Engstrom sitting in her office to express her fears to Osborne.

"I'm not supposed to be technical enough," says Engstrom. "This coming from a program manager who has never written code."

Osborne later summoned Engstrom into his office and told him he was leery of Engstrom's previous job-hopping—Osborne's political way of saying he didn't believe Engstrom possessed technical savvy. Osborne would not have hired Engstrom had it not been for Eisler, who, never revealing his friendship, convinced Breslauer that "this Engstrom guy" was the real deal.

"I had to do my best Jedi mind trick to get that done," Eisler says.

Engstrom was relieved. "Things changed for me," he recalls. "And Microsoft was fun again."

The three friends from the gym were now inside Gates's multimedia fort.

5

THE BEASTIE BOYS

Based on the feedback they received from the "Taking Fun Seriously" white paper, Eisler, St. John, and now Engstrom realized they needed to go shopping for a 3-D engine, a crucial alloy for forging quality computer games. Computerized 3-D animation is complex digital alchemy. Objects such as monsters and the worlds they inhabit must be described in terms of 3-D geometry, moved about in space, drawn in perspective by projecting the 3-D objects onto a 2-D screen, and then actually drawn and redrawn in a process known as rasterization. A 3-D engine is used to speed up rasterization for smoother animation. To achieve game-quality animation, a computer system must have this type of rendering capability. Eisler, Engstrom, and St. John didn't have a 3-D engine for games at their disposal, and it was way too late to make one from scratch to be ready for Christmas sales in 1995, when consumers would be hungry for Windows 95 software. The three proposed buying RenderMorphics Ltd., a London-based specialist in 3-D programming tools, specifically for its flagship 3-D engine, Reality Lab.

To buy a company, however, the three needed approval from Paul Maritz, group vice president for Applications and Systems and a member of Gates's five-person Office of the President. Eisler, Engstrom, and St. John didn't have computer-game experience and 3-D credentials on their résumés, and so, they didn't have the credibility to persuade Maritz to buy an entire company. However, Michael Abrash, Microsoft's most valuable player in 3-D graphics programming, did possess this credibility. Abrash, who had written books on 3-D programming, was a program manager in the multimedia group, working on 3D-DDI, the 3-D device driver interface—software that communicates directly with video hardware and boosts performance of 3-D graphics. Maritz told Eisler, Engstrom, and St. John that if Abrash gave his blessing, Microsoft would buy RenderMorphics.

Abrash, however, wasn't concerned about computer games. He was more consumed with developing Microsoft's first low-cost 3-D accelerator hardware for Windows NT, the industrial-strength version of Windows designed for corporations. To win Abrash's favor on the RenderMorphics deal, Eisler, Engstrom, and St. John decided they had to soften him up.

"We would go into his office every day," says St. John. "We drove him nuts with cooperation. He could not leave his office, he could not go to a meeting, without us being invited to help articulate whatever his point of view was. He had no peace. No privacy. He couldn't say anything that we couldn't take and carry further than he intended. We wouldn't make a decision without consulting him." St. John dubbed the practice "Abrashing."

The three also worked on bending Osborne to their will. They convinced him that adding RenderMorphics was necessary for the advancement of the company's games and multimedia efforts. Osborne, in turn, told Abrash that he could be in charge of Microsoft's 3-D graphics strategy if he endorsed the RenderMorphics deal.

Abrash acquiesced, Maritz gave the nod, and Microsoft bought RenderMorphics. One result of their feigned sycophancy was that Abrash quit Microsoft to work for id, the game maker.

"Abrash actually said that Eric and Craig were responsible for him quitting the company," one insider says. "That's kind of cool."

Abrash eventually returned to the Empire, but not before he and others would lead a private campaign to kill game technology built by Eisler, Engstrom, and St. John.

By September 1994, Windows 95 was already months behind its original launch date. It would be another year before the celebrated operating system hit retail shelves. Management called all hands on deck to accelerate work on Win95, but the bugs lurking in the operating system's 15 million lines of code couldn't be killed fast enough. Eisler was called to fix problems with the operating system's joystick control as well as help correct flaws with Direct Control Interface or DCI, a joint Microsoft/Intel project for enhancing video performance. As far as Eisler was concerned, these projects were annoying distractions. He and his two conspirators were plotting to make Windows 95 the preeminent platform for computer games.

From September through December 1994, Eisler, Engstrom, and St. John initiated their bold scheme without authorization—a rogue undertaking they called "the Manhattan Project," named after America's World War II atom bomb effort. The cabal was essentially a company within a company. The chaos to get Windows 95 shipped created cover of sorts for the trio, who initially worked on their project under the company's managerial radar. By the time the three took the wraps off their plan, too much time and money had been invested to abort it. Moreover, St. John had been leaking details of the technology to the trade journals, building unauthorized buzz and making it more difficult for Microsoft to kill.

In December 1994, unbeknownst to most Microsoft executives, the trio hosted about thirty of the industry's top game developers to a technical design review at the Redmond campus. By the end of the day, the developers knew more about what was up the sleeves of Eisler, Engstrom, and St. John than did most of Microsoft management. As an evangelist, St. John enjoyed enormous freedom and had no problem booking the Developer Relations Group's special conference center at Building 12 for the design review. The review was run like any conventional conference—attendees paid their own hotel and plane fare and were issued customary visitor's passes.

Microsoft hosts dozens if not hundreds of business and family visitors on any given day. Thirty or so representatives from the computer-game industry would hardly have caught anyone's notice.

Design reviews are techno show-and-tell sessions, often thrown together using video and other visual sleight of hand rather than using real code. They're meant to show the possibility of a technology, not necessarily the technology itself. On the eve of the review, the stress of the self-imposed deadline and fatigue conspired against the trio, who stayed up until three o'clock that morning, readying their PowerPoint slide presentation. In the predawn hours—a time when stupidity often is mistaken for inspiration—they thought it would be hilarious if each computerized slide were a different shade of radiation green, Day-Glo orange, fuchsia, and whatever other obnoxious hue came to their weary heads. By the harsh light of day, however, the hilarity of the idea was somehow lost.

"No one thought it was hilarious," Engstrom says, shaking his head.

Developers did, however, like the idea of technology that would make it easy to write games that would run well on Windows. They also liked the giveaway black MANHATTAN PROJECT T-shirts with the mushroom-shaped cloud logo and slogan, "Shall we play a game?" The slogan came from the Matthew Broderick movie *WarGames,* where a Department of Defense computer runs amok and nearly launches global thermonuclear war.

Eisler, Engstrom, and St. John had as yet no actual code written for their new technology. But they did have a road map outlining a plan of attack. After the design review, the three embarked on their five-pronged assault—a suite of application programming interfaces designed not only to improve game performance on Windows, but to simplify the task of writing games for Microsoft's flagship operating system. The arsenal—a series of application programming interfaces that communicated between the operating system and hardware—included DirectDraw for faster video playback; DirectInput for swifter joystick control, DirectPlay for playing games with others over a network such as the Internet, and DirectSound for better playback of prerecorded sounds. Later they would add the most controversial of the bunch, Direct3D, the RenderMorphics 3-D engine to make games more lifelike. Others inside Microsoft's Windows NT group were championing another type of 3-D engine—OpenGL—triggering an internal power struggle that eventually fueled a near-religious battle in the gaming community.

Similarly, DirectDraw would compete with DCI, the joint Microsoft/Intel technology for enhancing video performance. DirectDraw allowed game developers to exploit all the capabilities of a computer's video card, the little circuit board that controls high-resolution imaging, mapping textures on objects, and high-speed animation. DirectDraw gave developers access to this digital treasure without having to configure extra code for all the multitude of different video cards on the market.

DirectInput was derivative of the work Eisler had done on fixing joystick support for Windows. A computer system that won't accommodate a joystick is virtually useless for many games. Under DOS, then the standard computer-game platform, developers had to write code addressing every brand of joystick on the market. Again, DirectInput freed game programmers from this drudgery.

DirectPlay was the answer to the game community's plea for better support for multiplayer games. It took care of all the digital bookkeeping and connections tasks, so game programmers didn't have to write code for network or modem play. It also let players enter and leave multiplayer games in progress without crashing the game for others—a problem with DOS because of all the various compatibility issues.

DirectSound was similar to DirectDraw in that it allowed programmers deep access to all the capabilities available on the myriad sound cards on the market.

The significance of the trio's assault cannot be understated. Microsoft would be trying to move the entire PC-using world off of DOS and primitive versions of Windows and onto Windows 95. Eisler, Engstrom, and St. John were working on a plan that would give game developers and a vast segment of computer users reasons to buy into Windows 95.

The three decided on the "Direct" monikers because their technology would give programmers a standard way to write Windows games directly to hardware such as video and sound cards. A trade-press wag, amused by all the references to "Direct," later called the collection of APIs Direct "X," the variable suffix used in the computer industry to connote a future, indeterminable software update.

"They made fun of us, calling it the 'DirectX APIs,'" Eisler recalls. "We liked that, so we took it."

The DirectX campaign would become so successful that Microsoft marketers later wanted to use the name for a whole raft of new multimedia APIs other groups built. Eisler, Engstrom, and St. John bristled at the idea of having their technology co-opted and encouraged the company to come up with another branding campaign. Thus the "ActiveX" APIs were born.

"We always joked that 'ActiveX' meant all the crap that wasn't worthy of being called 'DirectX,'" Engstrom says.

Eisler, whose superfast reflexes had earned him the nickname Twitchy, was in charge of the unglamorous but crucial heavy-lifting job of coding, which he did mostly in the computer language C and some assembly language. Engstrom was the program manager, who drew up specifications of what should be included in DirectX, made sure Eisler had enough bodies and resources, and later, explained to managers what he and his two companions had schemed. St. John was the face man, the guy who would pitch the technology to the game-development community and the press. While St. John's job was primarily marketing, he played a key role early on in the development of the technology. Several APIs were developed by programmers under St. John at Developer Relations Group. As these aspects of the project grew, St. John moved them to the Systems group, where they came under Engstrom's control. St. John also supervised the teams that wrote the first games for Windows 95.

Eisler, Engstrom, and St. John soon realized they needed more developers to help build the technology, but weren't given authorization by Osborne. They had grown to dislike Osborne and didn't bother telling him what they were hatching. Segal, the director of multimedia evangelism at Developer Relations Group, helped route one or two programmers through DRG, but soon declined to help further.

"Segal told me, 'If you want something, don't ask, 'cause the answer will be no. Just do it and don't ask,' " St. John says. "So we would just hire contractors or commandeer developers we didn't have permission to talk to and convince them to make stuff for us and then hope they didn't get fired by the time their reviews came up. We'd already built much of [DirectX] with nobody's permission."

St. John would take full advantage of the freedom bestowed on evangelists and quietly funneled $1.7 million of Developer Relations Group money to pay for developers' salaries that managers in the Systems group refused to authorize.

The first version of DirectX was by seven contractors, a couple of full-timers brave enough to venture into the fray, and Eisler, who did the lion's share of coding. Later, about sixty programmers, many of whom were outside contractors, helped build second and third generations of DirectX. Some of those pressed into service worked near St. John in Building 12.

"I housed a number of contractors for Eric because it was easier to do from DRG," St. John says.

Others were stationed near Engstrom and Eisler inside Building 4. They later would move to Building 27, and eventually settle in Building 30, a three-story, brick-and-glass box located away from the center of the Microsoft metropolis. More than one hundred programmers would eventually be assigned to DirectX. But that would be years away. What mattered most in the beginning was producing working code, and Eisler, Engstrom, and St. John confronted a demanding deadline.

Eisler began coding on the Manhattan Project on December 24, 1994. It seemed perfectly natural for him to begin the biggest project of his career on Christmas Eve. He had, after all, just four months to finish the task. The three had promised game developers that Microsoft would hand out beta or test versions of the technology at the Computer Game Developers Conference in Santa Clara, California, the third week of April 1995. The technology would be packaged in what's known as a software development kit, or SDK for short, a collection of tools to build other technology—in this case games. Microsoft had still not authorized the Manhattan Project. Moreover, St. John had not even arranged for floor space or speaking times with conference officials in Santa Clara. And the sands of the hourglass were slipping.

"I had no clue how any of it would get done by April," Eisler says. "Every day I'd say, 'I'm so fucked, I'm so fucked,' and just write more code."

Engstrom and St. John say it may not have been so dire. Eisler usually regarded (and described) everything as an impossible problem, if only to ensure that his colleagues were duly impressed when he solved it.

As he feverishly coded, his concentration was broken one day in February 1995 when Segal burst in and told him they had to go pay an unannounced visit to Bill Gates.

Gates was huddled in his war room with his team of legal advisers and senior executives, plotting how to return fire against Apple, which had just filed another lawsuit against the Redmond company. On February 9, Apple accused Microsoft and Intel of stealing code from QuickTime, Apple's popular program that plays small movies on a computer, and using it in Video for Windows and DCI, the joint Microsoft/Intel project Eisler had been called on to help fix several weeks prior. It's worth noting that Apple controlled just 8.6 percent of the global personal computer market at the time, while IBM "clones" loaded with Microsoft software dominated 80 percent. One of Apple's core strengths was multimedia. Apple was seeking an injunction to prevent Microsoft from shipping *any* products with DCI, a not-so-veiled ploy to hobble the launch of Windows 95.

"We cannot and will not stand by and watch the fruits of our research and development efforts being plundered, and our hard-fought advances in the marketplace being unfairly undermined," fumed David Nagel, senior vice president and general manager of AppleSoft, an Apple subsidiary.

Tim Bajarin, president of Creative Strategies, a market research and consulting firm based in Santa Clara, expressed the opinion of many of the techno-pundits: "This could pull the wind out of Windows 95."

This was the second time Apple had accused Microsoft of stealing. In March 1988, three years after Microsoft had rolled out its first version of Windows, Apple's then-CEO John Sculley authorized the filing of an eleven-page lawsuit against the Redmond company for allegedly pilfering the "look and feel" of Apple's graphical user interface. Both lawsuits eventually proved fruitless for Apple. Nonetheless, they managed to frustrate Gates and distract everyone at Microsoft involved with the projects that were under fire.

Four days after filing the DCI suit, Apple executives sent a damaging thirty-six-page letter to federal judge Stanley Sporkin, on the eve of his decision whether to negate a tentative antitrust settlement between the Justice Department and Microsoft. The Justice Department, spurred on by Microsoft competitors, had accused the company of malevolent monopolistic business practices, such as courting would-be software partners only to jilt them after peeking at their code and quickly developing a similar product. In fact, exactly a year prior to this, a federal jury had concluded that Microsoft had wrongfully incorporated data-compression technology into DOS 6.0. Microsoft had failed to win licensing rights for the technology from tiny San Diego–based Stac Inc. Microsoft plugged the technology into its then-newest operating system anyway. Stac sued. The jury awarded Stac more than $100 million.

The letter to Sporkin stated Gates had made a "thinly veiled" threat to stop producing software for the Macintosh unless Apple dropped its look-and-feel copyright lawsuit against the Redmond company and discontinued development of software that competed with Microsoft's. The letter had its intended effect. Rather than kill the case, the judge kept the antitrust probe alive.

The mood inside Gates's chamber was as foul as the swollen Northwest skies when Segal and Eisler barged into the room. Gates had been formulating his counterattack to the DCI lawsuit when Segal and Eisler interrupted. Eisler had never met Gates before and his timing couldn't have been worse.

Segal knew Microsoft had never filched code from QuickTime and thought that the company should offer blanket legal protection for software developers who were writing DCI programs for Windows. Segal needed Gates's signature on a letter to indemnify the developers from potential legal harm by Apple. Eisler, because he had worked on fixing DCI, was in tow to provide technical support for Segal. Indeed, Eisler knew for certain DCI didn't contain Apple programming—he thought Intel's work was so bad that he had rewritten virtually every line of DCI code.

"We're pretty busy here," Gates said when Segal and Eisler bounded into the room. "What is it?"

Segal apologized for interrupting, but insisted that the letter of indemnification needed to go out that day.

"We did not recycle *any* QuickTime code," Segal says. "This was one of those rare times where we were clean."

Gates, who would rather fight than flee, signed the letter. Soon afterward he penned a letter of his own to Apple's then–chief executive, Michael Spindler, and faxed it to newspapers and magazines. In it, Gates called Spindler a liar.

"I am writing to make it clear how disappointed I am in the lack of candor and honesty Apple has shown in dealing with Microsoft during the last several months," Gates wrote. "I feel more straightforward communication from Apple to Microsoft is called for."

Apple relented and dropped the DCI lawsuit in October—two months after the release of Windows 95. Microsoft readily agreed not to use any of the disputed code. By then Eisler's fine-tuning had rendered it obsolete.

"Gates was pissed because he knew what Apple was doing," Segal says.

Eisler mostly watched during that February war-room encounter, as Gates ranted in his tinny voice about countersuing.

"That's when I first met Bill," recalls Eisler. "Over Apple suing us over fucking DCI. It was, um, unpleasant."

But Eisler didn't allow the DCI lawsuit to distract him from his primary goal: DirectX. The project was not only destined to change the computer-game industry, it also reinforced the bond among Eisler, Engstrom, and St. John, who were becoming inseparable. When they weren't spending hundred-hour weeks at work, they were lifting weights in the mornings at the Pro Club. Emboldened by their near-religious crusade to kill DOS games, coupled with pressure of the April DirectX deadline, the three developed a savage brashness in the corridors of Microsoft. They were on a mission, and those in the trenches who questioned their ideas were dismissed as clueless and hit with the mantra "Computer games represent a five-billion-dollar market. Five *billion* dollars."

Heidi "Brussels Sprouts" Breslauer, the Microsoft program manager, left her position in the multimedia group in February 1995. Steve Banfield, a former NCR Corp. programmer and Microsoft technical evangelist, took her place. St. John had urged him to take the position, hoping he would be a willing ally. Despite the upward career move, it would not be a good year for Banfield. Not long after joining multimedia, he and other managers in the group were called before Vice President Brad Silverberg, who blamed them for delaying Windows 95. Silverberg fumed that the group had failed to fix compatibility problems and that older DOS titles wouldn't run on the new operating system.

"His message was pretty clear: 'You guys suck. We're pissed off and I'm going to take it out on you,' " Banfield says. "Then he said, 'Oh, yeah, Steve, welcome to the team.' I was a little worried what I had dumped myself into."

It would get worse.

Banfield's mother died of cancer. His sister died suddenly of heart failure. Before the deaths he had looked forward to working on Windows 95, but was instead called to help deal with the lawsuit Apple had filed over DCI.

Oh, and he was also in charge of supervising Engstrom.

The Apple lawsuit distracted Banfield from establishing control over his new charges. Banfield was one of the first, but by no means the only, program manager to have trouble with Engstrom. Engstrom and his two friends did not respond well to authority, especially if it interfered with the Manhattan Project. Gates was trying to ship Windows 95, at the time the most important product in company history, but Eisler, Engstrom, and St. John had their own agenda. Banfield says he sometimes ordered them to fix a certain problem with Windows 95 only to be met with mumbled obscenities about what a "piece of shit" Windows was.

"They didn't care who they pissed off. They figured they were on a mission from God," Banfield says. "You were either with them or you were an infidel.

"Nobody in multimedia liked these guys," he adds. "They had this attitude that all the other multimedia guys couldn't design their way out of a paper bag, that they all sucked. They were not shy about telling someone to his face, 'You're an idiot.' "

Gates is blunt with people and isn't afraid to tell his employees, "That's the dumbest idea I've ever heard." But Eisler, Engstrom, and St. John, for all their considerable brainpower, are not Bill Gates. Fellow Microsoft employees, understandably, resented their brutal candor.

"A lot of times I felt a large part of my job was walking behind Eric with a dustpan," Banfield says. "He was like a bull in a china shop. He'd go busting in and I'd have to clean things up."

Many resented a condescending mannerism they all shared of squinting while bringing their forefinger and thumb to their forehead, as if struggling to make themselves understood by inferior beings. This was followed by an exaggerated gesture, ripping their hand away from their head to emphasize the point they were trying to make.

"It was almost like they were pulling a piece of their brain out and they were going to hand it to you," recalls Banfield. "Like they were saying, 'You know, you're just so stupid, I'm going to give you a piece of my brain.' "

Some referred to the trio as the Multimedia Mafia. Others called them the Beastie Boys, a name that stuck.

Eisler, Engstrom, and St. John did not corner the market on bluntness at Microsoft—they merely took it to an extreme.

"There's blunt and there's brutally blunt with a little contempt and arrogance thrown in," St. John explains. "We improved . . . over time, but not before bruising a lot of people."

In a company where titles often don't mean as much as credibility, being blunt is a way to establish dominance. The company was rife with pecking-order gamesmanship, such as not answering E-mail or chronically arriving late to meetings.

"The dominance game was to be the last one to walk into a meeting, tell everyone what you've decided, and claim you have to run to something more important," St. John says. "It was used by all the executives and emulated by the underlings."

Eisler, Engstrom, and St. John acknowledge today that their behavior was barbaric, but they offer no apologies. St. John laughs when reminded he used to plod through the hallways with a plastic battle-ax, his unkempt reddish beard and his three-hundred-pound bulk adding a certain primitive menace.

Yet the three maintain that nobody outside Developer Relations Group suspected they were close friends. They believed that by masquerading as enemies, their real enemies inside the Systems group would reveal themselves. The three believed they would be able to advance DirectX and their careers by surreptitiously gathering information from identified adversaries.

"A lot of people didn't know how good of friends we were, so they would piss and moan about the other guy to one of us," says Eisler.

"We would play up that we didn't get along. People really didn't get it. People still don't get it. It's very powerful to have that perception that we didn't like each other because people would spill their guts to one of us.

The three even scripted mock arguments as a means to manipulate managers.

"We'd agree to disagree vehemently on the things that didn't matter, then we'd 'spontaneously' unify, but with great contempt, over the three things we originally set out to do," says St. John. "We'd get together the night before and plan all this out. To make peace, [managers] would agree to the issues where we had found 'common ground.' "

St. John says this subterfuge was necessary because they faced resistance to their Manhattan Project. There wasn't a burning desire to drastically change course at the multimedia group, says St. John. With Osborne in "rest and vest mode" and the company focused on Windows 95, there was little incentive to spend even more hours and effort creating new technology, especially if it meant helping the Beastie Boys.

"The company has a very narrow focus on its profitable business. . . . I'm not saying that's bad," says St. John. "But it does preclude you from doing any dramatic thinking, doing any dramatic innovation.

"We'd come and say, 'Here's the right thing to do,' and no, it wouldn't happen," he adds. "If no is not an acceptable answer to you, then what do you do next? We just wanted to make cool technology."

Banfield, Segal, and others familiar with the situation shake their heads at the notion nobody knew the Beastie Boys were buddies.

"They had this delusional belief that they threw up this huge matrix where everybody believed they were enemies," says Segal, laughing. "The real trick is to find somebody in the company that didn't know this was going on. If you find that person, let human resources know, because they're stupid and should be fired."

Banfield, a Kentuckian who possesses his own matter-of-fact,

Southern bluntness, concurs. "The idea that they didn't like each other . . . and that no one was any the wiser, I think, is horseshit."

During development of DirectX, Eisler had moved out of Building 40 and into another nearby office where he could code without distraction. But his absence from multimedia group's headquarters led Osborne to give Eisler a relatively poor performance review. Engstrom received a better review, despite the fact that Eisler was doing most of the work on the innovative game technology. Eisler threatened to quit. Engstrom, out of loyalty, made the same threat.

"Because of the nature of what I did, I was always in Paul's office, going over specs," Engstrom says. "He didn't have a lot of contact with Craig. Paul was almost impossible to work for."

The Beastie Boys, nerd warriors whose naked ambitions were matched only by their IQs and egos, were raising hell in the halls of Redmond. Banfield says the only reason they didn't get fired then was because too many game companies were making business plans in anticipation of the Manhattan Project. Without Eisler, Engstrom, and St. John, the project couldn't get finished, thus making them virtually impervious. Or so they thought.

Weeks before the Computer Game Developers Conference in April, Microsoft vice president Brad Silverberg hauled Engstrom and Eisler into his office and angrily demanded to know why everyone was complaining about their behavior, why they couldn't get along with anybody, and why they wasted so much money on this thing indelicately called the Manhattan Project.

"You could cease to exist at Microsoft tomorrow," Silverberg railed at them.

Eisler, Engstrom, and St. John say that, up to then, it was the closest they had come to getting fired at Microsoft.

Moreover, Silverberg declared he was killing the name Manhattan Project and didn't buy Eisler's explanation that "the Manhattan Project changed the world, for good or bad—and we really like nuclear explosions."

Perhaps. But the Japanese had a huge presence in the game industry. An unamused Silverberg worried that computer-industry leaders there would take offense to naming technology after the World War II project that had rained nuclear terror on their nation. Some also worried that protesters might picket the company.

Silverberg suggested that the trio call their collective technology by the less incendiary name Windows Multimedia.

"We didn't want to call it Windows Multimedia because we all knew what people thought of Microsoft's multimedia," says Eisler. "Brad, to his credit, listened to us. He didn't like it, but we ended up calling it a game SDK [software development kit]."

Much later they also reached a compromise on the logo, eventually replacing the mushroom-shaped cloud with a variation of a radiation symbol.

"Brad came to appreciate our sense of humor," Eisler says.

Soon after the showdown in Silverberg's office, Engstrom returned to demonstrate the game Super Bubsy running on Windows 95. The computer screen filled with fast-motion, high-resolution characters bopping around a 3-D environment. Nothing like it had ever been seen on a Windows 95 prototype.

"Silverberg nearly fell out of his chair and said, 'Oh my God. Whatever that is, I want Windows to do more of that,' " Engstrom recalls. Silverberg became an instant champion of the new technology "and all the hard work really was over," Engstrom adds.

Eisler received an improved review. The Beastie Boys went back to work. But the session with Silverberg did nothing to change their attack-dog ways. Shortly before the Computer Game Developers Conference—DirectX's coming-out party—the Beastie Boys leaked details of DirectX to *PCWeek* magazine, which referred to the code name Manhattan Project. The leak is a time-honored way of manipulating the press. It inflates a reporter's sense of self-importance and lust for exclusivity, while serving the self-interest of the source. St. John soon became a master at the well-timed, self-serving leak.

Brad Chase, Microsoft's top marketing executive, was enraged and fired off memos expressing his displeasure. St. John leaked that as well. As a result, members of the trade press and game developers came to regard DirectX as a maverick skunk works that was defying the Empire.

"This trick worked for us on many levels because it made using Microsoft technology 'cool' among developers for the first time, and it lit a fire under the PR department's butt to clean up the mess I'd created for them with the press," St. John says. "Our management just thought we were nerds with no clue about the media and that it was all PR's fault. We could always count on being underestimated."

By sidestepping official Microsoft PR channels and arranging for DirectX to be splashed in the pages of one of the industry's leading trade publications, St. John was buying additional insurance that Microsoft wouldn't kill the project—not that there was any evidence the company wanted to do so at this late stage. St. John calls this technique "tar babying" the technology.

" 'Tar baby' means you have to get Microsoft stuck to it so that they can't ungum themselves from it," St. John explains. "If it's not public, you can kill it. If it becomes public, and you have Microsoft committed to it on record, Microsoft executives get glued to the technology."

Banfield almost came unglued when he read the article.

" 'Manhattan Project' was never supposed to have gotten outside the company," Banfield says. "Eric Engstrom, Craig Eisler, and Alex took great joy in getting that name out there. I thought they were being stupid for stupid's sake. There's something to be said for flying the pirate flag as a motivational technique. And then there's something to be said for walking too close to the edge and getting killed."

St. John had encouraged Banfield to take the supervisor's job at multimedia with the expectation he would serve the Beastie Boy cause. That plan backfired miserably. Banfield had grown tired of cleaning up after Engstrom's explosions with coworkers and confided in St. John that he was considering firing Engstrom. St. John informed Engstrom, hoping his friend would change his ways and conduct himself more diplomatically. Instead, Engstrom confronted Banfield, blasting him for unprofessional gossiping.

Another interesting subplot had developed. As the games evangelist and cocreator of DirectX, St. John influenced the quiet asphyxiation of WinG, Hecker's project that allowed games to work better on Windows 3.1 and the very technology Microsoft had trumpeted for Windows 95. True, WinG was almost experimental technology and had limitations. But WinG also showed promise. Games such as WinDoom, Freddi Fish, King's Quest VII, and Jump Raven used WinG. Yet with Engstrom and Eisler driving DirectX and St. John wielding the evangelical megaphone, WinG eventually faded into oblivion, as did its embattled counterpart, DCI, the Microsoft/Intel venture to boost digital video playback.

"Hecker had annoyed us to the extent that, like the Egyptians did to hated pharaohs, we set out to erase his cartouche from the tombs," St. John says.

It should be noted that Intel's experimenting with multimedia didn't die with DCI. Intel, desperate for the software industry to develop applications that forced consumers to upgrade to faster computers and frustrated with Microsoft's efforts in this regard, embarked on developing something called Native Signal Processing, a central-processing-unit chip that could run game animation. It was being engineered to replace video, sound cards, and 3-D rendering—which threatened not only makers of those types of hardware, but the as-yet-unborn DirectX technology. Native Signal Processing, or NSP, highlighted the uncomfortable symbiosis between Microsoft and Intel. St. John and others likened the relationship between the companies to two escaped convicts shackled at the ankles—they made okay progress when running in stride, but stumbled when one suddenly bolted in another direction.

Intel had invited Engstrom and Microsoft colleagues Carl Stork and Marshall Brumer to a Windows and Hardware Engineers Conference held just prior to the computer-game trade show. Intel wanted the Empire to see how aggressively it was promoting NSP, which triggered the "Cuban missile crisis" of multimedia between the two companies, illustrated by the following internal Intel E-mail.

From: Gerald S Holzhammer

[Gerald_S_Holzhammer@ccm.jf.intel.com]

Sent: Thursday, April 13, 1995 2:40 AM

To:. . . Claude_M_Leglise@ccm.sc.intel.com;Bill_R_Miller@ccm
11.sc.intel.com;Robert_Sullivan@ccm11.sc.intel.com;Ronald_J_
Whittier@ccm11.sc.intel.com;Craig_Kinnie@ccm.jf.intel.com;
mcg@ibeam.intel.com;Ken_Rhodes@ccm.jf.intel.com;Murali_
Veeramoney@ccm.jf.intel.com;Joe_Casey@ccm11.sc.intel.com;
Frank_T_Ehrig@ccm.sc.intel.com

Subject: Microsoft Face to Face Summary

Text item: Text_1

Bottom-Line:

—Based on W95 experience MS finds that they need to
own all drivers

—Expect no real cooperation from MS on NSP or media;
input/education is welcome, of course

—At Games developer's conference focus on "Design scal-
able games for Pentium" message; DON'T make a half-hearted
attempt to push Native audio without a compelling ISV story
(current POR). MS messages are tuned for this audience;
we'd come across defensive at best

—Bill, let's do the Native Audio press release before [Game
Developers Conference]; it won't harm our MS relationship:-)

Details:

We met with Carl Stork, Marshall Brumer, and Eric Engstrom
for 3 hours. WinHEC clearly opened their eyes regarding the
scope of NSP. They are upset with us being in "their" OS
space—no surprise there. Interestingly, they have evolved
their thinking on what their "space" needs to be.

. . . A recurring theme was that nobody but MS is qualified
to do good driver [software]. In their mind, [Windows 95] was
delayed 9 months by 3rd party driver dependence.

. . . Stork openly admitted that MS has completely missed the boat on developing a compelling state of the art media subsystem for Windows95.

. . . I don't expect MS to openly attack NSP at the [Game Developers Conference], BUT their thrust is clearly counter NSP. . . .

Not only would NSP have usurped multimedia from Microsoft, "it was also a really bad idea because it would run [games] about as fast as a manatee on tranquilizers," St. John says.

Ironically, Intel's NSP project fueled Microsoft management support for DirectX. Microsoft dispatched evangelists and executives to dissuade Intel from developing NSP, explaining it duplicated many features of DirectX.

"It was a weird sort of 'competition,'" says St. John, "because Intel was more than happy in some respects to finally have Microsoft devoting so much attention to multimedia, even if it was to crush their own NSP initiative."

Meanwhile, St. John went about quashing a Microsoft marketing effort to have the Beastie Boys' game-software developer kit renamed WinG 2.0. Walt Disney Co. saw its foray into computer games blow up in its face when they released the infamous Lion King CD-ROM game for Christmas '94. Compaq had shipped computers containing an untested driver with WinG, which didn't run the game and left legions of children sobbing on Christmas Day. Tens of thousands of angry parents demanded to know what was wrong. Disney was unprepared for the wave of consumer angst.

"I had mixed feelings about it," St. John says. "I wanted to have game companies be successful, but at the same time I was happy to be proven right about WinG's inadequacy. I used the Lion King incident to kill changing the name of our technology to WinG 2.0."

Microsoft—rather St. John—spared no expense hyping DirectX at the Computer Game Developers Conference that spring, despite the fact conference officials tried to block Microsoft's presence. Event officials initially declined to provide time for Microsoft speakers, or suite space for seminars and demonstrations, St. John says. CGDC officials finally relented and gave the company a small demonstration suite and some time at the rostrum when St. John threatened to "commandeer" the event with the full weight of Microsoft marketing money.

St. John launched a full assault. The CGDC staff, realizing their mistake, relented and offered to be more accommodating. But by that time it was too late to recall the missiles.

"My job was to see DirectX launched successfully," St. John says. "I concluded that if we set up a session or a suite at the conference itself, no one would come. Microsoft would have to do something so spectacular that it couldn't be ignored."

St. John used Microsoft's checkbook to rent out Paramount's Great America theme park across the street from the CGDC the day after the official conference ended. St. John used the official conference as a marketing platform for his own show, passing out invitations, hanging banners, the works. The seminar and party were collectively dubbed Ground Zero, in keeping with DirectX's original theme of nuclear war. Most everyone who attended the conference stayed for the DirectX show on Bill Gates's tab. And it was quite a show, both onstage and behind the scenes.

During the CGDC, Eisler and Engstrom engaged in a shouting match with St. John because he had set up demonstrations of WinG and other multimedia technologies in addition to DirectX. Eisler and Engstrom thought St. John diluted their technology's impact by having it wedged in with other demos. St. John explained there weren't enough DirectX tools and demos to fill the room and he needed the other stuff for padding.

Eisler and Engstrom were not on speaking terms with St. John the day they stepped onstage at Great America's thousand-seat amphitheater for DirectX's official public demonstration. They both wore lab coats for theater, mad-scientist props in keeping with the Manhattan Project roots. As Engstrom began explaining the concept of DirectX to the game developers, the crowd started chanting, "DOS, DOS, DOS." Engstrom tried to talk over the chant, but it was useless.

As the din reached a crescendo, Engstrom bellowed, "This is what DirectX can do for you!" He stopped speaking. On cue, Eisler pushed up the acceleration on the Super Bubsy demo running on Windows 95. The game whirred at eighty-three frames per second—faster than the motion picture standard of twenty-four frames per second. DirectX did to the gamers what it had done to Microsoft vice president Brad Silverberg. There was an audible, collective gasp from the crowd, then stunned silence.

6

BEYOND GROUND ZERO

After the demo, the Beastie Boys sat with their legs dangling off the edge of the Great America stage as a crowd of newly converted developers converged to ask about DirectX. Engstrom directed a crush of marketing questions to St. John; St. John referred technical inquiries to Eisler; if there was something Eisler couldn't answer, he pointed people to Engstrom. All three handed out black T-shirts and free beta copies of the DirectX software development kit on CD-ROMs—pressed just hours before the event. Not only had Ground Zero been a success for DirectX, it was cathartic for the trio, who were again on high-fiving terms. Eisler and Engstrom, impressed with the turnout, forgave St. John. When the crowd began to thin, the Beastie Boys climbed aboard a roller coaster and craned to see the fireworks display St. John had slipped into the event's budget. After the celebration, the three returned to Redmond to finish what they had started.

Eisler continued his mad-paced coding. Engstrom continued rounding up internal support and kept the project focused. St. John schemed ways to promote what was becoming a press darling. While most of the world's media focused on the long-overdue arrival of Windows 95 and its attendant business applications, numerous anticipatory articles about DirectX emerged. Gates helped fuel this interest when he announced that Microsoft would build its own 3-D action and adventure games in partnership with Dreamworks, the Spielberg/Geffen/Katzenberg Hollywood studio.

"Win95 will be a watershed for multimedia," gushed *PCWeek* in June 1995. "Millions of households that previously bought video-game consoles will buy Windows 95 PCs instead."

That same month *Computer Gaming World* wrote that it had tested beta versions of DirectX 1.0 and Windows 95. The verdict?

"Windows 95 has incredible potential—for good and bad—but three months before the announced August release, it looks as if the chips will fall on the side of the good. Of course, if things do not shape up the way Microsoft hopes they will, we will have the same kind of muddled confusion that prevails in software today. But if things do happen according to plan, gaming could have its next hot new gaming platform."

Not bad PR for the Beastie Boys.

"Ultimately, where all the power came from was talking to developers and making what they felt they wanted," says Engstrom. "But there was a spin to that. We gave them what they wanted on our terms."

More good news for the company as a whole was in the offing. At an August 21 hearing, three days before the launch of Windows 95, U.S. district court judge Thomas Penfield Jackson declared an end to the Justice Department's five-year probe of Microsoft. Jackson signed a now-famous consent decree, settled in 1994 but delayed while previous presiding federal judge, Stanley Sporkin, whipsawed Justice to find more dirt on the company. An appeals court removed Sporkin from the case after it determined he had overstepped his legal authority.

Under the consent decree, Microsoft agreed to end its practice of charging computer makers licensing fees even if their machines weren't loaded with Microsoft software. The decree, which had a life span of six and a half years, also prevented Microsoft from requiring vendors to sign contracts lasting up to five years. Instead, Microsoft was to have one-year contracts with its vendors. The decree did not specifically address Windows NT—the industrial-strength operating system Microsoft would use to crack the corporate computing market. But the government noted in the decree that "successor versions of or products marketed as replacements" to Windows could be targeted later.

Many in the industry—including a consortium of competitors who wanted Justice to include NT—saw the decree as a mere slap on the wrist because it didn't prohibit Microsoft from bundling its Microsoft Network software with Windows. Microsoft Network, or MSN, was Microsoft's on-line service. Rivals such as America Online complained that this gave Microsoft an unfair edge because of its market dominance with operating systems—an argument that proved groundless. Microsoft Network never really challenged the dominance of AOL as an Internet service provider. Nonetheless, the government said it would keep constant vigil on Microsoft and monitor what the company plugged into its operating systems.

Windows 95 finally launched August 24, 1995, with all the global hype $100 million can buy. Microsoft reportedly paid $12 million to Mick Jagger and Keith Richards so the company could use the Rolling Stones' pop hit "Start Me Up" as Windows 95's official theme song. When Microsoft first approached Jagger with the request, he reportedly quoted a ludicrous amount of money thinking Microsoft would turn him down. But to his surprise, Gates opened the company's checkbook without hesitation.

Gates hired Jay Leno to stand onstage with him under a big white tent at the Redmond campus as the two demonstrated the new operating system. "He's not necessarily so different from the rest of us," Leno quipped of his host. "I went into his den last night and his VCR is still flashing 12:00."

The company also benefited from free publicity. The *Wall Street Journal* reported there were more than sixty-five hundred newspaper stories about the operating system just in the two months prior to the official launch date, and there had to have been at least that many television and radio features. Computer stores around the world opened at midnight on the twenty-fourth to exploit consumer hunger for an operating system that was about two years late, was bloated with more code than the software used to run the space shuttle, and was, by many accounts, inferior to Apple's operating system. Apple, although eclipsed by Microsoft in so many ways, didn't miss an opportunity to throw a wet blanket over Windows launch day. Apple placed a billboard near Microsoft's headquarters that read, "C: 1/4ONGRTLNS.W95," a nerdy insult of the technical limitations that plague file names in Microsoft programs.

For all the hype about Win95's multimedia capabilities, DirectX wasn't included with the operating system's initial release—for the simple reason it wasn't designed to be tied to the OS.

"DirectX was built to be parasitic," St. John explains. "It was carried around in games, not the operating system. We didn't have the support in the company to tie it to the OS."

No wonder. The Beastie Boys initially enjoyed more support from outside game developers than they did from many people inside Microsoft. Eisler, Engstrom, and St. John committed the sin of designing software without consulting or working in concert with established players who had created the innards of Windows.

"There were guys who designed the Win95 kernel and guys who worked on the core guts of WinNT and there were people in Microsoft who have been around awhile and their word on technical matters is pretty much gold," says Banfield. "If you come up with new technology, you better run it past these guys and they better give their blessing.

"[The Beastie Boys] had their own development process," he adds. "They decided they were going to be incompatible with anything done in the past. If there was a new idea that no one tried, they were putting it in there at the last minute. In terms of decorum, they broke every rule in the book."

That they created new gaming technology without collaborating with the masters of Windows is testimony not only to the arrogance of the Beastie Boys, but also to their brilliance.

Yet their success came at the price of alienating or offending many within the company, which did nothing to encourage collaboration with other groups working on multimedia or to help lead to a more cohesive multimedia strategy.

Meanwhile, the staggered release of DirectX angered and confused some in the industry. Video board manufacturers such as ATI Technologies Inc., Matrox, and Diamond had adopted DCI and made hundreds of thousands of DCI-enabled products, only to have Microsoft replace DCI with DirectDraw, one of the components of DirectX. The switch echoed the OS/2 debacle. Microsoft had declared that video board makers should design their products to work with DCI. Even the *Windows 95 Hardware Design Guide*, published by Microsoft Press, stated that when using DCI drivers, video cards running Windows 95 "will enhance playing back video or Windows 95–based games."

The Beastie Boys changed the rules. Although DirectDraw eventually proved better than DCI at improving video playback, many consumers had purchased video cards that were useless until DirectX shipped. Fred Dunne of Jon Peddie Associates, author of the *PC Graphics Report*, said, "Microsoft went around preaching that DCI is life itself—now it's dead. Now they are saying DirectDraw is life itself. [These next] few months are going to be confusing."

Dunne noted, "As multimedia manufacturers and game developers wait in limbo until DirectDraw is finalized, they're afraid of hurting Christmas sales. . . . Board manufacturers are miffed at being held hostage until DirectDraw ships."

Still another trade publication said, "The reason behind the removal of DCI from Windows 95 is still a mystery."

No mystery at all. The Beastie Boys killed DCI because of the Apple lawsuit and because DCI was inherently unstable.

Engstrom says at no time did Microsoft say shipment of DirectX would coincide with the launch of Windows 95.

"We shipped right on schedule. Well, six weeks late," he says. "When we shipped it, we were clacking our mugs in the hall, until we read the article that said the SDK guys were so slow they had to be pushed out of Windows 95. We were never part of Windows 95."

The Beastie Boys and their pack of developers did more than clack celebratory mugs. They initiated a Chinese food fight of epic proportions, nearly blinding one of the software contractors with hot mustard and trashing a Microsoft conference room. Senior VP Brad Silverberg authorized the clean-up bill and sent a note to Engstrom—"I hope you guys had fun."

Microsoft released the final version of DirectX 1.0 on September 29, 1995. Within a year, the three had built the weapon that killed DOS games and would be the framework for another, even larger jihad targeting the Internet.

"Through the efforts of a few Microsoft evangelists who actually play games, Windows 95 is poised to be THE game operating system of the coming years," *Computer Gaming World* wrote that month. The magazine was a victim of St. John's evangelism, for the Beastie Boys hadn't been big game players when they had embarked on their project in late 1994. But the magazine was correct in forecasting that people would start buying Windows PCs to play computer games, severely eroding market share of the television-based Nintendo or Sega game consoles.

To fuel DirectX, St. John engineered a Halloween theme party and trade show to be held at Microsoft's Redwest campus, the domain of former consumer division senior vice president Patty Stonesifer. Although she oversaw one of the most poorly performing groups in the company, she had insisted on having one of the finest buildings on campus. Redwest reflected her arty tastes and included the palatial European Café, complete with vaulted ceiling, a man-made pond fed by a man-made stream, and the expanse trimmed with natural wood beams said to be left over from the construction of Bill Gates's $50-million techno mansion in nearby Medina. Redwest was still under construction at this time and the underground parking lot was largely unused—a perfect spot for St. John's twisted trade show. Stonesifer objected, but St. John had secured approval from his more powerful masters at Developer Relations Group. He promptly orchestrated the construction of a two-story volcano inside her glorious cafeteria and turned her building's underground parking lot into a haunted house.

Judgment Day I, the second of St. John's demented marketing extravaganzas, came complete with bowls of fake blood, fake brains, and free T-shirts proclaiming that DOS was dead. Each room of the haunted house was designed by a game company to reflect a theme from one of its upcoming titles. For example, id brought the band GWAR, a group famous for its sadomasochistic raunchiness. The bandleader wore a four-foot-long costume penis, while another member was dressed as an eight-foot-tall toothy vagina covered with penile tentacles. Mounted atop this vaginal monster was a severed head of O. J. Simpson. They were a strange sight, but it was stranger still that of the two hundred or so journalists who filed by, none wrote a word about this particularly macabre scene.

Eisler and Engstrom came dressed as demons, while St. John, naturally, played Satan. Some of the fifteen hundred invited reporters and game developers entered a chamber where their hands were bound behind their back. They were then blindfolded and forced by hooded figures to kneel before a faux guillotine.

"One way for Microsoft to get rid of the competition," quipped one attendee.

The event made local headlines. Stonesifer was not amused. After the trade show, she fired off an angry memo to Bill Gates, informing him that St. John had disrupted her building for a week preparing for Judgment Day I. What's more, she had not been invited. Gates forwarded the mail without comment to St. John, who couldn't resist a rebuttal:

"Her division bleeds so much revenue that every week I shut them down I figure I save the company money."

St. John's party paid off. More than forty video game companies were represented at the show. The year before almost no games were planned for Windows. By Judgment Day, the Beastie Boys had helped marshal more than seventy-five game titles for Christmas, 1995.

St. John's madness manifested itself again at the Computer Game Developers Conference in April 1996. Like the year before, he attached his party and DirectX conference to the CGDC, using the official event as a marketing vehicle for his own show. He had dreamed up Pax Romana, a Roman-circus theme party that managed to enrage CGDC officials, annoy Microsoft executives, and even offend some game makers.

Sponsors included Intel, ATI, IBM, and NEC. Attendees were herded into buses and driven to San Jose State University, where they were issued togas and a bag of "gold" coins and ushered into a sports arena. Awaiting them were slave girls and bodybuilders in togas and four islands in the middle of the arena overflowing with turkey drumsticks, ribs, pasta, salad, fruit—an orgy of food and drink dispensed on broad aluminum plates. Two actual lions prowled behind bars. One of the beasts inexplicably escaped, but was quickly corralled before anyone was mauled.

St. John also invited Gillian Bonner, a Playboy Playmate turned soft-porn game developer, to appear at the toga party, which included a requisite slave auction and vomitorium.

Bonner, president of Black Dragon, had just unveiled her Riana Rouge title, a cyberlove adventure game for Windows 95, where users helped a vixen-warrior conquer alien worlds. Bonner was to play Cleopatra and auction off slaves for "senators" played by corporate sponsors. St. John touched off controversy days before the event when he responded in an on-line newsgroup to someone who suggested few women would attend Pax Romana. The following rec.games.programmer newsgroup post on April 6, 1996, triggered "Bunnygate," which never got press attention but became infamous in the gaming community:

Okay, you guys, this is Alex St. John, and Jason Robar, Microsoft's entertainment evangelists, here to address an issue or two.

First off, regarding the 0.01% female attendance level at

the Toga party. This may be true but one of the 0.01% females attending may be a Playboy bunny, which should more than compensate. Anybody who has been to Ground Zero, or Judgment Day out there, should be able to attest that the events us game evangelists plan don't suck.

Last issue: Is this useful or just marketing fluff and cheerleading? The party is marketing fluff and cheerleading, but we figure the 12,000 cans of Silly String, and other stuff going on, will make it completely painless. There are 4 sponsors (ATI, IBM, Intel, and us) plus 9 game companies and hardware companies just dying to spend a bunch of money entertaining you.

The Developer event the next day is designed to be hard core, we bring the guys who build the technology to explain themselves, and us marketing fluff types provide color for them so your head doesn't explode with too much raw data. We'll be giving out the developer SDK for the internet from the PDC, beta 3 of the DirectX II SDK (including Direct3D), beta 1 of the DirectX III SDK (including DirectPlay for the internet, Direct3D Sound), plus the ActiveMovie beta SDK, and the game sampler CD. And we're going to cover all of it, plus some technologies that we're announcing, and SoftImage stuff for NT.

PS> And I'll be 14.095% funnier then last year as well.

St. John had his defenders and detractors, who flocked to the rec.games.programmer newsgroup to vent.

"Those Neanderthals," huffed Diana Gruber, a longtime game programmer and Microsoft critic. "Alex St. John said the bunny's presence 'more than compensates' for my absence. In other words, she's a babe, and I'm an arf-arf, and that's all that matters. . . . Excuse me for being more offended than I have ever been in my life."

She derided the event as "DirectBeer" and likened it to a sophomoric frat party.

Others threatened to inform Bill Gates and questioned Microsoft's social enlightenment quotient.

"This is the most disturbing aspect," fumed game developer David B. Schultz. "If St. John doesn't realize the added responsibility that comes with a high-profile job (he is, for the purposes of that forum, Microsoft), then maybe they've got the wrong guy. My worst fear is that his attitude is not an aberration, but representative of his (oh, God, I hate this term!) corporate culture."

Other developers begged their contemporaries to lighten up, noting that the beer would be on Microsoft's tab.

A smiling St. John sat back and watched the sparks fly. There was nothing like a threatened boycott to boost event registration. Still, Microsoft had demanded St. John remove Bonner from participating.

"But I maintained a high level of obstinate refusal to the point of being nearly fired, as usual, right up to the day of the party," he says.

Capitulating on the day of the event, he scrapped the Cleopatra skit and instead had Bonner auction slaves to the audience onstage. If a slave got the thumbs-down, Bonner would have centurions throw them into a "pit of lions." Slaves jumped into the pit, landed on a mattress, and were escorted back to the circus. Meanwhile, a guy stationed in the pit would throw up severed body parts and pieces of a torn toga, while a *National Geographic* video of roaring lions tearing apart an antelope played on giant screens.

In the end, St. John was sold as a slave to the women in the audience for sixteen hundred gold pieces. The women freed the slave girls who had been feeding him grapes and forced him to apologize to everyone for being a pig.

In St. John's evangelical mind, he believed he had perfectly manipulated the controversy leading up to the event. But while the bickering and threatened boycotts raged outside of Microsoft, internal outrage was escalating. Executives were growing increasingly troubled with this rogue evangelist.

"The Beastie Boys disavowed all knowledge that they had gotten [the Playmate] to show up," says Banfield, the program manager who had by now lost any semblance of control over Engstrom and Eisler. "People inside the company were saying this isn't cool, we shouldn't be involved in this sort of thing. It's the wrong sort of image.

"But these are the guys who called the thing the Manhattan Project," he adds. "They went for that shit, every day all day long."

Even Doug Henrich, one of those at Developer Relations Group who had advocated hiring St. John, questioned his methods. It seemed to Henrich and others that St. John was doing more to promote himself than Microsoft's technology.

"Those events were too extreme," Henrich says. "More extreme than they needed to be."

Yet the Beastie Boys, emboldened by their sense of prominence within the company and acceptance in the gaming community, expected and demanded more from Microsoft. After the release of DirectX 1.0, St. John received a perfect 5.0 on his semiannual review. Every six months, Microsoft employees draft a list of goals, which are usually refined by a manager. At the end of six months, managers grade their employees on a scale of one to five, based on how well they have achieved their objectives. Chief among St. John's goals was to kill DOS games and make sure none appeared in the top-ten bestseller list during a certain time. Reportedly only senior executives, if not Bill Gates himself, can sign off on a 5.0 rating because such a stellar review comes with promotions and/or large quantities of stock options.

Reviews and the company's frequent reorganizations work in an intriguing dynamic. Reorgs, as they're known, provide an opportunity for groups to unload deadwood—unproductive employees who somehow manage to hurdle Microsoft's high standards for entry. No company likes firing people; it's demoralizing for those remaining and tends to be expensive in terms of recruiting, replacement, and training costs. At Microsoft there are always power-hungry managers eager to swell their head count and so are willing to take on deadwood during reorgs. This is countered by other executives who, in the interest of appearing cooperative, are equally eager to dump their underachievers.

Microsoft managers are generally supposed to allocate reviews according to the following ratios: 25 percent get 3.0 or lower; 40 percent get 3.5; and 35 percent get 4.0 or better. Employees with too many successive 3.0 reviews are given six months to find another position in the company or face termination. A manager who is top-heavy with valuable or talented people doesn't want to be forced to give them 3.0 reviews. So these managers kept a few extra slabs of deadwood around so as to save the higher reviews for the employees they want to keep. Moreover, when a reorg occurs, these crafty managers have some padding and, when attacked by a rival, can shed some deadwood to satisfy a predatory manager's appetite.

Eisler and Engstrom didn't get a 5.0 and were envious of St. John. Moreover, Engstrom had looked over the company's official chain-of-command hierarchy—levels ranging from 1 to 15—and demanded at least double jumps up the rung, something unheard of at Microsoft. He cited his belief that he and Eisler were the best multimedia developers in Redmond, that they were moving an entire industry off DOS-based games, and that they had created brand-new technology. Eisler was at Level 12. Engstrom, who once built a robot as part of a childhood scheme to get to the moon, was at Level 11 and requested a lunar leap to 13, the pay and authority equivalent of a general manager slot and not far below vice president. Level 15 is the equivalent of a vice president and a promotion only Gates himself could authorize.

Microsoft is a development-oriented company and respects results. Great programmers, for instance, don't have to stop programming and take on administrative roles and lead teams for career advancement. Really good developers can make Level 14 or perhaps higher, get paid the equivalent of a vice president, and still do nothing but code. Engstrom was on the administrative path. True to his Viking roots, he wanted to lead people and wield power.

"[Engstrom] came in and said, 'I've done all these things. Show me why I don't deserve this,' " says Banfield. "They were told that they were getting good reviews, but they were a management nightmare and that they had to start playing nice."

Eisler and Engstrom received one-step promotions, but no big payoff of stock options.

By 1996, Banfield, tired of dealing with the cantankerous trio and emotionally depleted by the deaths of his mother and sister, left Microsoft. Engstrom, who has since mellowed and matured, occasionally has lunch with him. That can't be said for most of the other program managers who took Banfield's place. One ersatz manager who thought he could control Engstrom was On Lee.

"His entire job as near as I can figure out was to try to become my boss," Engstrom says. "He 'needed to be responsible for DirectX,' direct quote. But he never actually tried to do anything useful for it— he just wanted to be responsible for it."

Lee walked into Engstrom's office one day and asked if Engstrom would ever work for him again.

" 'Not only am I not going to work for you,' " Engstrom recalls saying, " 'if you don't start doing some work in the group, I will find a way to terminate your existence in this organization.'

"He and I are two people who have not mended our ways," Engstrom says. "We never have lunch. I can't figure what value it would add in my life. He's one of those people where you wouldn't even try to make friends with because he makes for a perfect enemy."

Engstrom often said that 70 percent of his job time was spent defending his turf. He often used fear and intimidation to ward off threats, such as the face-to-face engagement with On Lee. Engstrom also found that discrediting interlopers worked well. If one challenged Engstrom's leadership, he would take the time to shine the light of truth on that individual's feeble contributions within the company, usually to great effect. Engstrom minced no words. He rarely backed down from a fight. And if somebody criticized him, he could rest assured his own faults would quickly be brought into evidence. Engstrom usually used these blunt tactics only when subtler means had failed first.

Engstrom made enemies more easily than he tended to make friends, a legacy of his mostly solitary upbringing in Oroville and nearby Omak. Omak's claim to fame is the World Famous Suicide Race, so named because riders stampede horses off steep bluffs into the Okanogan River, in an annual rite decidedly more hazardous for horse than for man. It's a rough place. Engstrom is a product of his environment.

As a college dropout, Engstrom was at risk of falling prey to the Northwest cliché. He might have worked in the woods until an injury put him on disability and spent his days in a dead-end job and his nights in poorly lit taverns, smoking generic cigarettes and drinking Rainier beer. Fortunately for the computer industry—and perhaps unfortunately for a few inside Microsoft—Engstrom did not bow to the stereotype.

After the release of DirectX, Engstrom had reason to feel brash. He and his two friends had overtaken the gaming industry and won press accolades. And he had bought his first Porsche, a twin-turbo 911—just like Eisler's. He and Eisler had been driving similar Mazda RX-7s. Then Eisler had switched gears and one day wheeled into Engstrom's driveway to show off his black Porsche. Engstrom remarked that "it's no different than a Mazda." Eisler let him hop in for a test-drive. After a couple of hours behind the wheel of the powerful German machine, Engstrom pulled into the same Porsche dealer where Eisler had purchased his and, that very day, bought the same model, only silver.

Not wanting to be left behind, but refusing to be a complete conformist, St. John bought a massive, customized, purple Humvee, complete with air-conditioning, CD player, and of course, snorkel exhaust for deep-water excursions. Oversized, loud, obnoxious—it was the perfect St. Johnmobile. And Microsoft, at the height of a building boom with no shortage of construction sites, was the perfect Humvee playground. To celebrate closing a deal to port DirectX to Sega's Dreamcast game console, St. John piled in Shoichiro Irimajiri, chairman and CEO of Sega America, and Bernard Stolar, the company's president, for a cross-country romp through Microsoft's manicured lawns and construction sites. On another occasion, he paid a visit to Intel's Seattle-area office to raise sponsor support for yet another DirectX promotional event. The Intel reps made the mistake of asking for a ride. St. John thought it would be fun to ply through an expanse of a nearby greenbelt. He pitched the massive truck over a three-foot concrete embankment, but instead of tearing through freshly mowed grass, he landed nose-first in a swamp. The back of the Hummer was hung up on the embankment. The front end was sinking into muck. Water lapped at the windshield. Horrified Intel reps sat wide-eyed at St. John's lapse of stupidity.

"Don't worry," St. John said. "It's watertight. The engine will run as long was the snorkel is above water."

The monster truck had self-inflating tires, which added a couple inches to the Hummer's height. On occasion St. John would forget to deflate the tires, and the elevated Humvee would smash into the WARNING: LOW CLEARANCE signs hanging in Microsoft's underground parking lots. St. John's reign of Humvee terror eventually came to an unceremonious end the day he jammed the truck into an overhang at Sea-Tac International Airport. Instead of terrifying computer industry officials, he had now outraged and inconvenienced innocent civilians. Realizing Seattle wasn't big enough for his Humvee, he sold it and bought a decidedly smaller Mitsubishi sports car.

Not long after the Beastie Boys' car-buying spree, the wheels started to fall off their DirectX ride. The Beastie Boys had released DirectX 2.0 in June 1996. The release included Direct3D, the RenderMorphics Reality Lab technology that allowed programmers to quickly create animation segments. Technologically, it was one of the most important ingredients in DirectX 2.0. The technology wasn't the only thing impressive and important about RenderMorphics. Microsoft had paid a lot of money to buy RenderMorphics and executives wanted to see some return on the investment. By that summer dozens of developers were making games and business applications using Direct3D—more than three hundred DirectX-based games were due that Christmas.

The maker of the hottest-selling games on the market, id Software, was among those that had pledged support for the new suite of technologies.

"Direct3D is a crucial technology for the rapid and widespread acceptance of 3-D acceleration hardware," John Carmack, id's founder and technical director, said in June.

But in December, Carmack, a titan in the computer game industry, suddenly reversed himself and threw his influential weight behind OpenGL, competing technology that had by now been transported to the PC from high-end workstation computers. Carmack's decision seemingly came out of nowhere. The move threatened Direct3D and the career advancement of the Beastie Boys. If the industry followed id's lead and abandoned Direct3D, the trio would have to explain to Bill Gates and the executive staff why Microsoft had spent millions of dollars to buy and develop technology nobody was using.

It's no coincidence that rivals of the Beastie Boys inside Microsoft were working on developing OpenGL for Windows. Their old nemesis, Michael Abrash, had been convinced that the OpenGL technology the Windows NT group was developing was adequate for games. This had been the subject of violent debate inside Microsoft, with St. John strongly lobbying for the Direct3D API. Underscoring the fact one can never be too paranoid at Microsoft, the Beastie Boys suspected Abrash of defecting to id to sway Carmack on OpenGL, all in an effort to validate his long-held opinion that the technology was right for games.

St. John also suspected Microsoft employee Otto Berkes and others of making clandestine trips to help id—and Abrash—port an OpenGL version of Quake II to Windows.

Below is a sample of Carmack's letter to the developer community, which appeared in a public newsgroup. To preserve historical authenticity, the posting has not been edited for grammatical errors:

[idsoftware.com]
Login name: johnc In real life: John Carmack
Directory: /raid/nardo/johnc Shell: /bin/csh

On since Dec 15 01:19:05 6 days 2 hours Idle Time on ttyp2 from idnewt

On since Dec 17 01:05:12 4 days 19 hours Idle Time on ttyp3 from idcarmack

Plan:

. . . Direct-3D IM is a horribly broken API. It inflicts great pain and suffering on the programmers using it, without returning any significant advantages. I don't think there is ANY market segment that D3D is appropriate for, OpenGL seems to work just fine for everything from *quake* to soft-image. There is no good technical reason for the existance of D3D.

I'm sure D3D will suck less with each forthcoming version, but this is an opportunity to just bypass dragging the entire development community through the messy evolution of an ill-birthed API.

The surprise attack enraged Engstrom and Eisler.

"I see ID was completely and successfully evangelised," Engstrom deadpanned in an E-mail to Craig Eisler, Steve Lacey, Servan Keondjian, Alex St. John, Jason Robar, and Kate Seekings. Engstrom, knowing he'd have to explain this disquieting turn of events to Microsoft's executive staff, wanted verification that Otto Berkes made the clandestine trip to id.

Eisler was more forceful, blaming Carmack's 180-degree turn on "linear combinations of stupidity, ignorance, incompetence and outright lying" by those inside Microsoft.

Kate Seekings, who was assimilated by Microsoft in the Render-Morphics deal, confirmed her suspicions that rivals inside the Redmond company may have played a part in trying to torpedo Direct3D. Those rivals, she said in E-mail to Engstrom and Eisler, needed to be "shut down."

"We all know that our OGL team has been working against us," she noted.

Microsoft was pursuing a confusing 3-D strategy driven by internal political warring, which was dragging the entire computer-game industry into conflict. Enemies inside Microsoft wanted to see Eisler, Engstrom, and St. John perish. One way to hobble them would be to advance a competing technology—OpenGL. Rival executives, meanwhile, failed to get solidly behind either technology, telling the public OpenGL was great for high-end workstations and that Direct3D was good for making PC-based games. But, in the end, Microsoft would say, OpenGL was good for games, too. The industry's OpenGL/Direct3D debate would continue into late 1998. (Despite Carmack's defection, Direct3D survived and underwent inevitable refinement. Then again, so did OpenGL. Microsoft began work on converging those two technologies into a combined and compatible API, an initiative known as Fahrenheit.)

Morale among the Beastie Boys also took a hit when the company reorganized shortly after DirectX 3.0 shipped in September 1996.

Microsoft constantly boils with internal reorganizations, often causing monumental disruptions and sweeping realignment of duties. Gates is said to tolerate reorgs because they allow burned-out employees a chance to get recharged in new areas, which stokes competitive fires and keeps the giant company nimble.

Some joke that reorgs are used to force programmers to clear off their desks periodically.

The official reason for reorgs, however, is that by reallocating company resources, Microsoft can make better products.

"They're in response to market conditions and how we can best meet needs of customers," says Microsoft spokesman Tom Pilla. "This is a very fast-paced industry. Any company that isn't constantly reevaluating itself isn't going to be around very long."

A reasonable explanation, but one that might not penetrate far enough. Others inside the company say many Microsoft reorgs were the result of massive political tectonics and power grabbing between Brad Silverberg's Windows group and Jim Allchin's Windows NT army. This larger political battle inside Microsoft had shaped numerous skirmishes, including the OpenGL versus Direct3D conflict.

Reorgs also provided a gracious means to eliminate failed projects and disperse deadwood. Again, Nathan Myhrvold's Advanced Consumer Technology group was a prime example. In the early nineties, many Microsoft employees coveted positions at ACT because it presented an opportunity to work on nonconventional projects such as multimedia, WebTV set-top boxes, speech-recognition software, and other technologies.

"ACT produced lots of new vice presidents, but nothing that was ever commercially useful for anything," St. John says. "Nobody at Microsoft ever said, 'Wow! What a colossal waste of money. This was really a bad idea. Let's fire them all!'

"They just had a reorg and stuffed all the various random projects and teams into product groups."

Some of these "random" elements, as it turned out, would be dumped into the domain of the Beastie Boys.

The fall '96 reorg was partial fallout from Bill Gates's urgent refocus on the Internet.

Gates had put the company and the world on notice on May 26, 1995, when, in the now famous "Internet Tidal Wave" memo, he gave his executive staff marching orders to attack cyberspace. The Internet, Gates said, was more important to the computer industry than the graphical user interface and even the advent of the personal computer itself.

Consumers had been racing to the Web since the introduction of Netscape Communication Corp.'s first browser in 1994. The Web didn't care what operating system you used. You could browse the Web with a machine running Windows the same as you could using a Mac or OS/2 or Unix. Netscape's browser moved key application programming interfaces to any platform, threatening to turn the underlying operating system into a commodity. The Internet was the great equalizer. And a great threat to Windows and Microsoft. Bill Gates and his executives had seen what was happening to the great computer manufacturers of yore as their products became inter-changeable commodities—they were being crushed by upstart new-comers. The rulers of the Empire were determined that this would not be their fate.

"Now I assign the Internet the highest level of importance," Gates had declared. "I want to make clear that our focus on the Internet is critical to every part of our business. . . . I want every product plan to try and go overboard on Internet features."

Gates, of course, didn't suffer from tunnel vision. Before the fall '96 reorg he and St. John were making trips to Tokyo to negotiate a deal to put DirectX on Sega's Dreamcast game console. Nonetheless, the "Tidal Wave" memo thundered through Microsoft. The Beastie Boys would not be the only ones jostled by the ensuing tsunami.

Senior Vice Presidents Jim Allchin and Brad Silverberg were ele-vated into a new Executive Committee that included Gates, former Harvard buddy Steve Ballmer, former Proctor & Gamble executive Bob Herbold, and longtime Microsoft executives Pete Higgins, Paul Maritz, Nathan Myhrvold, and Jeff Raikes. But Silverberg lost control of Windows to Allchin, who would head the newly renamed Personal and Business Systems Group and be in charge of both Windows and Windows NT operating systems as well as the server applications divi-sion. Consolidating operating systems under Allchin failed to erase the tension between the Windows and Windows NT developers, how-ever. Microsoft had declared that Windows NT was the operating sys-tem of the future and that Windows 95 and eventually Windows 98 would be phased out. Many in the Windows camp, including devel-opers working on DirectX, suddenly felt like second-class citizens and fretted about job security.

Allchin had won this round. It would not be the last. Meanwhile, Silverberg, who had directed the release of Windows 95, would head the renamed Applications and Internet Client Group, which contained some of Microsoft's most high-profile projects, such as the Microsoft Office software suite and the Internet Explorer browser. Silverberg's new group included the Desktop Applications Division,

Internet Client and Collaboration Division, Tools Division, Web Authoring Product Unit, and Developer Relations Group.

John Ludwig and David Cole would be under Silverberg and lead the development side of the Internet Client and Collaboration Division, while Brad Chase would assume command of Developer Relations Group. Chase, the man who loathed St. John and once demanded that he be fired, would be St. John's ultimate manager. Rick Segal, St. John's immediate supervisor and political heat shield, had long since quit Microsoft. Doug Henrich, who had helped hire St. John and had replaced Segal as the forgiving superior, reportedly disliked Chase and moved to another part of Microsoft. In Henrich's place would step Tod Nielsen, a doppelgänger of Chase who failed to appreciate St. John's particular talent for mayhem.

This sort of massive executive musical chairs was unusual in one regard. Where reorganizations were usually handled quietly by internal E-mail, this time whole divisions were shuttled to a nearby conference center for face-to-face meetings.

The reorg followed on the heels of Microsoft's August 1996 release of the Internet Explorer 3.0 Web browser, beating rival Netscape's 3.0 version of Navigator out the door by a week. Microsoft had shipped its first Internet Explorer browser just in time for the Windows 95 launch. It borrowed heavily from technology licensed from Chicago-based Spyglass. And Spyglass based most of its browser technology on Mosaic, the original graphical browser developed in part by Marc Andreessen at the National Center for Supercomputing Applications at the University of Illinois in Champaign-Urbana. Andreessen went on to become Netscape's senior vice president of technology, completing an incestuous competitive circle common in the software industry.

Microsoft ended up giving its IE 3.0 browser away, along with free T-shirts for the first ten thousand people who downloaded the software off the Web, which clogged Microsoft's download apparatus and triggered network traffic jams.

Microsoft also announced it would bundle future versions of the browser with Windows. Netscape had an 80 percent browser market share, according to widely reported estimates. Microsoft, with but 15 percent, would battle for browser market share by leveraging Windows.

The bundling announcement prompted Netscape attorney and longtime Microsoft enemy Gary Reback to fire off an eight-page letter to the U.S. Department of Justice accusing Microsoft of violating the 1995 consent decree, as well as trampling antitrust laws. Netscape claimed Microsoft gave "clandestine side payments," as well as software, hardware, and advertising discounts, to computer makers, Internet service providers, resellers, and large corporations in exchange for using Internet Explorer.

Netscape said Microsoft's decision to bundle its browser with Windows 95 was anticompetitive. Computer makers, Netscape said, were charged $3 more for Windows 95 if they placed non-Microsoft browser icons on their PCs. Finally, Netscape also said that by giving Internet Explorer away, Microsoft was engaging in predatory pricing.

Microsoft defender Doug Rutherford of the Redwood City, California, Internet-analyst firm Zona Research Inc., likened Microsoft's tactics to Soviet-era muscle flexing.

"Kirkenes is a town on the northernmost Norwegian/Russian border," Rutherford explained in a company newsletter. "During the Cold War, the Soviet troops would mass a hundred or so tanks and pieces of armor and then rev the engines and charge at breakneck speed toward the border. Just before crossing into Norwegian territory and World War III, they would slam on the brakes and screech to a halt. Illegal? No. Aggressive and provocative? Absolutely."

The browser war was heating up, and DirectX had become part of Microsoft's Internet arsenal. As a result, Engstrom and Eisler had control over much of DirectX stripped from them, when the company's upper management rushed to take ownership of what had become successful multimedia technology.

The putsch highlighted the Microsoft myth of individual empowerment. Initiatives at Microsoft typically come from above and are provisioned by senior executives who can take credit for such projects. If they fail, of course, there's always the reorg option. While it is acceptable for developers to suggest how code should work, it was alien at Microsoft to have rank-and-file developers starting large-scale projects, let alone fueling them through brash force of will, political subterfuge, and massive infusions of cash from sympathetic forces inside DRG.

"Why would any powerful Microsoft executive support a successful project they couldn't get any credit for?" St. John says. "Better to kill it, or acquire it."

Jay Torborg, a former vice president at now defunct SuperMac Technology and an executive at Alliant Computer Systems, arrived to take command over much of DirectX. Everything that was tied to hardware—DirectDraw, DirectSound, DirectInput, and Direct3D—became the province of Torborg and was dubbed DirectX Foundation. A full-on browser war, coupled with the success of DirectX, gave Torborg—an ally of Nathan Myhrvold—an entrée into this commercially valid multimedia project via the reorg.

Engstrom and Eisler were given control of the related media layer that sat atop the foundation and included DirectShow, DirectModel, DirectAnimation, DirectPlay, and Direct3D Retained Mode. This technology allowed developers to create a variety of multimedia for playback in several applications, including NetShow or Windows Media Player, a Microsoft product that played video and audio via the Web.

Torborg came to the group championing Talisman, a hardware chip design that was supposed to improve 3-D graphics. It was the brainchild of Nathan Myhrvold, Microsoft's chief technology guru and master visionary. Yet many inside and out of the company saw Talisman as yet another masturbatory research exercise run amok.

It fell to Engstrom to choose who among his group would go help Torborg. Engstrom took advantage of the reorg and, to be cooperative, shed a few of his developers, keeping some of the better ones for himself.

Torborg assembled a team of about fifty developers to create a proof-of-concept plan called Escalante, an "everything but the kitchen sink" multimedia card that would implement the Talisman ideas. Talisman would render only those objects that changed in an animation scene in any given frame, rather than rerendering the entire scene every frame. This would be accomplished by several processes including "chunking," which divided images into pixel regions, rendered each chunk independently, and reduced on-chip memory requirements.

It was all complex, unnecessary, and confusing. The OpenGL versus Direct3D debate was raging. Now, here came Microsoft, a software company, announcing that it would introduce a new hardware "solution."

"It's not like we're hitting a wall in 3-D [graphics cards]," Phil Eisler, director of product marketing for ATI, told *Multimedia Week* magazine. "We're tripling performance every year."

Tension ratcheted inside the company as well.

"We were skeptical about Talisman," says Colin McCartney, a DirectX developer. "The actual projected cost of the boards was extremely high, about five hundred dollars, when a board should cost about ten bucks to be competitive."

Torborg had also been brought in to impose order on what was considered a disorganized group. The DirectX team tended to "fly by the seat of its pants" according to developers inside and out of the organization, a reputation the Beastie Boys nurtured. Although some inside DirectX conceded that some order was needed, most, if not all, chafed under the new commander.

"There was a feeling that the Torborg guys didn't understand the game community—they didn't get games," McCartney says. "There was the feeling that members of the Talisman team were being favored."

Amid all of this, Engstrom and Eisler threatened to quit over having someone else put in charge of DirectX. Despite his best efforts, St. John failed to calm the two and sought the help of John Ludwig, the new vice president in the Internet Platform and Tools Division.

"You can't let these guys quit," St. John begged Ludwig.

Ludwig liked Eisler and Engstrom. He admired their drive. And he appreciated their differences. Both were passionate about making technology, but Eisler was more analytical while Engstrom was more emotional. Eisler judges software in terms of how well it performs specified functions; Engstrom thinks in terms of how people will love certain features and talk about them with friends. "They sparked my thinking," Ludwig says of the two. Moreover, they reminded him of himself. Ludwig recalls the time at another company when he and his first boss were giving a presentation. A junior executive from the host firm asked what Ludwig deemed an asinine question and Ludwig laid into him. After the meeting Ludwig's boss hauled him aside and said he needed to develop another weapon besides the bazooka.

"That's what Craig and Eric needed to work on," Ludwig says.

Ludwig told St. John he'd agree to intercede and summoned the two Beastie Boys to his office for what would be the first in a series of weekly, one-hour sessions. Those sessions, which occurred over six months, marked the beginning of Eisler's and Engstrom's slow maturation within the company. Ludwig encouraged Eisler and Engstrom to identify goals and determine measured steps needed to accomplish them. They didn't need to use a machete when a scalpel would work just fine, Ludwig counseled. Moreover, he stressed that although Microsoft seemed immense, it was still a small world in many ways, "and you never know who you might be forced to work with one of these days."

Although Ludwig's lessons sometimes failed to sink in, the two learned from Ludwig how to smile at their perceived enemies, rather than club them with insults.

"He explained to us how the world works," Engstrom says. "He'd say, 'Here's what the executives think about this issue, that issue. You guys spend all your time looking up from the bottom of the ship. If you're Paul Maritz or Bill Gates, you're up here at the top of the mast, looking at the horizon.

" 'You should learn to look at the ship from their angle,' "

Engstrom continues. " 'Just run up the ladder, take a look, and go back down and fix the boat.'

"That was the best example of mentoring at Microsoft I ever encountered and it doesn't happen that often. John spent an hour a week that he could have spent making his career better. For all the good it will do him in the future, he made us very loyal to him," Engstrom says.

Yet for all Ludwig's counseling, he could not make Engstrom, Eisler, and Torborg like one another. Through the prism of time, Engstrom realizes working with the Beastie Boys was no easy task.

"As bad as it was for us, it was just as bad for Jay," Engstrom says. "No one was high-fiving in the halls. No one was smiling. [Torborg] wasn't saying, 'I get to have those two people working for me. God, I'm so happy.' "

7

CHROME, THE NEW EXCALIBUR

As 1996 drew to a close, the Beastie Boys' wild DirectX ride as they knew it was nearly over. The technology was put on a long-term maintenance schedule. The next updated version of DirectX—DirectX 5—wouldn't be released until summer 1997. Microsoft would skip the release of DirectX 4. Although the technology was ready by December '96, the timing was bad. Eisler and Engstrom had achieved what most in Microsoft fail to do—ship product on or ahead of schedule. His system was to have three versions of DirectX in early, middle, and late stages of development in parallel with each other, enabling the company to pump out DirectX about every year. But in this instance, the Beastie Boys would have saturated developers, who were just rounding the learning curve of DirectX 3. Moreover, it was deep into Christmas season—too late for game companies to plug the technology into new titles and too late even for a marketer like St. John to orchestrate any meaningful promotional event.

Because of the yawning time span since the previous release, the company decided to call the next iteration DirectX 5. No matter. DOS was dead. Eisler and Engstrom, warriors who had captured new terrain, now found themselves relegated to caretaker roles. Even St. John, the golden pit bull with the 5.0 review under his collar, would find himself muzzled by the very company that had unleashed him. He had planned one more insane marketing stunt to show the world Microsoft's prowess in the computer-game world. But higher-ups would abort St. John's coda, costing the company millions of dollars and, in the end, triggering a bizarre "hostage" situation.

By November 1996, St. John had spent $2 million of Microsoft's money to rent an abandoned hangar at California's Alameda Naval Air Station and have Swiss design artist H. R. Giger conceive an interior mock-up of a spacecraft like the one he had created for the movie *Alien*. St. John's plan was to hold a computer-game developers conference at a nearby hotel. During the last session, "armed" G-men would storm in, herd all the unsuspecting attendees at gunpoint into buses, and cart them to a hangar called, of course, Area 51. Some three thousand vendors, developers, and members of the press were to walk through a misty tracheal tube dripping with slime and emerge inside the "spaceship"—unwitting participants in a faux alien abduction. At the far end of the elaborate, football-field-sized exposition hall would be a stage, where a videotaped Bill Gates would appear, give a talk on technology, company growth projections, the coming new world order, and then . . . rip off his "Bill" mask to reveal a gray, bug-eyed alien. In fact, Gates had already been filmed for the event. David Duchovny and Gillian Anderson of *X-Files* fame were scheduled to make an appearance. Actor Richard Dreyfuss somehow found out about St. John's show and called to see if he could get in on the act.

This was Judgment Day II, a P. T. Barnum–scale spectacle to promote the third iteration of Microsoft's DirectX software development kit. JDII, as the event was to be called, was to be one of the most audacious marketing extravaganzas St. John had ever brewed, a testimony to both the power—and limits of that power—he had amassed while at Microsoft.

St. John's new boss, Tod Nielsen, general manager of platform marketing and Developer Relations Group, pulled the plug on St. John's bright idea just two weeks before the big show. Nielsen is blessed with one of those all-American, fresh-scrubbed faces like those found in circa-1950s yearbooks. He wears his hair slicked back, each strand marshaled into exact position. His expensive suits are testimonies to tailoring precision. If St. John—with his tarp-sized T-shirts forever untucked and beard draped from his jowls that increasingly resembled rusted steel wool—was the epitome of a Beastie Boy, Nielsen was the antithesis . . . a preppy boy.

Microsoft event personnel told Nielsen that St. John was "out of control" and that they believed no press would attend the abduction, plans for which had been in the works for about a year. In previous years, St. John had often ordered around Microsoft's event planners, engendering considerable resentment among them. For Judgment Day II, he dealt Microsoft planners the ultimate insult and replaced them with an outside contractor.

"They were even more determined to get [the event] stopped," St. John says. "Mind you, the show *was* out of control, but no more so than the three successful ones I'd done before."

The same event planners who had futilely complained about St. John to Rick Segal and Doug Henrich so many times before suddenly found receptive ears with Nielsen. Without ever meeting St. John, Nielsen issued a stop-work order while attending the annual Comdex computer convention in Las Vegas, oblivious to the surreal drama he would unleash.

Contractors who were assembling the spaceship were contractually obligated to stay with their equipment. But members of the Teamsters, who were in charge of moving the equipment, didn't take kindly to the stop-work order and weren't about to let the contractors remove the ship until the union got paid. The contract with the base required the facility to be locked at certain times, so everyone, about fifty in all, allowed themselves to be shut inside the hangar that night. Nielsen could not be reached when the hangar doors slammed shut, so the cell-phone call went to St. John, who was bumping along in his Humvee. Initially amused, St. John joked that Microsoft "doesn't negotiate with terrorists, and if they lay down their weapons, we may let them live." When he realized the situation was serious, he asked if anyone had been threatened with violence.

"No, no, not at all," said one event official at the scene. "But I can't be held responsible for anything that might happen should someone try to remove that equipment."

Now that sounded ominous. Because the incident was on military property, calling civilian police was not an option. The next morning, St. John ordered breakfast catered to everyone inside the hangar and made contact with the base commander.

"So, is it customary for you to allow civilians to take over sections of your base?" St. John asked.

The unamused commander said he wouldn't lift a finger to help until the base was paid the $60,000 owed for rental of the hangar. St. John had a check written up and asked his top superior, none other than Brad Chase, for a signature.

"If I sign this," said Chase, glaring, "I never want to hear about this again."

St. John promised the problem would go away.

Indeed, the incident ended quietly after the base got its money from Microsoft. Military police cleared the hangar. Eventually, the Teamsters and independent contractors got paid. The $2-million spaceship remained in storage as this book went to print.

"I still own it," Nielsen says.

St. John notes that it cost $4 million to cancel the event. But, with third-party sponsorship, it would have cost Microsoft just $2.6 million to let the show go on.

Clearly, Microsoft had changed. Where once St. John's antics would have been tolerated, the company was now more inclined to muzzle him. Microsoft had almost doubled in size since St. John's arrival in 1992, from about seven thousand employees in Washington state alone to about twelve thousand by the end of 1996. As Microsoft became more of a societal icon, the company, while agile for its size, became less like a feisty start-up and in many ways more like a conservative corporation. And that tended to be bad for renegades within the company.

Nonetheless, as 1997 dawned, the Beastie Boys could still wave their plastic swords and battle axes in triumph. Despite the canceled conference and the jarring reorg, the three had succeeded not only in driving a stake through the heart of DOS-written games, they helped boost the sales of Windows 95. They had changed an industry and looked forward to the rewards that they were certain would follow. Their expectations, however, collided with corporate reality—games were not a priority among Microsoft executives. The Internet had grabbed their attention. Although the Beastie Boys had identified and seized new technological terrain for Microsoft, in the end they realized they had played out DirectX for all it was worth to them. The trio would have to mount another offensive to claim the lucrative bonuses and stock options they believed they deserved.

"When we made DirectX, the whole idea was to make neat technology that would solve a whole lot of problems," St. John says. "We did that. We spent years of our lives, lived in our offices, we worked our asses off, and we had all these developers out there adopt our technology. We changed the market, and the net effect on our careers was, 'Thank you very much.'"

Eisler, Engstrom, and St. John now confronted a turning point, as they mutually reassessed their careers. St. John's power had evaporated when Nielsen and Brad Chase took command at Developer Relations Group. Eisler and Engstrom were now working under Torborg. The Beastie Boys, who all at one time harbored fantasies of becoming vice presidents, realized that probably wasn't going to happen. St. John was growing disenchanted with his job and distracted with his troubled marriage. Eisler was also having marital woes, and both he and Engstrom chafed at having had DirectX taken from them. They could all have just quit, but leaving Microsoft and $1.5 million a year in stock options was like freeing yourself by gnawing off your own arm. Besides, they had tasted power and wanted more. St. John says the three concluded that only one of them would have a realistic shot of advancing to the upper echelons at Microsoft, and that man was Engstrom. Eisler allegedly argued that he should be the one the others got behind.

"Eric has what it takes to be vice president," St. John said. "We should get behind him and push."

St. John says Eisler begrudgingly agreed. Eisler and Engstrom say this never happened.

Nonetheless, the three concurred it would be a good idea to get along better with supervisors and coworkers. Engstrom began taking management courses. To curb their tendency to disparage others, the Beastie Boys agreed to pay each other a fine of $5 each time one of them talked ill of fellow human beings. This old habit was particularly hard to break, however, and the three usually ended up swapping the same $5 bill back and forth.

But the migration from making cool technology to trying to make Microsoft managers happy was painful for the Beastie Boys. It was also short-lived. Their discussions increasingly turned to how they could build technology so innovative, so impressive, so important to the company and to the world, that they could not go unrewarded. Yet to achieve the type of fame they coveted would require more than building application programming interfaces, which were necessary but unglamorous pieces of software plumbing.

With DirectX they had proved themselves to be very capable plumbers. They knew they would have to build something that would be more of a stand-alone product, technology that lived as an entity if not apart from Windows, then at least as a companion—software that could be hyped on the front of shrink-wrapped merchandise testifying to Beastie Boys authorship. Relatively few Microsoft programmers are in the position to innovate. Their charter is largely to work on Windows, Office, and such—bolt tightening, it's called—and stack new features on existing products. Building something from scratch, however, and creating a stand-alone product was, as Engstrom says, "an engineer's dream."

So, taking their cue from Gates, the Beastie Boys set their sights on cyberspace.

Gates's "Tidal Wave" memo had set the entire company on an Internet course. Eisler, Engstrom, and St. John were eager to exploit that and in January began a series of brainstorming sessions on how to marry some of the elements of DirectX with Microsoft's latent obsession with the Web. Over beers and sodas—Engstrom had injured his back while lifting weights and the three no longer worked out at the Pro Club—ideas about bringing fast, high-quality 3-D graphics to the Web began to coalesce.

The three saw the Web as a plodding means of communication, constrained by inherent limitations of piping text, graphics, sound, and other digital data through phone lines designed to carry analog voice messages. Eisler, Engstrom, and St. John were used to the fast world of games, where motion occurred at thirty-plus frames per second with high-fidelity sound. But the three had no experience with the Internet. The closest experience any of them had with the Web was perhaps posting a message on a newsgroup or sending correspondence via the company's internal E-mail network, Microsoft's central nervous system. Certainly none had ever authored any Web pages. As with computer-game technology, they were setting out to take unfamiliar ground. And as in the realm of games, they thought there was vast room for improvement.

"We looked at the Internet and said, 'It's shitty. It takes forever. We're bored. What a primitive paradigm,'" St. John recalls. "We in games lived in a much faster world."

They wanted to use the 3-D animation power of DirectX, which Microsoft was bolting into the new Windows 98 operating system, and couple it with the Web. What they had in mind was something fast and something flashy—a browser that could deliver animated-game-like 3-D images and sound, an ultimate multimedia browser . . . a "browser on steroids."

St. John originally hit on the idea of a flag that could flap in a virtual breeze. But the original concept soon evolved into much more. Drawing on their recent experience with games, the Beastie Boys incorporated the concept of a "collaborative" browser, where groups of people could interact with and manipulate the same Web page at the same time—much like multiplayer computer games. They also thought about adding a simple authoring tool, software that enabled users to draw primitive 3-D shapes, add color, texture, and shading. With the authoring tool sprang the idea that the browser could be used as a medium for exchanging more complex 3-D images and pictures on the fly. Instead of using text, people could use images and graphics to convey certain concepts, giving high-tech meaning to the phrase "a picture is worth a thousand words."

With these rough ideas in mind, Engstrom enlisted two veteran developers from DirectX—Bob Heddle, a skinny Canadian, and Colin McCartney, a cherubic Scotsman with a voracious appetite for diet Pepsi and Mountain Dew. Heddle and McCartney were still working on DirectX, but quickly grasped the Beastie Boys' vision and became willing Chrome recruits. The two would carry St. John's waving-flag example further than he envisioned and would be the core developers—the spelunkers who would rappel into the guts of the new technology. Engstrom would play the commanding managerial role. Eisler would play a lesser role. He would grow eager to try his hand as an administrator rather than a coder and slowly migrated to the project's periphery.

As a technology and project, DirectX enjoyed a good reputation within the company, even if the creators were viewed as obnoxious lunatics. The success of DirectX helped lure programmers to work on Chrome. Moreover, executives liked the idea behind the project. That kind of buzz whetted the appetites of the ambitious, who asked to be reassigned. Programmers, program managers, marketers, and others within Microsoft can pick up and leave for other assignments. Managers can stop them, but that sort of authority is rarely exercised—detaining people against their will can hurt a group's performance. Chrome's initial staff of a dozen or so would eventually swell to about a hundred.

"Most came to me because it was the coolest thing at Microsoft," Engstrom says, noting that working on a way to bring dazzling new 3-D multimedia to the Internet was far more rewarding than, say, tinkering on yet another upgrade of Word or testing SQL Server.

St. John, meanwhile, would be haunted and distracted by his failed marriage. His estranged wife, Kelley, wanted to punctuate their separation with an official divorce, forcing the procrastinating St. John to deal with the inevitable. With his American Dream in ruins, he would eventually want out of Microsoft, but didn't want to lose $5 million in unvested stock options. The dilemma would set up one of the most celebrated and notorious escapes ever recorded at Microsoft.

Heddle and McCartney were not burdened with such distractions and took an enthusiastic shine to Chrome. They soon incorporated concepts of 3-D objects that, when clicked, could change color, texture, or shape. An icon of an elephant, say, when clicked could morph into a Web page about elephants complete with live links to other Web pages about pachyderms. The Web page resided in the 3-D object, opening a new realm of interactivity. Heddle and McCartney envisioned Web pages that could be mapped to a cube that could spin and reveal more Web pages—six pages for the download price of one, in essence. In another scenario, sections of a Web page could swing back like a door, revealing more valuable screen real estate. Inspired by their work with computer-game technology, they toyed with the notion of bringing interactive, 3-D cartoon characters to the Web—characters that could talk and walk about a page. They saw how 3-D could deliver unique page transitions—pond ripples, shattering glass, sophisticated fades, and the like. They saw the potential to have the Web deliver exploding, shocking, bombarding graphics like those seen on *Monday Night Football.* The Chrome team believed that such hi-fi interactivity could mount real competition for TV advertising. Internet ad revenue was just approaching $1 billion a year in 1998, while television had hauled in more than $23 billion in ad revenue the year before. But advertising on the Web was growing faster than TV revenue—Chrome could hasten a narrowing of the gap.

Indeed, the technology could do for the Web what color did for television—make it more interesting and appealing. This could in turn pull more users on-line, increase computer purchases, and in the end, deliver more revenue for Microsoft and others in the industry. Not only would the technology be fast and flashy, it would be functional.

Initially referred to by the lackluster name "multimedia browser," McCartney started calling the technology Burning Chrome, the title of a William Gibson book about a pair of renegade hackers who plot a way to break into a mob-run computer.

The technology's name was soon shortened to just Chrome, "after the shiny stuff on cars." Engstrom's business manager, Chris Phillips, paid a young developer in Oregon $15,000 for the rights to use the name. Coincidentally, the developer had used the moniker for a 3-D authoring tool kit he had invented. The name Chrome would survive up until two weeks before it was finally unveiled ahead of schedule in the summer of 1998.

But to ship, the nascent Chrome team would have to overcome significant technical and business-strategy hurdles, not to mention Microsoft's internal political minefield.

John Ludwig, the mentoring vice president in the Internet Platform and Tools Division, was growing impatient with the Chrome team's initial lack of progress. Engstrom, Heddle, McCartney, fellow Chrome member and DirectX veteran Cristiano Pierry, and occasionally Eisler were now meeting every Monday morning at nine with Ludwig, who would ask for progress reports on the project. The weekly meetings were becoming more painful as the Chrome team had little to show Ludwig. Chagrined, McCartney spent an entire weekend drafting a 130-page specification report—a spec in software parlance—detailing Chrome. Specs are to software what architectural drawings are to buildings. Specs outline what the technology is about, what it will do, why it is important, what the deadlines are, and provide enough information so that developers can code the desired features.

That next Monday, McCartney was prepared. However, Heddle didn't think the spec was ready and told Ludwig that the team might have one in a week or so.

"John was clearly unhappy," McCartney recalls. "Then I pulled out the programming spec and laid it on the table. That started the ball rolling."

The first and most obvious technical obstacle was overcoming the limitations of existing bandwidth, that is, how much information a phone line, coaxial cable, or any other type of network can carry. Images, movies, animation, and graphics are notorious bandwidth hogs. As cyberspace drew more users, digital traffic jams resulted, leading many to dub the World Wide Web the World Wide Wait. In early 1997, most phone modems pulled in data at 28.8 kilobits per second, expressed as 28.8K. Even the more expensive 56K modems rarely achieved anything above 38K. Cable modems, which delivered data at superhigh speeds through cable-TV lines, were only useful in a few major cities, and even then their adoption was limited. Other high-speed transmission lines such as Integrated Services Digital Networks (ISDNs) and Digital Subscriber Lines (DSLs), which could deliver data over existing copper phone lines twenty-five to fifty times faster than 56K modems, were expensive, not widely available, and poorly marketed. None of the high-speed options had become as ubiquitous as conventional hookups. The Beastie Boys were betting that the promise of greater bandwidth would be years if not a decade away.

"People always assume that the wire, the infrastructure, is going to solve the bandwidth problem. Not true," says St. John. "Infrastructure needed to get that bandwidth to everybody will take years. To simply say we can solve our inefficient use of our existing bandwidth by adding more is false. You'll simply use that bandwidth inefficiently as well.

"Rather than waiting for greater bandwidth and bigger modems, which was five years away, we thought, why don't we make existing bandwidth more efficient."

But how?

Instead of Internet bandwidth, Chrome would find its power inside the internal bandwidth of the computer itself. The Beastie Boys would leverage Moore's Law, coined by Intel cofounder Gordon Moore, who stated in 1965 that the number of transistors on a computer processing chip would double every year. He later revised that to eighteen months. The more transistors, the faster the processing chip. His revised law has proved accurate. As a result, computers could process information a thousand times faster than the Internet could deliver data. Yet, as a rule, computers, with all their computational power, sat mostly idle as Web pages trickled in. The Beastie Boys would change the rules . . . again. When it came to downloading Web pages, Chrome would have the computer do most of the work.

Recognizing that computers, rather than bandwidth, would do the heavy lifting, Engstrom approached Intel early on requesting the company tweak its newer Pentium II and the future Pentium III processor chips, code-named Katmai, to optimize Chrome. Intel readily agreed. Most software applications don't need superfast chips. A word processor or Web browser, for example, work fine on a computer running at the pedestrian speed of ninety megahertz. Chip makers Intel, Advanced Micro Devices, Motorola Inc., and others are desperate for applications that justify superfast chips. Other than games, speech recognition, and a few other selected applications, there was little market justification for faster, more expensive chips housed in correspondingly pricier PCs. At a time when demand for cheap, sub-$1,000 computers was at an all-time high, Chrome would represent a reason for people to plop down more money for the higher-margin, faster machines. Intel's role would prove to be crucial in more ways than Engstrom imagined. In fact, the liaison would inadvertently rescue Chrome when Microsoft managers tried to kill the technology in the spring of 1998.

As in game animation, Web elements authored with Chrome would start out as a series or mesh of polygons. The skeletal framework of the image would be piped to a Windows-based computer equipped with Chrome, which would then apply the specified color, texture, shading, motion, and other behaviors to the object. Chrome's secret was a sort of compression. If you had to move a house over a narrow, rickety bridge, it would be nice if all you had to carry over was the frame and have carpenters on the other side slap on the walls and roof and install the plumbing and electricity. Chrome was like the carpenter on the other side of the bridge. The amount of data that actually needed to be downloaded would be dramatically smaller than a complete image sent in standard compression format known as JPEG files (Joint Photographic Experts Group) or their bulkier cousins, GIF files.

Heddle and McCartney initially wanted to use a variety of highly customized HTML tags as a basis for scripting or authoring Chrome. HTML, or hypertext markup language, is the language that browsers use to display text and images and create links to other Web pages. You can use the <bold> tag to display text in bold, or <font size> to display a restricted range of font sizes or set up tables and other simple formats. HTML tags are generic, easy to use, and thus necessarily limited in what they can do.

Heddle and McCartney—and legions of other developers—saw creation of custom tags as a means around the limitations of HTML. But custom tags could only be read by browsers that support them. In customizing HTML tags, Heddle and McCartney were running into an unforeseen buzz saw. Many in the Web-development industry were not happy that Microsoft and Netscape were releasing browsers that didn't support the same HTML tags. Layouts and designs that worked in one browser often didn't work well in another, forcing developers to write Web pages with both browsers in mind, driving up development costs. The industry wanted a commitment to standards.

The industry got that commitment in June of '97. Microsoft and Netscape reached a rare truce and agreed to support only standard HTML tags as defined by the World Wide Web Consortium, or W3C, the standards body composed of industry representatives—including Microsoft—and academia. The so-called Web Interoperability Pledge took Heddle and McCartney by surprise. If Heddle and McCartney couldn't use their custom HTML to implement Chrome, then the nascent technology was doomed before it ever left the womb.

"The initial spec [for Chrome] was HTML-based," says McCartney, his Scottish accent rendering the word Chrome as *Kruuum.* "Shortly after we introduced that spec, Microsoft said it would not release HTML that was not W3C-compliant. Bob and I at that point panicked."

Chrome was dead before arrival. Or so it seemed.

"Bob went on a hunt and came across XML," McCartney says. "He came back and said, 'That might be just what we need.' "

Indeed, extensible markup language, or XML, would prove to be perfect for Chrome. Developed by on-line publishing experts from industry and academia under the auspices of a W3C working group, XML enabled users to create custom tags and more finely separate content from presentation formats. If HTML were a blunt collection of nouns, XML represented the verbs and adjectives that allowed for nuance.

That XML wasn't even a standard yet didn't really matter. There was critical mass to get it adopted, with heavy support coming from the standards-setting W3C. Microsoft's initial interest in XML was its ability to support Channel Definition Format, a standard proposed by the Redmond company for "pushing" content to its Web channels on the Windows Active Desktop. The Active Desktop, yet another offspring of Microsoft's Internet quest, included a list of Web icons from major partners such as Disney and America Online running down the right side of the screen. Using push, content from selected sites was continuously updated and fed to a user's computer. Many Microsoft employees use push to keep track of stock fluctuations.

"XML gives users the ability to manipulate and input data efficiently, with minimal load on the server," said John Ludwig. "The result will be faster, richer, and more interactive information on the Web."

As it turns out, a majority of computer users didn't use push technology. Most users don't remain on-line hours on end at work and watch their stock portfolios. And corporate information-technology administrators complained that uninterrupted flows of pushed content clogged internal networks.

Still, XML had obvious advantages over HTML, and Heddle and the Chrome team were eager to take advantage of this emerging standard.

More important, implementing Chrome with XML was relatively easy. It took significant programming skill to use DirectX, limiting its use to a smaller number of developers. But with Chrome's use of XML, the riches of DirectX were unlocked for vast legions of Web developers.

"It was fortuitous that XML came along," McCartney says.

Armed with the spec, the Chrome developers now had a way to deploy Chrome content and had theoretically figured out a way to cheat the limitations of Internet bandwidth. But that created another problem. Chrome would demand superfast computer processors, machines that ran at four hundred megahertz or faster—computers that could process information at a minimum of 400 million cycles per second. Computers, it should be noted, that didn't even exist at the time. Microsoft had never built and marketed technology targeting a nonexistent install base. The Chrome team conferred with Intel and other hardware and computer makers and were told that faster machines would be rolling out sometime in 1998. Despite those assurances, the Chrome team would be shooting at a moving target, or at least one that lay over the immediate horizon.

Critics complain that Microsoft doesn't innovate; that it has gotten to where it is by acquiring other companies and copying the successes of other, more innovative minds. This could not be said of Chrome. In fact, it could be argued that no other software company but Microsoft, with its billions in assets and near monopoly in the PC operating system market, could afford to build and market software for computers that didn't yet exist.

Initially, the plan was to sell Chrome as a premium multimedia browser, bundled only with deluxe versions of Windows 98 and future versions of Windows NT. Microsoft had been giving away its Internet Explorer via CDs and downloads over the Internet. The company was planning to sidestep that channel and bundle the IE 4 browser with all versions of Windows. That strategy would prove fateful for

Microsoft and eventually force Engstrom to alter the marketing scheme for Chrome.

But for the time being, Chrome was to be the one Microsoft browser consumers would have to pay for at a price yet to be determined. But with that cost came reward. For the first time, high-end computers would be able to display more interesting Web content than low-end machines, for up till then Web pages looked the same on a $700 computer as they did on a $2,000 model. Because Chrome would at least initially be proprietary—it wouldn't run on a Mac, say—the technology possessed branding appeal and gave users another reason to buy high-end Windows machines.

Over the long term, the price of high-end computers would drop as the processing chips became faster—the addendum to Moore's Law. Intel was talking about producing chips that churned at 550 MHz by early 1999. The high-priced computers of 1998 would be the cheap computers of the near future. Over time, the argument went, Chrome would become ubiquitous . . . at least on Windows-based machines.

Even if the Chrome team were relatively certain faster computers were in the offing, it had no such assurance that Web developers would use Chrome. And without Chrome content, the technology would be stalled on the information superhighway. This highlighted the intersection where technology and marketing meet. The Beastie Boys and the Chrome team would need the cooperation of the company's Developer Relations Group to convince Web authors to build Chrome sites.

Yet without an existing install base, even Microsoft's own Developer Relations Group hesitated to evangelize Chrome. Early on, Engstrom pleaded for evangelism support. DRG was supposed to evangelize leading-edge technology and Engstrom pressed this argument hard. But DRG was no longer the cowboy outfit it had once been. Microsoft had already conquered much of the computing frontier by 1997. Brad Chase, who came from a pure marketing background, was now at the helm. Developer Relations Group had lost a lot of its aggressive edge and was much more cautious since when Engstrom had been an evangelist, and DRG balked.

DRG manager Morris Beton told Engstrom that he wasn't convinced Chrome had market appeal and was skeptical about its revenue potential.

Another DRG operative said Engstrom had a "poorly articulated vision."

Eisler had a different take: "There's a lot more comfort in evangelizing Windows NT 5 and established technologies. There's a lot less comfort to evangelize something where you have to get a lot of [independent software vendors] aboard. In the face of a tougher job, fewer people are inclined to do it.

"Back when I was evangelizing NT, no one wanted it," Eisler adds. "Now, it's all people want to do. They don't want to evangelize new technology unless they're sure it's a sure win. Chrome is hard to see as a sure win."

Yet Chrome had its high-level supporters within Microsoft, including Nathan Myhrvold and Bill Gates. While DRG would drag its heals, Heddle had Microsoft video developers produce a concept video to demo for senior executives. The video included the flapping flag, a sailing ship on a virtual sea, parts of the screen flapping back to reveal more monitor space, and a little 3-D stick character that tore off a Netscape logo and shimmied down a Web page. Like DirectX, Chrome was pitched to management as a way to leapfrog the competition.

Indeed, Chrome was a Web weapon aimed at many targets. It didn't require users to waste time downloading special software called plug-ins, used to view animation or video or hear sound files and the like. As a result, it was a threat to Macromedia Inc., the company that produced the Shockwave plug-in that enabled browsers to see animation.

Because of its ease of use and the fast download of animated 3-D graphics, Chrome challenged some uses of Java, the complex programming language used to make banner ads on the Web.

Chrome's 3-D ability also put VRML in the crosshairs, although Microsoft made contorted arguments that Chrome wouldn't compete with it. VRML, or virtual reality modeling language, is the specification for a 3-D graphics language for the Web. After downloading a VRML page, its contents can be viewed, rotated, and manipulated, and simulated rooms or interiors can be "walked into." VRML's complexity was one reason it had never captured the interest of most Web developers. In contrast, simplicity was one of Chrome's features. Still, Microsoft took pains to convince VRML developers that they had nothing to fear.

"Chrome is an interactive media browser that is designed to integrate 3D graphics objects, animations and 3D (user interface) elements within Web pages and to add intelligent navigation, interactivity and impact," a Microsoft report concluded. "VRML is primarily targeted at 3D Internet solutions and fully immersive 3D worlds with limited media integration. . . . There is ample room for VRML, Chrome and other multimedia technologies to coexist."

But the two fattest targets were Netscape and, once again, Apple's QuickTime. Because the foundation of Chrome was based on DirectX—which was owned wholly by Microsoft—and tied to the Windows operating system, neither Netscape nor Apple would have anything like it.

"It always seemed like we were always trying to catch up to [Apple]," Heddle says of the Cupertino company. "We showed Microsoft taking a leadership role in a technology area where our competitors really would not be able to or have a very hard time equaling or even taking the lead from us."

In many ways Chrome was a paradox. Here was technology that could blow away rivals Netscape and Apple. It also gave reasons for people to buy high-end computers. Yet because Chrome didn't target an existing install base, key factions at Microsoft were skittish about supporting it.

"People wanted to know what our Netscape and Windows 3.1 story was," Eisler recalls. "People forget that we make our fucking money from Windows. There's no money to be made from making commodity technology."

In the 1990s, leveraging the market dominance of Windows was what Microsoft was all about. It's the reason the Department of Justice continued its battle against the company when Microsoft made good on its promise to bundle the IE 4 browser with Windows 95. And in the end, that's why key executives at Microsoft supported Chrome.

Although Microsoft—mindful of an antitrust probe—would eventually market Chrome as a Windows 98 "enhancement" that could improve 3-D graphics delivery from CD-ROMs and their more robust cousins DVDs, the technology was squarely aimed at conquering the Web.

"Chrome was one of many ideas that we could actually sell to Microsoft executives, because it was a big, fat, bloated technology feature," St. John says. "Microsoft just loves that because it tangles everyone in your technology forever. It had 'Internet' in the sentence and did that mystical multimedia shit that Engstrom, Eisler, and I controlled.

"We knew we had the magic formula."

Indeed, although Microsoft was making inroads into Netscape's browser market share, it came at a cost. Microsoft was giving away its browser. Zona Research reported in January '97 that Microsoft's Internet Explorer had more than tripled its market share against Netscape's Navigator since August, jumping to 28 percent from 8 percent. Netscape's market share had fallen to 70 percent from 83 percent according to Zona, which asked 211 businesses to name their "primary" browser.

Netscape sold Navigator for $49.50 and would later sell its more robust Communicator browser, which included E-mail, newsgroup, and Web-page-authoring software, for $59.50. But Netscape would be forced to give away the browsers in the face of Microsoft's growing market grab.

Gates hated the idea of giving away technology. Chrome, however, could be marketed as a premium, upscale browser. Unlike the standard Internet Explorer browser, Microsoft could hang a price tag on Chrome. It was a way Microsoft could reverse the freebie trend, yet retain existing gains in market share.

"Finally," Gates reportedly said, "a way to make some money off the damn Net."

8

ST. JOHN'S WATERLOO

A s Project Chrome began to coalesce, Alex St. John soon found himself confronting an old enemy—Chris Hecker, the former WinG wunderkind. Hecker, who had since left Microsoft to found his own game company called Definition Six, was leading a group of game makers in an attack against Direct3D, the 3-D rendering component in DirectX. Hecker and allies inside and out of Microsoft wanted the company to offer more support for OpenGL, the competing technology first developed by Silicon Graphics. OpenGL enjoyed marquee credibility—Hollywood has used it to make *Jurassic Park, Mask,* and other special-effects blockbusters. Plus, Direct3D was too complicated and too poorly documented to use, complained Hecker and his cabal, including game guru John Carmack.

By now Microsoft was definitely supporting OpenGL in Windows NT—targeted for corporate users—and to a lesser degree, it was offering some support in Windows 95. Microsoft was advocating OpenGL for high-end, complex computer animation, once the sole province of Unix-based workstation computers. But Microsoft saved all the mainstream technology that game developers needed for Direct3D and positioned it as the solution for games for personal computers. Direct3D allowed Windows to take full advantage of the new breed of inexpensive 3-D graphics and accelerator chips coming to market. Microsoft did not offer that same support for OpenGL, making it harder for chipmakers to write OpenGL drivers that would work well with Windows. Yet, continuing to muddle the message on this subject, Microsoft also said if developers wanted to, they could use OpenGL for games.

It was a confusing strategy and one that Hecker—with aid from friendly contacts inside Microsoft—exploited to publicly push for full OpenGL support on Windows 95 and the upcoming Windows 98 operating system, code-named Memphis.

St. John had at one time advocated supporting OpenGL in Windows 95, and he had even asked the Windows NT group for help in writing the necessary software to plug it in. But the NT group wasn't interested in PC games, forcing St. John and his fellow Beastie Boys Engstrom and Eisler to look elsewhere. That led to the purchase of RenderMorphics, which produced the foundation for Direct3D.

After going through all that, having a competing application programming interface for PC-based games was unacceptable to St. John. He had spent too much time, effort, and Microsoft money evangelizing DirectX—as flawed as it initially was—to allow Hecker or anyone else to attack the Beastie Boys' achievements. His first order of business was to quash OpenGL inside the company.

Yet as St. John prepared to slay the OpenGL movement inside Microsoft, his failed marriage reappeared to haunt him. After being separated for three years, Kelley St. John had pressed for an official divorce. St. John was forced to confront something he didn't want to deal with. He was now fighting a multifront war. Historically, warring nations that spread themselves too thin eventually collapse. Dealing with divorce lawyers and fighting enemies inside and out of Microsoft were becoming too much. St. John realized he would implode if something didn't give.

The distraction of the divorce proceedings "fucked with my ability to be productive," he says. "The threat that some or all of my [stock] options would be taken away from me left little incentive for me to get up in the morning and come to work. It's very hard when you have your wife and kids leave to try to figure out what the motivation is to work hard for a future you don't have anymore."

Paradoxically, those very unvested stock options, worth an estimated $5 million, were too seductive for him to abandon. He didn't have the mettle to just quit. So, he says, he eventually hit on the novel idea of forcing Microsoft to fire him. Microsoft rarely fires people. The company spends as much as $20,000 recruiting each new hire, an investment in intellectual capital that human resources managers hate to see disappear. Rarer still were instances where fired Microsoft employees got to keep portions or all of their unvested stock. If St. John quit, there was no chance he'd get to keep any of his unvested options. If he was fired, he believed he had a chance to see some of that money.

Resolving to get fired freed him to launch an aggressive internal campaign against what he felt were the key threats against the Beastie Boys' technical and career agendas—OpenGL and Talisman, Microsoft's own ill-fated 3-D chip design. The noise he'd generate would have the collateral benefit of helping Chrome.

In the spring of '97, Chrome was still in its infancy. It had not yet been "tar babied" and could be killed by competing factions within Microsoft, particularly the Internet Explorer group. The IE team, understandably, thought any technology having to do with Web browsing should be under its domain. The Beastie Boys were attempting to infiltrate one of the most important assets of the company—the browser market—and were at risk of being ordered to work on Chrome under the direction of another group or, worse, having their new technology simply taken from them.

St. John reasoned that he could serve as a political heat shield for Chrome by waging a diversionary, no-holds-barred internal battle. St. John believed that by kicking up a storm, Engstrom and his team could advance Chrome at least to the tar-baby stage, get it stuck to somebody or something important enough to Microsoft to increase markedly its chance for survival.

St. John told Eisler and Engstrom that "I would go destroy OGL and Talisman and make life miserable for [Windows multimedia group manager] Jay Torborg."

St. John soon got an opportunity to launch his personal jihad.

Otto Berkes, the Microsoft employee suspected of helping id port an OpenGL version of Quake to Windows, was to speak before the Computer Game Developers Conference in April '97. St. John found out about it and moved to kill Berkes's appearance. He told Developer Relations Group manager Morris Beton that Berkes was about to undermine the company's entire Direct3D message.

The company's 3-D multimedia strategy was in disarray. Beton fired off E-mail to Berkes and Torborg, inquiring just what it was Berkes was going to say at the game developers conference. "I keep hearing conflicting opinions on whether we're in sync" with regard to OpenGL and Direct3D, Beton wrote.

Torborg, more consumed with advancing Nathan Myhrvold's Talisman dream, offered little clarity on the issue.

He admitted he was "a little nervous" about the presentation. Nonetheless, Torborg said Microsoft should tell developers not to use OGL for games, but if they really wanted to use it, the company should offer suggestions how best to implement it for Windows.

A few days later, Berkes sent E-mail stating that he had decided not to give his presentation because "talking about OpenGL at the Game Developers Conference is, by simple association, talking about OpenGL as used with games."

This was exactly what St. John had told Beton. St. John won round one.

St. John could not have engaged in his internecine battle in a more tumultuous year for Microsoft—a year in which the browser war escalated, competitors increased their attack on the Redmond company, and the government stepped up its antitrust campaign.

In February, Texas became the first state to launch its own probe of Microsoft's business practices, paralleling an ongoing Justice Department investigation that had begun the previous summer at Netscape's behest. Netscape accused Microsoft of charging personal-computer makers less money for Windows 95 if they didn't install Netscape's Navigator software.

In March, three U.S. senators, unhappy with the pace of the Justice Department probe, asked the Federal Trade Commission to grab control of the Microsoft inquiry. Republican senators Conrad Burns of Montana, Ted Stevens of Alaska, and Craig Thomas of Wyoming wrote the FTC after receiving complaints from Netscape and South Dakota–based computer maker Gateway. The FTC demurred. The letter's authorship is queer in a number of respects: Bears probably outnumber software developers in Montana, Alaska, and Wyoming, and Republicans are generally card-carrying free-market capitalists. Yet the letter was significant because it marked the first time Congress had joined the fight between Microsoft and its competitors and foreshadowed more government scrutiny later that year.

That same month, IBM, Sun, Oracle, and Netscape said they would develop common standards for network computers and related software. Unlike personal computers that had their own hard drives and software, network computers or NCs were essentially keyboards and display monitors linked to a central computer. Oracle was pushing NCs as a cheaper alternative to personal computers running Windows.

It seemed that for every bit of good news to come along, bad was almost sure to follow. Microsoft's browser market share continued to make gains on Netscape, and the Redmond company's stock kept Wall Street happy. The Software Publishers Association even awarded Microsoft's IE 3.0 browser a Codie—the software industry's version of an Oscar—in the Best New Software Product category. But less than a week after the award was presented, the browser was found to have serious security flaws that allowed hackers to get access to the inner workings of computers that visited booby-trapped Web sites. Microsoft had been gearing to release beta test versions of its IE 4.0 browser on St. Patrick's Day. But the discovery of the bug forced Microsoft to delay the release, allowing Netscape to unveil its Communicator 4.0 browser first.

Amid this climate of increasing competition, industry hostility, and mounting government investigations, St. John embarked on his suicide mission to flame out and take as many internal enemies as he could down with him. On April 25, he fired his first major salvo at Deborah Black, Microsoft's director of systems division. He didn't just shoot over her bow, but bombarded her with a three-page, single-spaced E-mail detailing the company's failed 3-D strategy and warning her about those inside and out of Microsoft who were trying to torpedo Direct3D.

St. John told Black he was worried by what was going on with Microsoft's "new improved" 3-D strategy. He acknowledged that he was not an unbiased observer due to his ties to DirectX. Nonetheless, he said he had credible evidence to support his belief that members of Black's group were leaking details of Microsoft's internal debate about Direct3D and OpenGL. Black's team, St. John claimed, fed information to Michael Abrash and Chris Hecker, among others, in an effort to generate enough controversy to force Microsoft to adopt a friendlier posture toward OpenGL. Hecker had posted much of this internal conflict on the public rec.games.programmer Internet newsgroup, flurries of which were there even as this book went to press. In one instance, Hecker wrote:

> . . . two [3-D] APIs fairly competing would be the best thing overall for the industry. However, it doesn't appear that will be allowed to happen inside Microsoft, which is a shame and basically an insult to 3D game programmers. Already, I've heard rumors that the MS OpenGL team will no longer be allowed to innovate on the API, meaning they can't propose extensions nor implement them. Also, the fate of the DirectDraw bindings (which I believe are finished code-wise) seems to be up in the air for purely political reasons.

St. John grew more forceful in his correspondence to Black, pointedly telling her that there was no demand in the game-development community for OpenGL, other than from those directly funded by Silicon Graphics, Inc., the creators of OpenGL.

"There is no OGL vs. D3D debate that we aren't creating," St. John said, adding that members of her team were conducting their own evangelism directly competing with his efforts.

Stop the leaks, St. John admonished, particularly to Silicon Graphics, id Software, and Hecker.

Despite St. John's warning, Chris Hecker continued to gain access to Microsoft officials, including Deborah Black. Meanwhile, St. John continued to erect his career dolmen by needling upper management—and drawing unwanted attention away from Chrome. On May 20 he sent mail to Gates and Senior Vice Presidents Brad Silverberg, Paul Maritz, and Brad Chase, showing that in March, for the first time ever, all top-ten-selling PC games were written for Windows using DirectX.

"We just win if we keep our platform stable and innovate in our drivers," St. John wrote in a not-so-veiled stab at the company's 3-D Talisman chip and OpenGL efforts. "Everybody getting this?"

Three days later he shot E-mail to Talisman project leader Jim Veres, Torborg, Gates, and more than a dozen other executives belittling the Talisman project as irrelevant.

For St. John, the company's aim should be to do one thing—to make the PC the number one multimedia machine.

"We've got more multimedia marketshare and ISV's [independent software vendors] than Sega, Sony, Nintendo, Apple or SGI," St. John said. The war, as far as he was concerned, was over. Now, he was working to solidify Microsoft's position in the game industry, and Talisman did anything but help him manage that.

St. John was never shy about voicing his opinion, but had become even more bellicose since deciding to get himself fired from the world's most powerful software company. Despite his harangues, or perhaps because of them, his pleadings about the futility of Talisman and repeated warnings about the suspected OpenGL leaks from inside the company went unheeded. Which is why St. John took private perverse satisfaction when Hecker hit Microsoft with a bombshell. On June 9, Hecker met with Black and told her he had orchestrated a petition in the form of an open letter to Microsoft, demanding that the company include support for OpenGL in Windows 98. If Microsoft didn't yield, then Hecker would give the letter to targeted media. Hecker told Black that Microsoft evangelists—i.e., St. John—were lying to Microsoft managers about the lack of developer demand for OpenGL.

Hecker told Black that while it was true that some of the developers on his petition were using Direct3D, they were doing so because they had no other choice.

"That's what the letter is all about," Hecker told Black. "We want to be able to choose OpenGL, and we'd like Microsoft's support in this decision."

The petition, signed by some fifty game developers, including id's John Carmack, was a toned-down reprise of Carmack's anti-DirectX letter from the previous year. However, this time the letter would be getting greater public exposure in the trade press. Black sent E-mail to Maritz asking for direction.

In it, she said Hecker would postpone sending the letter, which he intended to issue as a press release, until she had time to confer with Maritz. She also said that "every indication" was that OGL was superior to Direct3D, and warned that it was "entirely possible that OGL will gain broad support."

Hecker had tried to gain audience with Maritz. But Maritz blew off Hecker and referred him to Black. Maritz, who clearly didn't want to be bothered by the former Microsoft programmer, essentially instructed Black to ignore Hecker.

"Chris is somewhat of a strange animal—mixture of chutzpah and naivete," Maritz said.

And so, on June 13, Hecker released his letter, which read in part:

"We . . . call on Microsoft to continue its active OpenGL development. . . . As developers, we believe the choice of which 3D API to support for our games should be ours alone.

"We recognize Microsoft must take part in creating this technically competitive environment because of their control over the operating system. . . ."

After several publications and Web magazines printed Hecker's petition, St. John unleashed a series of scorching E-mails up the Microsoft chain of command, essentially accusing Black and other executives of incompetence. He also expressed bitterness about not being informed of Hecker's meeting with Black and her ensuing

E-mail dialog with Maritz. It's doubtful Microsoft senior management had ever received such brazenly bellicose mail before, at least from employees. And it's doubtful they ever will again. St. John had a knack for burying the knife deep.

He accused Black of "spewing" leaks to Hecker and others outside the company and deliberately "subverting" his evangelism work in the computer-game community. "I can't work against this kind of BS," he told her. "I'm fed up with trying to help you here."

Less than an hour later St. John sent E-mail directly to Gates, Maritz, and Torborg, among others, saying the petition was the result of "some really poor evangelism and account management, a little bad media handling, a really screwed-up 3D strategy for too long and a proactive effort on the part of some current and former Microsoft employees."

Maritz promptly responded, telling St. John he was completely out of line. Maritz acknowledged that he received E-mail from Hecker requesting a meeting. Maritz ignored the message, and later passed it on to Black, instructing her to meet with Hecker to try to pacify him. At any rate, Maritz said, Microsoft was going to support Direct3D based on feedback it received from Developer Relations Group—St. John's own people.

"We may very well have had other folks leaking stuff outside of MS during this process," Maritz told St. John. "But it is not Deb, and you owe Deb an apology."

St. John "apologized" all right—an apology dripping with so much bleeding sarcasm that it has become legendary inside the company. Employees scrambled to get copies of it to post in the hallways and on office doors of the Redmond campus, even as Microsoft lawyers issued orders that the E-mail was to be destroyed.

St. John verbally attacked Maritz and Black for failing to include him in any of the meetings or discussions regarding the Direct3D debate. St. John was particularly furious that he was told of Hecker's open letter to Microsoft only after it was published.

"HOW DO YOU EXPECT ME TO MANAGE THESE ISVs or manage the media on something like this when nobody is communicating with me or DirectX marketing?" St. John fumed. "Isn't developer relations my job?"

St. John said Microsoft was ignoring his "tremendous" wealth of knowledge and experience in the game community.

"While I'm shouting 'Look out for the rocks!' at the top of my lungs, you're telling me to apologize for getting angry and frustrated with Deborah for running the ship aground," he said.

His three-page, single-spaced tirade segued to sardonic apology.

"I'm sorry I personally promised so much technology and support to so many ISVs and IHVs and lived to see them burned so badly by our blundering and lack of focus," he began.

"I'm sorry I falsely accused Deborah of maliciously leaking internal information to Chris Hecker. It's clear to me now that it was just a foolish mistake that she made despite being warned," he said in another passage. "My humble apologies."

He went on to "apologize" to Tony Garcia, Bruce Jacobson and Patty Stonesifer for their contributions to "dull, uninspired multimedia titles."

He apologized to Paul Osborne, a "nice, well-intentioned guy" who did his best by "pursuing the uninspired strategy of doing whatever Apple did."

To Alistair Banks, for trying to stop him from announcing the development of Quartz, a stillborn challenger to QuickTime. "I see now that my effort was futile, and challenging your video architecture just made its inevitable failure more stressful for everybody without actually solving anything."

St. John included Mike Van Flandern for the run-in the two had over the aborted "Raptor" joystick project. "Your group still can't seem to make a simple joystick driver work, let alone the vastly complex one you envisioned delivering one day, told all of the game developers about, and never wrote a line of code for."

To Mike Abrash, On Lee, Otto Berkes, Steve Wright, Hock San Lee, and all the other 3-D developers. "With so many people working on so many different API's and drivers how could we help but stumble onto a solution one day."

And finally, St. John tipped his hat to Chris Hecker, who taught him that "the only way to get WinG to ship after promising it to 300 developers and not finishing it was to have Craig Eisler sit on him to get it done. And really, really piss him off."

He apologized to Jay Torborg, Mark Kenworthy and Jim Veres, "three great worker bees who did their level best to satisfy their management, and justify massive R&D investment."

To Colin Campbell and Salim AbiEzzi: "I'm sorry I gave Active-Animation such a hard time for being useless and having no identifiable customers."

Bill Gates has said publicly that Microsoft "has to attract a lot of people who think in different ways, it has to allow a lot of dissent." But clearly Paul Maritz and the rest of the executive staff had had enough of St. John's dissent. St. John had gone too far. The day after the "apology," Morris Beton, group manager at DRG, called St. John in for a chat. If Microsoft managers have something to say to employees, they'll usually do it via E-mail. When they have to fire someone, they call the doomed employee in for a talk. This allows Microsoft security officers to swoop in when the employee is out of the office, sweep the room for any sensitive documents, and lock down the computer to prevent sensitive files from leaving.

St. John knew his days at Microsoft were coming to a close and anticipated the time when Beton or Black or any number of executives would call him over for the final good-bye.

Before leaving his office for the last time, St. John grabbed a handful of Hershey's chocolate kisses from Engstrom's office and scribbled a note saying "Help yourself!" for the security guards.

A beaming St. John walked into Beton's office and plopped an apple on his desk, like a proud grade-schooler sucking up to a teacher.

"What's that for?" Beton asked.

"That's so you can have a funny anecdote to tell people when you talk about how you fired me," St. John said.

Morris put on his bureaucratic game face and told St. John that he had failed to improve on his performance over the last six months—

which was untrue but necessary for legal reasons. St. John's lowest review during his tenure at Microsoft was a 4.0.

"I'm supposed to advise you strongly that it's time for you to pursue other interests," Beton finally said.

And with that, St. John strode off the Microsoft campus a free man. For the first time in five years, St. John felt relief, like a techno-indentured servant who had put in his last day at the digital factory. He never did get his $5 million in unvested stock. But he viewed that as the price he had to pay to get his life back.

"I didn't have to choose to walk away from five million dollars," St. John says. "Microsoft made the decision for me, which made it easier."

Others in the company still debate whether Microsoft should have fired St. John.

"If he hadn't grown so powerful so quickly with his own ISV audience, he might have learned that he had to behave differently with . . . other development teams and senior management," says Alistair Banks, one of Microsoft's original evangelists. "I'm sure he was a loss to Microsoft, but considering all things, he was doing more damage than good at that time. Something had to change, and the whole of the rest of the hierarchy wasn't about to leave."

Yet St. John's impact could not be understated. At one time Microsoft had eighty evangelists urging software makers to build programs for Windows 95. Of the scores of Windows 95 applications that were built during St. John's tenure, he claims to have ushered more than 60 percent of those on his own by evangelizing DirectX.

Ken Fowles, the Harley-riding evangelist who had strongly backed hiring St. John in '92, believes Microsoft reacted too corporately.

"Five years earlier he wouldn't have gotten fired," says Fowles, recalling the Microsoft of the early 1990s. "There was this siege mentality when I joined. Microsoft was attacking all these different market segments. Evangelists were fearless. They would get on a plane to descend on people and didn't even ask if it was okay to go."

Fowles says the company grew more conservative, in the pejorative sense. Frequent reorganizations may have played a part, creating inertia as many hunkered down, hoping to dodge the expected disruptions and dismantling and reconstruction of product teams. Moreover, because of its size and power, many—but by no means all—at Microsoft had lost the taste for the hunt, that desire to conquer new markets. At the same time, size made the company self-conscious—particularly after the Department of Justice attacked—and some inside Microsoft were hesitant to gun for certain markets for fear of drawing antitrust fire.

"Now there's this attitude that, 'Well, we can't do that kind of thing because of what the company is,' and I never heard that when I first joined, this complacency," Fowles says.

He says where once St. John's vitriolic E-mail would have triggered a "flame war that would have flamed out," such spirited candor was now considered insubordination.

"This guy single-handedly moved an industry," Fowles adds. "The thought of getting rid of a guy like that baffles me. The company changed—Alex didn't."

That was fine with St. John. He was able to wrap up his divorce and shed sixty pounds within two months after leaving Microsoft. He started making social contacts again and took an extended vacation to the South Pacific. What's more, the day after he was fired, Microsoft acknowledged that it had canceled its Talisman reference design for 3-D chips. Although Microsoft vowed to keep elements of Talisman alive, no trace of it ever appeared.

Score a TKO for St. John.

But best of all for the other two Beastie Boys, St. John's noisy war game had helped keep the wolves at bay while Project Chrome gained momentum.

9

INVITE TO A "REVOLUTION"

St. John's noisy exodus cleared some of the internal political land mines for Eisler and Engstrom. Others who might have ambushed Chrome were engaged with their own skirmishes as well as St. John's spectacular career suicide. Eisler, Engstrom, and team Chrome took advantage of some of this to stage their hopeful invasion of the Web. But to stage a revolution, you need people waging battle in the streets, in this case developers who would actually build Web sites with the new technology.

The Chrome team believed developers would embrace the technology if it was easy to use; that's why Heddle and McCartney wanted it to author as easily as HTML. Eisler and Engstrom reasoned that one way to simplify Chrome would be to provide a tool that would help developers build Chrome sites. With Microsoft money in hand, Engstrom took the lead and went shopping for a tools company.

Unlike the RenderMorphics deal, this time he would not need to curry the favor of Michael Abrash, the 3-D graphics guru who had defected from Microsoft to join id, only to return to Gates's Empire. Engstrom's credibility at the company, if not his popularity, had risen with the growing market adoption of DirectX. That technology, developed by a skunk works, had gone mainstream—it had been plugged into Internet Explorer browsers and would be hardwired to Memphis, code name for Windows 98.

So Engstrom thought he would have little trouble when he wanted to assimilate San Francisco–based Dimension X and add it to the fledgling Chrome arsenal.

Dimension X, founded in 1995, billed itself as the computer industry's first start-up to build and market Java-based products. Its claim to fame was Liquid Motion, a Java-based authoring tool, which enabled programmers to make 3-D and multimedia Web content such as banner ads, animated graphics, and the like, as well as Liquid Reality, a Java-based VRML (virtual reality modeling language) browser. Microsoft had already licensed some of Dimension X's technology for the IE browser. With the acquisition of the forty-employee company, Dimension X's Liquid products and technology would be integrated further into DirectX multimedia, which enabled developers to incorporate video, audio, 3-D, 2-D, and animation into applications for Windows.

A couple of stars throttled into alignment to help Engstrom win approval for the acquisition, even though the odds initially appeared stacked against him.

Tod Nielsen, the manager of multimedia at Developer Relations Group who had canceled St. John's alien-abduction event, was advancing a project known as iHammer, code name for a set of canned multimedia special effects for Internet Explorer 4. Engstrom privately derided iHammer "as a world unto itself" and not nearly as functional as the multimedia authoring technology Dimension X had developed. More to the point, Engstrom viewed iHammer as a competitive threat to Chrome because iHammer siphoned from the same pool of resources and duplicated some of the elements of his work. Under ordinary circumstances, trying to sink a general manager's project would appear reckless and futile. But in typical Engstrom fashion, he marshaled information to his advantage.

In February, Engstrom alerted superiors that Sun's JavaSoft division was two weeks from making its own play for Dimension X, and made a compelling, if not Byzantine, argument that Microsoft should do what was necessary to thwart this acquisition. JavaSoft was aligned with its spin-off Marimba Inc. of Mountain View, California. Engstrom said that JavaSoft and Marimba were poised to partner with Netscape to provide it with key multimedia authoring tools hoarded from Dimension X.

"Given how important iHammer is to TodN, I would think derailing the iHammer equivalent for Netscape would be a HUGE thing," Engstrom wrote Senior Vice President Brad Silverberg. "We could achieve a big tactical win here by removing their key tool."

Depriving Netscape of a weapon was an argument that played well with senior management, even if it came at an estimated cost of $20 million. Microsoft authorized the purchase.

But pulling the rug out from Netscape wasn't entirely Engstrom's point.

"The whole point . . . was to vector Tod Nielsen's support for iHammer into the Dimension X acquisition," Engstrom says. "Quite frankly, iHammer was a project I wanted to kill at Microsoft, but I needed Tod Nielsen's support [for the acquisition]."

Moreover, Dimension X came with more than a dozen highly skilled Java programmers.

"We desperately need good 3D talent . . . to make Chrome happen faster," Engstrom wrote to members of his staff.

With the assimilation of Dimension X, Engstrom predicted that by mid-1998, Microsoft would be "churning out AWESOME demonstrations of the power of Chrome."

Still, Engstrom's acquisition didn't sit entirely well with key members of his team.

"With Liquid Motion, the Chrome authoring tool, he never bothered to ask the Chrome leads if this is something they needed or wanted," says Heddle, Chrome's lead program manager. "That decision took a lot of time out of our schedules to interview a lot of people. There were times we needed to get ahold of Eric and he was off trying to close the Dimension X deal.

"He actually hindered Chrome at some stages."

Nonetheless, the acquisition earned Engstrom glowing accolades from Microsoft executives, who saw the Java programming language—which promised to run on any operating system—as a threat to Windows. Microsoft would much rather absorb an innovative Java company such as Dimension X than compete against it.

Now that he had his Java, Engstrom wanted his Caffeine, a poor man's version of Liquid Motion. Where Liquid Motion would be a separate tool to provide sophisticated transitions and effects, Engstrom intended Caffeine to be included with Chrome to supply simple 3-D shapes and the like. This generated more gripes from Heddle and McCartney, who believed that Engstrom not only piled on too much work, but also suffered from "feature-itis," the insatiable desire to add on features to a technology.

"When Eric approached me to work on Chrome, it was with the understanding it was a team effort, there would be a lot more people involved," McCartney says. "In fact when we first started working on it, it was just Bob and I. Eric managed to give us about thirteen other tasks as well, mostly all DirectX stuff.

"We didn't do a particularly good job of starting Chrome because of the other responsibilities," he adds.

McCartney tried to keep all the balls in the air, while Heddle dropped most of his DirectX duties and focused on Chrome, creating another source of tension between Engstrom and his lead Chrome developer.

At one point Engstrom outlined no less than eight initial features that he wanted crammed into the first version of Chrome, including hi-fi sound, 2-D rendering, 3-D rendering, and Caffeine, among others. Heddle and McCartney wondered who was going to do all the work to get all these features into Chrome's first release, initially slated for June 1998.

"None of the people I talked to who were supposed to do some of this stuff could explain how it was going to work," says Heddle. "They said they understood when Eric was in the room explaining it. But were at a loss later. They were victims of what I call the 'Engstrom reality distortion field.' "

Engstrom has a way of imposing his will. He debates methodically, persistently, and enjoys arguing someone out of his position, then arguing him back in—sometimes just for the pleasure of beating him again, Heddle says. Engstrom was the guy, remember, who convinced an astronomer that Venus, not Polaris, was the North Star. That takes remarkable rhetorical skill. It can also take up a lot of time.

Heddle and McCartney would argue that certain features in Chrome were beyond the scope of what the first release should contain. The first iteration of Chrome, as conceived by the ambitious Engstrom, was just too big. Engstrom initially refused to ditch all the added features, and the ensuing arguments, Heddle says, delayed the project.

"We'd say, 'Eric, the stick's too long!' and he'd break the stick and say, 'Measure again,' " says Heddle. "Sometimes he was right, you could actually squeeze more in. But other times it was impossible. Like pi, right, is 3.14. But Eric would say, 'Measure again.' Some things you can't change."

Heddle was also disappointed with St. John, who had failed to secure the licensing rights for the THX logo, the initials for Lucasfilm's motion-picture sound technology. Heddle wanted a right to use the metallic, futuristic logo in a demonstration video because it had wide brand recognition—it materialized at the beginning of some of Hollywood's biggest movies—and was a large, simple shape to render. But St. John flamed out before finishing the job.

"That was my one big request of Alex and Alex didn't come through," Heddle says. "That was the extent of his involvement in Chrome. Yeah, Chrome may have been his idea, but [McCartney and I] were the ones who did all the implementation. Having an idea is one thing. Actually executing it is another."

But Heddle and McCartney were busy working deep inside the hull of Chrome and did not see the bigger political, strategic, and personal battles St. John had been engaged in on the upper deck.

The two were also harboring resentment toward Eisler, who they thought wasn't pulling his weight. Eisler often was absent day to day when his expertise could have been useful. But he would make appearances at Chrome meetings when company bigwigs were attending.

"There was a common perception that Craig wasn't doing much," McCartney says. "He decoupled himself from Chrome. There was a fair degree of resentment for that. There was work that needed to get done. He came to these vice president meetings, but he wasn't involved in the preparation. I answered all the technical questions."

Heddle, McCartney, and others didn't fully appreciate that Eisler, the master coder of DirectX and the recipient of no less than eleven patents, was undergoing a rite of the overworked—divorce. His six-year marriage had collapsed while he toiled for the Empire and the riches such work promised.

While he dismisses the divorce as not much of a distraction, others, including Engstrom, beg to differ.

"It was massively distracting to Craig," Engstrom says. "He downplays his divorce and that leads people to believe that he must not have cared, right? In his effort to make himself look strong he may look indifferent.

"There was a good two-month period in there where Craig was going through his divorce where he did nothing and that was fine," Engstrom adds. "I didn't expect anything from him."

Engstrom could relate. Eisler's internal hiatus mirrored the one Engstrom had taken after his own marriage plans had collapsed and he went to hide inside the company's Advanced Consumer Technology group. Moreover, Eisler had grown tired of working under Engstrom. Although Eisler and Engstrom thought themselves kindred spirits, in the end Engstrom actually had more in common with St. John. Both were built like hay bales. Like St. John, Engstrom never earned a four-year degree, a noncredential that bestowed a certain renegade status in the degreed realm of Microsoft. And like St. John, Engstrom seemed to be more of a risk-taker than Eisler. Engstrom and St. John stayed in touch socially. Eisler, however, distanced himself from St. John for political reasons. The smallest of the Beastie Boys entertained bigger plans to advance his career, and associating with St. John and lingering on the fringes of DirectX and Chrome weren't going to get him there. So Eisler drifted toward the margin of Chrome—and away from the other two Beastie Boys—as he recalibrated his career compass at Microsoft.

Despite the ill will toward Eisler and to a lesser extent Engstrom, the Chrome team made progress. Heddle and McCartney were busy solving the thorny problem of getting Chrome to interpret digital instructions sent via a phone line and then to reconstruct the data into animated 3-D images. Meanwhile, Netscape did its best to keep Microsoft executives focused on the browser war.

The same month St. John and Microsoft parted ways, Netscape released its official version of Communicator 4.0, a bruiser of a browser that allowed users to compose Web pages, send Web pages via E-mail, and read and post messages on newsgroups, among other things. While some decried the browser as bloated—no other browser to date had such a broad range of capabilities—the press gave Communicator rave reviews, noting that the official release of Microsoft's Internet Explorer 4.0 was still some four months off.

But Microsoft could not let the challenge go unanswered, even if it didn't have any real return ammunition at the moment. The day Netscape released Communicator, Microsoft unleashed an advertising blitz touting the coming of IE 4—a typical and perfectly legal Microsoft ploy to persuade consumers to delay purchasing or downloading a rival product. Netscape responded with predictable outrage.

"Customers buy our products, not promises of future resources, not promises of future products, not all that fear, uncertainty, and doubt that Microsoft is the best in the world at spreading," blasted Jim Barksdale, Netscape's chief executive.

For all its bluster, Netscape was running scared, having seen its browser market share tumble from nearly 90 percent to below 70 percent in less than a year. By June '97 Netscape's stock price had imploded as well, dropping to about $29 a share, a free fall from a high of $78 a share in January 1996, adjusted for splits.

The market share for Microsoft's free IE 3 browser had surged to about 30 percent—despite the bad publicity associated with the discovery of a security bug in the program. The security flaw had delayed the release of IE 4 and undoubtedly slowed Microsoft's relentless grab at Netscape market share. Still, Microsoft's IE team, which hung "Refuse to Use" Netscape bumper stickers in the halls of Redmond in reference to the "Refuse to Lose" slogan of the '95 Seattle Mariners, had reason to rejoice.

Netscape, it turned out, wasn't immune to bugs. Shortly after Communicator's release, Web developers in Denmark discovered a security flaw in Netscape's new and previous browsers, giving Microsoft inadvertent momentum.

Netscape, which had exploded onto the scene with the first commercial Web browser, was trying to wean itself from reliance on consumer browser sales. By 1997 it was targeting corporate "intranets," in-house versions of the Internet that let employees E-mail files and Web documents on internal, presumably secure networks. The potential size of the intranet market was expected to exceed $10 billion by the year 2000. Yet the corporate enterprise was Sun, IBM, and to a growing extent, Microsoft territory. Microsoft had been forging deep into the corporate realm with Windows NT. And IBM, reinforced with the 1995 acquisition of Lotus and its groupware, enjoyed an entrenched presence in corporate America.

"We may not be cool [like Netscape], but we are trusted," quipped Dr. Irving Wladwasky-Berger, head of Internet at IBM.

Competing against Microsoft was tough enough, but to attack it where it was strong bordered on the insane. And Netscape wasn't just any competitor. This was the company that had beat Microsoft to the Internet and championed its software as the weapon that would render Windows irrelevant. Bolder and more foolish still was Marc Andreessen, Netscape's senior vice president of technology, who publicly ridiculed Windows 95 as a mediocre, bug-laden device-driver layer. The truth does more than hurt; it tends to make people mad. Andreessen's bad-mouthing of Windows 95 angered not only Microsoft executives, but riled Engstrom as well.

"It's like Andreessen found this sword in the forest and held it up to a great samurai and said, 'Look! I have one, too,' " Engstrom says. "Netscape's problem was it just made too much noise. We couldn't ignore it so we had to use our own sword."

That sword was Windows, the operating system used on about 90 percent of the world's personal computers. In a few months Microsoft would piggyback the IE 4 browser onto Windows 95. Microsoft planned to fully integrate the browser with Memphis, aka Windows 98—all in the name of making life easier for consumers.

The government, however, began to argue that the company was trying to use its Windows monopoly to dominate the Web. The stage was being set for a showdown.

When Microsoft previewed Windows 98 for the press in July '97, the world saw what it was like to graft a browser to an operating system. Windows 98 would look and work more like a browser; users would open files and navigate on the hard drive in much the same way they would surf the Net. Indeed, users would be able to find and display Web pages by using Windows rather than separate software, such as Netscape's browser. Windows and its conjoined companion Internet Explorer could become a de facto Web device, a prospect that drew fire from competitors and government trustbusters.

"Microsoft is trying to reach out and kill the browser market," complained Microsoft critic Gary Reback, the anti-Microsoft attorney with Wilson, Sonsini, Goodrich & Rosati in Palo Alto, California, which represented Netscape and other Redmond competitors. His remarks would later resonate in a massive government antitrust probe.

As all this controversy exploded overhead, team Chrome was in the bunker toiling in relative and fortuitous obscurity.

Chrome dovetailed well with Microsoft's overarching Internet mission. The technology would only work on Windows computers, it was

Web-based, and it was tied directly to the operating system. The paradox was that Chrome was controversial for some of those very same reasons. Some familiar with Chrome started calling the project "the Netscape killer." Engstrom, who was becoming increasingly sensitive to internal and external political threats, quickly doused that moniker. In fact he and others stopped calling it a browser altogether—Chrome became a Windows 98 "enhancement." This shift was the result of Microsoft's larger strategy of redefining the operating system to include the IE 4 browser—insisting that a browser was not a separate piece of software but a part of Windows. Microsoft competitors and the Justice Department, however, were becoming increasingly vocal in their criticism of Microsoft's plans to fuse a browser to Windows and accused the company of doing so with the sole intent of obliterating Netscape's market share.

"Chrome is not a 'Netscape killer,' " Engstrom admonished in one E-mail. "It's a new paradigm for conveying information."

McCartney concurred: "We never set out to build a 'Netscape killer.' That was never our mission. Our mission was to make Windows *the* platform to doing Web stuff."

Engstrom had matured since the DirectX days. Where he might once have sanctioned NETSCAPE KILLER T-shirts, he was now learning to play it more low-key. Engstrom's mellowing was in part the result of the weekly mentoring consultations he and Eisler had had with John Ludwig. But political considerations also forced Engstrom to advance with more diplomacy. Whereas DirectX targeted an identifiable market, Chrome's market—high-end computers running at the superfast rate of 450-plus megahertz—didn't even exist yet. Unlike with DirectX, he couldn't boast that he was attacking a "FIVE-BILLION-DOLLAR MARKET." While DirectX had been about seizing new ground through brute force, Chrome was more a finesse game. Given the increasing likelihood of antitrust litigation, Engstrom and Eisler toned down the message that Chrome was a weapon against Netscape and other Internet rivals. The two found themselves walking a delicate line. If they called too much attention to the technology, they ran the risk of having it attacked by rivals inside Microsoft, not to mention capturing the premature interest of antitrust investigators. On the other hand, if they didn't nurture it with enough internal hype, it could die before getting a chance to bloom.

Despite the bumpy start and the internal dissent, by the end of summer '97 Chrome had several things going in its favor. Dimension X and its Liquid Motion were inside the fort. The Chrome team had a simple standard language, XML, to deploy a new breed of Web content. And Intel was on board to support the technology. Engstrom and Eisler, in a move to boost morale, bet that they would shave their heads if a DirectX team could produce more working code within a couple of weeks. The team met the deadline and Engstrom and Eisler were forced to become "Chrome domes."

What Project Chrome needed now was actual product. It's been said that content is king when it comes to the Web. Eisler and Engstrom didn't have anyone outside the company building Chrome content. They needed independent software vendors building Chrome sites to validate the new technology. Wedding others to your technology is, after all, another way of tar babying it. The two Beastie Boys knew just where to turn.

In a scene reminiscent of the Godfather coming to collect on an old favor, Eisler and Engstrom first approached Monolith Productions, a computer-game company just down the freeway from Microsoft.

Monolith was founded in 1995 by Jason Hall and a half dozen other former developers at Edmark Corp., a Redmond-based educational-software firm. Hall and his partners had wanted to get into the more lucrative computer-game business and had built a demonstration multimedia CD-ROM in '95 that caught the eye of St. John. The Beastie Boys commissioned Hall and his crew to write a game sampler CD for Windows 95 using the then-new DirectX technologies. Hall, a former marine, teenage stockbroker, and computer hacker, used the commission money to seed Monolith.

The arrangement worked well. For Hall and his Monolith employees, making games such as Blood was far more fun and profitable than making educational CD-ROMs. Conversely, the Beastie Boys had a reliable ally using DirectX.

The Beastie Boys had helped Hall become a wealthy man. So when Engstrom asked, Hall obliged in developing content for Chrome, a technology ideally suited for game Web sites. Game companies use the Web to showcase upcoming titles in development and to give fans a sort of behind-the-scenes look at production. Games, with their 3-D worlds and fast action, dovetailed well with the potential of Chrome. Monolith received $25,000 from Microsoft to build "Chrome-plated" demo Web sites. Monolith leveraged the contract by building sites based on its new game, code-named Riot.

"The money wasn't that great, but we like to keep up with new technology," recalls Karen Burger, one of Monolith's project managers. "And maybe other companies will come to us for creative designs."

Yet signing on to build prototype Chrome sites entailed obvious risks. Although Monolith was paid for developing Chrome content, the exercise would siphon time and resources from other projects. Because the technology was so new, it would be poorly documented and contain a nest of bugs. The first Monolith demos didn't even use Chrome, but a patchwork of scripts and VRML (virtual reality modeling language) coding.

"It was a little frustrating," Burger says. "Microsoft asked us for a very flashy demo—'cool' was the term they used. To do cool we had to use VRML."

Moreover, because Chrome would be built for computers that didn't exist commercially at the time, there was no guarantee a critical mass of Web developers would embrace the new technology, dooming or at least hampering it before it had a chance to grow legs.

However, the payoff could be handsome, as Monolith had discovered with DirectX. As early adopters, Monolith and a handful of other Chrome recruits would have at least a six-month lead on competitors who took a shine to Chrome. In Internet time, six months can be as good as six years. By working with Microsoft early on, initial developers could get better at squashing bugs and advancing the technology's potential. And, if widely adopted, Chrome could change the way the world viewed the Web—in 3-D and in stereo. In the end, Monolith realized that Chrome could do for the Web what DirectX had done for Windows.

Or as Adam Ketola, one of Monolith's Web artists, mused, "Hey, this could ultimately revolutionize the entire Web industry."

10

MERCENARIES OF THE EMPIRE

Eisler and Engstrom would need more than Monolith, however. The two Beastie Boys needed more bodies to build compelling Chrome demos. Reinforcements would arrive from an unlikely source some two thousand miles away. A seemingly random series of events would reintroduce Eisler and Engstrom to Paul Scholz, a casual acquaintance they had met years before at computer trade shows. In the end, Scholz and his small team would build more prototype Chrome Web sites than anyone else inside or out of Microsoft—demos that would impress Bill Gates and would eventually be showcased at the coming-out party for Windows 98.

In the fall of 1997, inside a monastic office carpeted in software manuals and CD-ROMs, Scholz hunched at his keyboard and composed another E-mail. The modern Beethoven tucked gray locks behind an ear and playfully surrendered to an impulsive muse, oblivious to the stain on his jeans from the previous night's meal of a cheeseburger and fries. He shifted in his rickety armchair, an aged and hazardous device that nearly spilled him backward at times. The chair was companion to a folding desk, which, missing a support beam, bowed under the weight of a seventeen-inch computer monitor. His appearance and his furniture, though shabby, were a pragmatist's testimony to function over form. For inside this unassuming workspace, he was linked digitally and contractually to the most powerful software company on the planet.

Scholz was owner and president of flashCast Communications Corp., a four-man Web-development firm in Dayton, Ohio. Scholz had scrounged in the bitter autumn of 1996, pleading with banks for venture-capital loans never approved. In less than a year, however, he had earned the respect of some inside Microsoft and was corresponding with the likes of Steve Ballmer, then the Empire's executive vice president of sales and support and one of Bill Gates's most trusted generals.

Original Message——
From: pscholz@flashcast.com [SMTP:pscholz@flashcast.com]
Sent: Tuesday, September 16, 1997 10:09 AM
To: Steve Ballmer
Subject: SteveB's Shakespearean Creed

"And we charge, that in our marches through the country, that nothing be compelled from our customers, nothing taken but paid for, no one from Netscape or Sun upbraided or abused in disdainful language. For when levity and cruelty play for a kingdom, the gentler gamester is the soonest winner."

The next day came Ballmer's two-word reply: "Sounds right."

No one accused Microsoft of being "the gentler gamester," particularly by 1997 during the height of the browser war. But that really was not the point. That Ballmer had time to respond, let alone read Scholz's bastardization of the Bard, served as inspiration. After losing precious time during the eighties—the decade of decadence, cocaine, and excess—the forty-two-year-old Scholz had achieved more than self-made success.

"In the browser war, flashCast is the most forward-leading element in Microsoft's army," Scholz boasted in the late summer of 1997.

Scholz's march to battle began, appropriately enough, in the military. In 1975, the same year that Gates and Paul Allen had launched

Microsoft in Albuquerque, New Mexico, Scholz had enlisted as a cavalry scout in the U.S. army. He became a commissioned officer and was assigned to the Chemical Corps at Ft. McClellan, Alabama, where he calculated combat casualties from simulated chemical warfare. He shed army fatigues for civilian clothes in 1981 and spent the next fifteen years as a computer consultant for corporations from Baltimore to the Bay Area. Then the Internet wave arrived, and Scholz, "tired of working for people dumber than me," formed his own Web company.

Initially, flashCast was going to build Web sites that delivered audio and video content via PointCast or other "push" technology. The good news was flashCast received numerous business inquiries. The bad news was that all too many of those calls were from pornography vendors charmed by the idea of streaming smut to desktops—flashCast turned them all down.

"I'm all for free speech and everything, man, but we didn't want to get involved in that stuff," says Scholz, a nonpracticing Christian. "Think of the kind of people you'd have to deal with."

As a result, his start-up company faced insolvency shortly after its inception in June 1996. Yet within a year, his business had become one of only two companies in the world to help build initial content for Chrome. Ask about his reversal of fortune, and Scholz says, "You've seen *Henry V,* right?" referring to the Kenneth Branagh screen adaptation of Shakespeare's play. No matter your answer, Scholz briefs you on Agincourt.

The battle of Agincourt was waged five centuries ago and some four thousand miles from Dayton. For Scholz, the battle remains immortal. Outmanned more than three to one, England's young warrior-king Henry V faced certain annihilation. He had pushed his expeditionary force of six thousand archers and men at arms deep into France in a highly mobile and up-to-then victorious campaign. His troops had fought bravely, but a 250-mile return march in just seventeen days had left the men fatigued and ill. Morale hit a wall. And, wouldn't you know, it was raining. Aware of the grim odds and wanting his troops well rested, Henry ordered absolute silence in camp that chilly eve of battle, October 24, 1415. Meanwhile, more than twenty thousand French troops, believing their numerical superiority had frightened off the English, partied all night.

Henry, dressed in complete armor except headgear so his men could see his face, led a thousand troops onto the sodden battlefield that next morning, while five thousand of his archers hung back. Within an hour thousands of French corpses littered the field. The English won.

How?

Superior technology and a better game plan. The English maneuvered the enemy into a killing zone then rained arrows from longbows, a weapon the French lacked and one that could launch ordnance with enough velocity to pierce armor.

Scholz insists there is a parable. In the summer of 1996, the men of flashCast faced grim odds against a numerically and financially stronger adversary, Datalytics Inc. In those days, few serious Web firms were competing in Dayton. Despite Scholz's technical credentials— Visual C++ programmer, Windows specialist, chemical-warfare analyst, among a long list of others—the fledgling flashCast didn't have the client base to make payroll. To pay his troops and get the company off the ground, Scholz sold his vintage 1946 Globe Swift airplane for $18,000, less than half what it was worth. His company, as he puts it, "was doing Web sites for food." In fact, to establish itself and gain clientele, flashCast built some Web sites for free. Although flashCast's initial struggle for survival was not unlike that of countless other start-ups, Scholz blames part of his company's woes on Datalytics, which he alleges reneged on its part of a deal to feed flashCast Web business. Worse, according to Scholz, Datalytics had threatened to use its established presence and bigger market share to bury flashCast.

But Scholz, who keeps *Henry V* at the ready by his VCR, is not easily defeated. By the end of 1997, Datalytics had folded, Microsoft had signed flashCast to work on Chrome, and Scholz's accounts receivable had swelled to more than $100,000. Scholz, who once helped program the largest computer war game ever devised for the Defense Advanced

Research Projects Agency, frames the world in military terms. That flashCast outlasted Datalytics prompts him to compare his company to the English at Agincourt.

"Superior technology and a smarter strategy," Scholz says, guffawing. "We're mercenaries of the Empire."

Scholz, in fact, had little to do with the demise of Datalytics, a company that once joined former Ohio governor George Voinovich on a technology junket to India, a favored spot for corporate headhunters seeking programmers who will work for less pay than their American counterparts. Datalytics climbed into its own grave when it hired more people than it needed, stuffed its downtown office suites with expensive furniture it couldn't afford, and invested in data-compression and other Web tools no one bought.

Meanwhile, through the remainder of 1996 and into 1997, Scholz laid the groundwork that would put flashCast in the trenches of the browser war.

When flashCast built a Web site, it promoted Microsoft and always included icons with links to Redmond's browser. A prolific E-mail writer, Scholz made sure field representatives from the Microsoft Site Developer Network knew about his evangelism by firing off flattering messages extolling his "service to the Empire."

flashCast's home page, with its signature art deco man emerging from a radioactive cloud, earned a Microsoft Network Pick of the Week in October 1996. Scholz seized the marketing opportunity and pasted the award icon on the flashCast site as a badge of glory. Later that month one of flashCast's sites, a freebie built for Dayton's retro burger joint The Diner on St. Clair, was among fifty finalists in Microsoft's Activate the Internet '96 contest. Scholz's business won $1,000 in free software, some of which it shared with The Diner. More important, his small company's work grabbed the attention of Microsoft officials in Redmond. The software giant bestowed upon flashCast the status of Level 3 Microsoft Site Builder, the highest membership ranking within the global Microsoft Site Developer Network. Level 3 status meant—at least in Microsoft's estimation—

you were among the best at building high-end Web pages, ones that used databases, animation, sound, the latest coding tricks. There were only about two hundred Level 3 site builders worldwide back in October 1996, and as late as summer 1997 flashCast was only one of two companies in all of Ohio to have the designation. Scholz even persuaded Microsoft to waive the annual $2,500 membership fee, an extremely rare, if not singular, honor.

"Back in those days we were getting so much crap submitted to us," says Eric Ewing, then product manager for the Microsoft Site Developer Network. "Paul's Web sites really stood out."

Although just five feet seven inches tall, Scholz had a way of standing out, of grabbing attention in a world of giants. Before leaving a bar in New York's SoHo neighborhood one day, he cinched his overcoat, approached the owner, and sotto voce, told him, "We're here for the envelope."

"You could make alotta money doin' dat round heeah," the owner said, laughing, slapping Scholz on the shoulder. "You could get killed, too."

When Site Developer Network representatives paid visits to flashCast, Scholz treated them like royalty, sometimes draping them in a gilded $600 tapestry he had bought in Tysons Corner, Virginia.

Sometimes Scholz acted younger than his first batch of young employees—David J. Culberston, twenty-four at the time, who goes by the high school nickname Inky; Dustin Tiemeier, who was seventeen when he started at flashCast; and Geoff Porter, a twentysomething database programmer.

Scott Bateman, former director of Cox Interactive Media in Dayton and the one in charge of Web sites for the *Dayton Daily News* and other Cox media outlets in the area, recalls a business lunch where Scholz started shooting spit wads at a waitress.

"You know what he's like? He's like a twelve-year-old trapped in the body of an adult," Bateman says.

Still, that didn't stop Bateman and others from doing business with Scholz. His growing client list included Dow Chemical Inc., Motorola

Inc., and perhaps most important, Lexis-Nexis, home to one of the world's largest warehouses of on-line legal documents. In the months before he started flashCast, Scholz had worked as a Web-server consultant for Dayton-based Lexis-Nexis. flashCast later constructed Web pages for the company and its parent, Reed Elsevier PLC, a $30-million partner with Microsoft. Although Scholz refers to the British/Dutch-owned Lexis-Nexis as "a real Dilbert outfit" because of its management-heavy organization, the work flashCast did there lofted the company's star sharply into Microsoft's view.

Based on flashCast's work at Lexis-Nexis, and because it was a Level 3 Site Builder and Activate the Internet finalist, in May 1997 Microsoft invited Scholz's company and a select group of outside developers to help fine-tune infant or alpha versions of Internet Explorer 4, Redmond's answer to Netscape's Navigator, then the market-leading browser. Both browsers featured advanced E-mail capabilities, better ways to jump back and forth to previously viewed pages, and simple Web-page-authoring tools. Both also offered competing, noncompatible versions of Dynamic HTML, which among other things can handle animation faster. flashCast emerged as a specialist with Microsoft's version of Dynamic HTML. flashCast's Inky, named for his drawing acumen and because he used to chew on pens till they splurted ink as a ruse to get out of taking geography tests, has a deserved reputation for showing up late. He customarily awakes at the crack of noon. He still didn't have a driver's license at age twenty-three. As tardy as he is in much of his life, Inky became one of the first to use DHTML to create what's called a collapsible tool bar. Built for Reed Elsevier's RELive Web initiative, the bar or channel guide was a standard row of links to other areas of the Reed Web suite. The bar would appear when the cursor was pushed to the right of the screen, then would disappear when moved off, saving valuable screen space.

Inky says infighting among the eighteen divisions at Reed Elsevier drove him to create the tool bar. Reed Elsevier exercised centralized control over the RELive site. But most of the divisions involved wanted "one hundred percent of the screen real estate in their control," Inky says. "They didn't want to give up any screen real estate."

Marc Kuperstein, a senior director at Lexis-Nexis, served as a buffer of sorts between flashCast and the competing divisional heads at Reed. Yet the heads still called flashCast to jockey for position on the site. Kuperstein, it needs to be mentioned, would soon play a part in Chrome's initial content coding, then would later take a job at Microsoft to become part of a group opposed to the technology.

After "a lot of pacing," Inky hit upon the solution of Solomon—the collapsible tool bar. All divisions would disappear from sight until called upon by the user. But that only triggered another round of bickering and backstabbing.

"They were partners but actually got along worse than most business competitors," Inky recalls. "They all wanted to be listed first in the channel guide. We were offered bribes by some of them to list them on top—vague insinuations like 'you'd never be out of work,' that kind of thing."

Despite the internal conflicts at Reed, flashCast finished the site on time. Scholz and Inky believed the experience, although a headache, gave flashCast the seasoning it would need to woo and capture other large corporate accounts.

Inky had no way of realizing that his creation would later grab the attention of two driven men at Microsoft, forever changing the fortunes of flashCast. Yet, in strange serendipity, had it not been for an experimental mouse project and a chance encounter in a Bellevue, Washington, hotel room, those ambitious men might never have seen Inky's collapsible tool bar and the history of flashCast might have been written quite differently.

Few people outside of Yellow Springs, Ohio, will have heard of Andrew Junker and his small company, Cyberlink Mind Systems Inc. Yet in many respects Junker is responsible for flashCast's ascension in the Microsoft Empire. Junker invented the Cyberlink Interface, which he claims is the world's first brain-wave-activated mouse. Worn as a headband, the mouse picks up voltages from the forehead as a result of facial gesturing and brain-wave activity, which in turn moves the cursor on the computer screen. Junker needed help with the mouse's virtual device driver and called upon Scholz in the summer of 1997. Scholz had responded to one of Junker's job ads a few years back and had seen him at a computer show in Dayton in April 1997. Scholz told Junker he was too busy building Web sites, but thought he might know someone who would be interested in the technology.

Scholz E-mailed his Microsoft acquaintances, none other than Eric Engstrom and Craig Eisler, to tell them about this new kind of mouse. Scholz had met Engstrom in 1993 at a computer trade show in Atlanta, while Engstrom was still an evangelist with Microsoft's Developer Relations Group. Scholz met Eisler later that year at a Microsoft convention in Los Angeles. Both Engstrom and Eisler recall being impressed by a technical programming manual Scholz had written and his expertise with Microsoft software tools. When Scholz left his job at Simulation Technologies Incorporated in early 1994, Eisler and Engstrom wanted to hire him as a C++ programmer and arranged for Scholz to fly out for an interview. A key personnel man in charge at the time, however, rejected Scholz, saying he "lacked technical depth."

"I kept talking to them about the Internet, the Internet. But nobody fuckin' listened to me," Scholz says. "I wound up bumming in Silicon Valley. I knew the Internet was coming, so I wanted to get 'technical depth' on it."

Scholz did more than bum. He got a job at QCS Corporation in Santa Clara, rigging what's called computer-telephony systems. Ironically, Bill Gates's famous "Internet Tidal Wave" memo to his executive staff a year later would bank Microsoft's future on the global network. Scholz would be there waiting.

He had kept in touch with both Engstrom and Eisler periodically via E-mail. Last he had heard, Engstrom and Eisler were involved in Microsoft's DirectX technology, the stuff that made games on Windows possible. He thought the two might be interested in a brain-wave mouse.

"They both wrote back saying, 'Fuck yes, we want one right now!' " Scholz recalls.

The ambitious at Microsoft are always looking for new technology, the next big, multibillion-dollar thing that will capture the masses.

Eisler and Engstrom were no exception, despite, by then, their deep involvement with Project Chrome.

Junker, excited that the Empire was interested in checking out his invention, made hasty plans to fly to Redmond and demonstrate the brain-wave mouse. Scholz, who couldn't resist a trip to Microsoft, went along for the ride.

"I shot myself in the foot before I could even get started," Junker says of the demonstration.

Project demos sometimes humble even the mighty. A Comdex 98 computer-conference crowd in Chicago watched with equal parts horror and joy as a Windows 98 system crashed while Bill Gates gave his keynote address. Junker knows Gates's pain.

"It was a disaster, really," Junker says of his demo. "I just brought my own installation disks and Microsoft works with the next-generation stuff of Windows. I had to do some quick software reconfiguring right off the bat."

His armpits moistened. His awkward attempts at conversation only heightened his anxiety. Engstrom and eight of his lieutenants watched with growing impatience as the man from Yellow Springs struggled to get his mouse to work.

"I was nervous," Junker continues. "And I was in this room with some pretty high-level people and I never got the mouse to work quite right. They said it wasn't a billion-dollar product and it wasn't going to replace the [conventional] mouse driver."

Engstrom and his colleagues said the brain-wave mouse was much too slow for games, but might have potential for those with severe disabilities. In fact, they hooked up Junker with folks at Microsoft's Accessibility Group.

Engstrom and Eisler invited Scholz to dinner that night, whetting the Ohioan's appetite with talk of salmon steaks and microbrew. More appetizing for Scholz, however, was his realization that his acquaintances had ascended to the managerial ranks at Microsoft.

"I didn't know they had been in charge of DirectX until that day," Scholz says.

He thought he might be able to leverage this to his advantage somehow in the future. The future arrived that evening, when Engstrom and Eisler drove their matching 911 twin-turbo Porches to pick him up at the Embassy Suites in Bellevue. Scholz was surprised to see that both men had shaved their heads. Scholz quickly recovered from the sight and, ever the opportunist, invited them to check out some flashCast Web sites on his Toshiba laptop. Engstrom and Eisler were reasonably impressed by flashCast's work. It didn't hurt that flashCast's site had an animated graphic of the Microsoft marketing slogan "Where do you want to go today?" spinning in 3-D, one of the features Chrome simplified. The two also enjoyed an inside laugh at flashCast's logo, whose art deco man emerging from a radioactive mushroom cloud was reminiscent of their original Manhattan Project logo. But what really caught their eyes was Inky's collapsible tool bar. Microsoft had developed a similar tool bar for Chrome, the only difference being the Microsoft prototype appeared on the left and didn't completely disappear—it just sort of folded back, like a door swung open.

Engstrom and Eisler exchanged a glance.

"Hey, Paul, we're working on a little project that may interest you," Engstrom said.

By the time Scholz flew home the next day, flashCast had been enlisted into the browser war.

11

BIG BILL VS. BIG BROTHER

Two thousand Apple faithful couldn't believe their eyes and ears that August 6 morning inside Boston's Park Plaza Hotel. There was Apple's charismatic cofounder and prodigal interim CEO Steve Jobs, onstage at the annual East Coast MacWorld Expo trade show, declaring an alliance with the enemy—Microsoft! Jobs had returned to Apple's helm the month before, with the ouster of the ineffective Gilbert Amelio. Although Jobs—who headed Pixar Animation Studios, maker of the hit movie *Toy Story*—agreed to remain only as temporary CEO, Apple followers at MacWorld greeted him with a hero's welcome.

And he responded in kind by electrifying the throng with the news that Apple had ditched its old board and replaced it with a dream team of industry leaders, including Oracle's iconoclast billionaire CEO, Larry Ellison. Jobs's appearance at MacWorld recalled the heady days of 1984, when the Macintosh debuted with a global TV ad campaign featuring a trim hammer-heaving heroine shattering the PC industry's bland conformity. But the initial euphoria of Jobs's return evaporated when he talked of an alliance with the devil. As he spoke, a thirty-foot-tall image of Bill Gates's smiling face, beamed via satellite, loomed to life on the stage's screen, dwarfing Jobs in an episode of perfect Orwellian surrealism.

Jobs now awkwardly tried to quiet the chorus of boos from the outraged and by now thoroughly confused crowd. Seemingly taken aback by the reaction, a chagrined and angry Jobs spoke over the din, telling the world that the two foes had entered a new era of détente. Microsoft would infuse $150 million into its ailing archenemy, acquiring 9 million nonvoting shares of the Cupertino company, plus paying a rumored $100 million for licensing Apple technology. Gates also pledged to make software—including the market-leading suite of Office products—for the Mac for the next five years. In return, Apple agreed to drop what was left of its failed "look-and-feel" Windows lawsuit initiated by former Apple CEO John Sculley. Moreover, Apple would make Internet Explorer the default browser on all Macs—the company had been using Netscape's Navigator—and would use Microsoft's version of the Java programming language, not the pure version from Java's founder, Sun Microsystems.

In this sweeping victory for Microsoft, the company not only gained more platforms on which to deploy its browser, but put a dagger in the heart of an unofficial anti-Microsoft Java alliance formed earlier by Apple, Sun, Netscape, and Oracle.

With Apple's market share declining, and the company bleeding more than $1.5 billion over the previous eighteen months, Jobs said the time had come to put an end to the feud with the Redmond giant.

"If we want to move forward, we have to let go of a few things," the demigod in denim said. "We have to let go of this notion that for Apple to win, Microsoft has to lose. . . . We need all the help we can get."

Apple executives would later utter dark accusations that Microsoft had coerced its struggling rival into inking the browser deal by threatening to stop making software for the Mac.

Apple faithful may not have liked the deal, but Wall Street did. The company's common stock surged 33 percent to close at $26 that day, adding nearly $830 million to Apple's stock value.

For many, the battle between Apple and Microsoft had been a holy war. To them, Microsoft was the Evil Empire, imposing its proprietary standards on the world by quashing or assimilating competitors. Apple represented a rebellious alternative—the innovative company that made pricier computers, as Jobs once said, "for the rest of us." Apple and Microsoft had locked horns since nearly the inception of the information age. Theirs were among the more storied and defining battles in the PC industry. Many believed the "Great Satan" Gates had filched the concept of Apple's point-and-click operating system, had done a better job of pricing and marketing it, and had nearly plowed Apple under. (In truth Apple was its own worst enemy. It made inept business decisions and chose to manufacture its own computers even if it meant higher prices. Meanwhile, Microsoft captured market share with a less elegant but a lower-priced operating system running on commodity PCs.)

Others saw the deal as a way to soothe Justice Department regulators, who were itching to prove Microsoft was using its near monopoly with Windows to attack and control the Internet and other markets.

"This is antitrust insurance," said Chris LeTocq, an analyst at Dataquest in San Jose. "It allows Microsoft to stand up and say, 'Hey, we're supporting alternative architectures.' "

Yet at its core, Apple's deal with Microsoft reflected the complex reality of the computer industry—despite what they say about each other in newspapers, many competing companies are simultaneously partners. Most of the software written for the Mac, for instance, was made at Microsoft. And contrary to the notion of two constantly warring camps, Apple and Microsoft routinely conducted meetings and negotiated deals far removed from the glare of public scrutiny.

Meetings such as the one Eric Engstrom attended in Apple's Cupertino headquarters in August '97—one of a series of meetings that would later hurl Engstrom into the chilling orbit of a massive and historic antitrust lawsuit.

The same month Jobs dropped his bombshell, Engstrom was promoted to general manager of DirectX multimedia. Among his growing list of duties—aside from nurturing Project Chrome—was to advance Microsoft's Internet multimedia technologies, including ActiveX Animation, DirectX3D Retained Mode, DirectPlay, and ActiveMovie, later renamed DirectShow.

DirectShow formed the core of the subsystem in Windows for the playback of audio and video content using a variety of formats. DirectShow and the rest of the DirectX media were collectively referred to as the "multimedia runtime" for Windows, the technology that allowed playback of multimedia delivered via the Internet. DirectShow's counterpart was NetShow, back-end server technology that piped content to desktop computers. NetShow was like the pitcher on the mound, throwing to the catcher. Engstrom played catcher and was in charge of the Windows Media Player, the so-called client software that appears on a user's PC and looks like a combination of a videocassette recorder and a television, with "play," "rewind," "fast-forward," and "stop" buttons and a viewing screen.

DirectAnimation, which had not yet been released, would allow developers to combine sounds, movies, 2-D and 3-D images, and text for the Web and time them with mouse clicks or other user-initiated events. Click on a picture of Mozart, for instance, and the computer plays *Requiem.* Craig Eisler, the more cautious and low-key Beastie Boy whose involvement with Chrome was increasingly on the wane, had been providing guidance on DirectAnimation.

DirectShow, the new entrée for Engstrom, was Microsoft's move to play back streaming and progressive video and audio feeds over the Web. Instead of waiting for an entire sound or video file to download, which could take minutes or even hours, streaming technology played back a file as it arrived without the file first being downloaded to a computer's hard drive. Streaming is the cousin of "progressive" downloading, which, as the name implies, begins playback of a file while it downloads to the computer. Unlike the Windows Media Player, Apple's QuickTime at the time only supported progressive downloading, not streaming.

In any event, the Web was still too slow to accommodate real-time video feeds—the images were grainy and jerky and the sound was often out of sync. Like silent movies of old, multimedia delivery over the Internet was in its infancy. Nonetheless, even 28.8K modem hookups could stream or progressively download audio reasonably well, and many radio stations were beginning to broadcast via the Internet.

Engstrom and his trusted business manager, Chris Phillips, were no strangers to Apple's headquarters. QuickTime and DirectX were competing technologies. Overall, Apple no longer represented the threat it once did to Microsoft. And given the intensity of government scrutiny, Microsoft did not want to be seen burying its once-chief rival. Within days of the announced groundbreaking deal with Apple, Microsoft directed Engstrom to redouble efforts to cut more deals where Apple was still strong—multimedia.

The multimedia fortunes of Apple and Microsoft became more intertwined with the development of delivering video and audio over the Web, and media players represented a growing market. Apple was said to be developing its own streaming multimedia player. And just days before Jobs's big announcement, Microsoft had purchased a 10 percent stake in Progressive Networks Inc., later known as RealNetworks, which was founded by ex-Microsoft executive Rob Glaser.

RealNetworks produced RealAudio and RealVideo, the most popular streaming software in cyberspace. It had been Microsoft's third major media acquisition in six months, including investments in VDOnet and VXtreme Inc. The investments complemented Redmond's own nascent NetShow and Windows Media Player technologies, but they also drew more attention from the Justice Department, which vowed to investigate.

In August, Engstrom and Phillips—a former Hewlett-Packard programmer turned marketing whiz and Engstrom's eyes, ears, and sometimes mouth within Microsoft—traveled to Cupertino to persuade Apple to swap codecs, a contraction of the phrase for the software routines that compress and decompress digital images and audio. Because of their large size, multimedia files need to go through this compression/decompression process to be piped through the Web efficiently.

From Engstrom's perspective, he was on a simple technology-sharing mission, paved in large part by the remarkable truce between Jobs and Gates.

"I went down there to sell them on swapping codecs so that we could play all of their stuff [on Windows Media Player] and they could play all of ours," says Engstrom. "The codec we're talking about are six years old or more, and it's a nuisance for our customers because if you didn't have our player or their QuickTime player, you can't use the other player. What I wanted to do was swap them our codec that causes problems with their QuickTime and vice versa.

"If you look at our shitty codec and their shitty codec, nobody in their right mind would use any of that anyway," Engstrom adds.

Streaming and progressive-downloading multimedia was a morass of incompatible formats and protocols—defined as the methods multimedia creators use to organize a set of data. Multimedia authors faced a Hobson's choice of developing content to support all file formats, which is expensive in terms of production time, or using a single format that not all multimedia software will be able to run. Apple's QuickTime player didn't use all the formats Windows supported, and as a result the player didn't function as well as it could or should on PCs. Some users would be apt to blame Windows, which is what motivated Microsoft to dispatch Engstrom to engage in talks with Apple.

Engstrom likened the situation of file-format incompatibility to a world where consumers had to buy one kind of television to receive UHF broadcasts, another type of TV to view VHF programming, and still another to view cable channels. Unless there was agreement on common standards that permitted all multimedia content to be played on a variety of media players, the desktop computer would remain a poor substitute for radio and TV. Engstrom saw the way to improvement was in widespread cross-licensing of codecs, a move Apple termed "codec détente."

Despite Jobs's jaw-dropping truce with Microsoft, however, Apple saw Engstrom as an enemy. In fact, to executives in Cupertino, Engstrom seemed to be pushing Apple to help Microsoft carve up the media-player market in an act more of collusion rather than of cooperation. An act, it must be noted, that would add fuel to the government's attack on Microsoft.

RealNetworks and Apple media players worked with various computer platforms and servers. Microsoft's Windows Media Player at the time, however, was proprietary technology in that it only worked with Microsoft NetShow servers and Windows-based PCs. Although Microsoft and RealNetworks—but not Apple—were among those working with the industry to standardize around an Internet streaming file format known as ASF 2, that didn't stop Apple from raising a dark question: Was Engstrom actually plotting to make cyberspace a place where only those using Microsoft products could explore and use the riches of the Internet?

The August 1997 meeting included Apple's Tim Schaaff, director of QuickTime engineering, and Peter Hoddie, senior QuickTime architect. According to them, Engstrom said Microsoft was troubled that QuickTime was being used on Windows, a transgression he allegedly viewed as trespassing on Windows turf. Engstrom reportedly told Apple that if it got out of the media player market, Microsoft would let Apple have free reign to forge software tools used for making multimedia content—a much smaller piece of the action.

Hoddie says he asked if Microsoft was proposing that Apple "knife the baby," referring to QuickTime, and that Chris Phillips said yes.

Engstrom denies that exchange ever took place and counters that he and Phillips were only exploring the possibility of Apple and Microsoft developing a unified multimedia runtime or playback technology for Windows—based on DirectX, of course, and incorporating certain QuickTime technologies. Engstrom also acknowledges that Microsoft was considering creating a version of DirectX for the Mac.

During this and other discussions, Apple officials were telling Engstrom that Microsoft should drop various parts of DirectX and adopt QuickTime instead—an absurd request considering the high body count the Beastie Boys had racked up building DirectX, not to mention its credential as a technology that had shifted the entire computer-game industry and that was now plugged into Windows.

Engstrom always had problems taking no for an answer. He

resumed his quest for codec swapping again in September, when Microsoft hosted a meeting at the Fairmont Hotel in San Jose to kick off its new Advanced Streaming Format, technology used in the company's new Windows Media Player.

Engstrom and Apple's Tim Schaaff slurped diet Coke and again talked about developing a unified multimedia player technology. Engstrom reiterated that it would have to be based on DirectX. Microsoft was burrowing DirectX deeper into Windows to make it a basic part of the operating system. QuickTime would be a poor substitute, Engstrom said. The two also brainstormed about ways Apple could make money off of QuickTime.

"I suggested that Apple consider developing a video editing tool," Engstrom says, arguing that Apple's massive brand recognition coupled with the growth of digital cameras made for a lucrative venture.

Engstrom says he was just trying to work cooperatively with Apple. Again, Apple's Schaaff has a different take. He recalls Engstrom stating that if Apple refused to abandon development of its QuickTime media player and didn't concentrate only on the multimedia authoring market, Microsoft would assign 150 engineers to make media authoring tools and run Apple out of the market.

"He assured . . . that if Microsoft needed to make an investment in providing authoring tools in order to push Apple out of the playback market, then Microsoft would devote all the necessary resources to accomplish this goal," Schaaff recalls.

Engstrom acknowledges he said "Microsoft would compete against any software that sought to duplicate the multimedia functionality in Windows," but denies trying to strong-arm Apple from making QuickTime for Windows.

As the summer of '97 gave way to fall, Microsoft had other things to worry about. Government officials, industry competitors, and critics were in a feeding frenzy because of the anticipated giveaway of IE 4, its bundling with Windows 95, and its tighter integration with the upcoming Windows 98. Many of the Empire's critics saw Microsoft's Web effort as a brutal assault on Netscape, rather than a business tactic to satisfy customer desires.

In late September, two days before Microsoft released the new browser, consumer savior Ralph Nader and his Consumer Project on Technology watchdog group circulated an on-line petition urging the Justice Department to investigate Microsoft for allegedly engaging in "predatory pricing" by giving away its browsers and illegally bundling the new version with Windows. Bad news for Naderites at Microsoft, who still had NADER FOR PRESIDENT bumper stickers on their cars.

The petition urged the DOJ to *protect* consumers by "taking action to prevent Microsoft from using anticompetitive practices to monopolize the market for Internet browsers."

Gates and his allies wondered why consumers needed protection from free software.

Trouble brewed on other fronts. Attorneys general in California, New York, and Connecticut joined those of Texas and Massachusetts in pursuing accusations that Microsoft might be violating federal antitrust laws. Capturing some of the anti-Microsoft sentiment resonating in the land was computer-industry columnist and pundit Nicholas Petreley: "I'm not one of those who think Bill Gates is the devil. I simply suspect that if Microsoft ever met up with the devil, it wouldn't need an interpreter."

Undeterred, Microsoft released IE 4 for download over the Web on October 1, 1997. The company claimed that more than 1 million copies of the browser were downloaded within forty-eight hours. The day of the launch, members of the IE team punctuated their celebration by rolling a giant, blue, lower-case *e*, IE's logo, onto the lawn of Netscape's Mountain View, California, headquarters. The plucky crew from Microsoft even posted pictures of their handiwork on the Web.

The celebration was short-lived.

On October 20, the Justice Department rolled out its anticipated antitrust lawsuit in federal court, accusing Microsoft of illegally bundling IE 4 with Windows 95 in violation of the 1995 consent decree. The government said that by forcing computer makers to install IE 4 with Windows 95, Microsoft broke the provision that prohibited the company from imposing anticompetitive licensing terms.

Much of the argument turned on a clause in the 1995 agreement that said Microsoft could not tie the sale of products such as Windows 95 to the purchase of another product, such as a Web browser. But the ambiguous clause also said Microsoft retained the right to integrate new functions into its software. Microsoft said its Web browser was a feature set of Windows 95.

"Internet Explorer is not a browser at all," declared Bob Herbold, Microsoft's vice president and chief operating officer. "It was a browser at one time. Sure, there's a separate icon for Internet Explorer on the computer desktop. But the browser really is an operating system, not a stand-alone application."

U.S. attorney general Janet Reno didn't buy it.

"Microsoft is unlawfully taking advantage of its Windows monopoly to protect and extend that monopoly and undermine consumer choice," she said. "The Department of Justice will not tolerate that kind of conduct."

Reno demanded that Microsoft stop requiring PC manufacturers to accept IE 4 as a condition of receiving Windows 95; that the company tell PC makers how to uninstall the IE 4 logo from the Windows 95 desktop screen; and that the court authorize a record fine of $1 million a day until Microsoft complied.

Assistant Attorney General Joel Klein advanced the government's case at a press conference by saying, "While trying to play catch-up here, Microsoft went over the line when it chose to use its monopoly power in Windows to coerce computer manufacturers to also take its browser."

Reno and Klein also hit at Microsoft's nondisclosure agreements, sort of an industry code of silence that required those who signed to inform Microsoft in the event they were subpoenaed by the DOJ. Klein said such agreements did not apply to the Justice Department and encouraged those who had complaints against Microsoft to come forward.

Klein and Reno didn't rule out probing other Microsoft business practices, including the impending integration of the IE 4 browser with Windows 98 and, though not revealed at the time, Engstrom's sorties to Apple.

Spurring on the inquiry was Senator Orrin Hatch, a Republican from Utah and chairman of the Senate Judiciary Committee, which oversees the Justice Department. The same day the DOJ unveiled its complaint, Hatch said he planned to go forward with the committee's broader examination of Microsoft's business practices.

Hatch said he applauded Microsoft's achievements, yet added, "Success in the operating-system market does not entitle it to a permanent, unchallenged monopoly, nor should it entitle Microsoft to a monopoly over desktop access to the Internet."

The government had fired its first shot. The smell of war was in the air. Microsoft, in the mood to fight, vowed to "vigorously defend" itself.

Meanwhile, Alex St. John, the cast-off evangelist who had recently returned from spending time with his ex-wife and children in Maine, was in the mood to party. He was writing kiss-and-tell columns and hosting a forum called AskAlex for *Boot,* a computer-industry print and on-line trade magazine. Although he enjoyed his role as the outside agitator who ridiculed Microsoft bureaucracy, more often than not he defended his former company like a protective sibling and thought the government's case was a foolish campaign.

"[Microsoft] is a monopoly, sure, but more specifically it's an American international monopoly!" he stated in one on-line discussion. "I'm not an economist, but I think that means that most of the money . . . [Microsoft] makes actually comes from other countries to us. I'd think those would be the kind of monopolies we'd want more of."

His departure from Microsoft did nothing to dim his appetite for extravagance, an appetite whetted when he'd crashed the Microsoft Christmas party back in '92. Despite no longer having access to Microsoft's bottomless checkbook, St. John orchestrated another outlandish Halloween bash reminiscent of his Judgment Day I party— this time at his own expense. He spent more than $12,000 and invited a couple hundred game developers and friends to a party at Seattle's famous Showbox nightclub. The likes of Duke Ellington, stripper Gypsy Rose Lee, and more recently Pearl Jam had strutted upon that venerable stage. Now it was St. John's turn. He had postcard invitations printed with his agape face morphed onto a fifties movie poster depicting a giant man hoisting a bus above his head. Passengers spilled out the bus windows and military guns trained their sights on the menace. "The Towering Terror from Hell! Starring: Alex St. John . . . Party of the Colossal Beast," the invitations read.

Headlining the evening's entertainment was the now-defunct Seattle rock trio the Presidents of the United States of America, known for its upbeat, irreverent tunes about cats, fruit, and seminude celebrities. That would probably have been enough to feed the bacchanalian tastes of most of the guests, but this was a St. John event, and he was compelled to add shock value.

Draped in a toga, St. John took to the stage that night and issued a challenge to the inebriated crowd: "When we were children, we had ghosts and goblins and monsters to frighten us on Halloween. Now that we're adults, how do we confront some new fear? I have a proposition. How many would volunteer to do something insane? How many of you are willing to come up here and do whatever I have planned without knowing beforehand what it is? Who's willing to take a real risk?"

A crowd, including several game-company executives, soon packed the stage.

"Okay," a smiling St. John said. "We're going to go streak GameWorks!"

Sega GameWorks was a struggling, multistoried video-game arcade in downtown Seattle. Streaking was St. John's inimitable way of helping an ally in the computer-game industry.

St. John handpicked the first group, including several game-company executives, and sent them out the door to a waiting limousine. Then he revealed a secret. The first group was merely the advance team, sent ahead to occupy the arcade's bouncers while the second group, whisked to the scene of the crime in a big black

Suburban, would do the dirty deed. To St. John's delight, everybody in the second group agreed to streak, even some of the more hefty, cellulited revelers who had trouble squirming out of elaborate costumes. St. John had accounted for slow-moving runners. The advance team of handlers was armed with trench coats to throw over any hapless streakers who happened to stumble or otherwise got caught in the GameWorks crowd.

St. John's reconnaissance of GameWorks and careful planning paid off. The streak was an unqualified success. St. John's streakers broke through the unsuspecting crowd, which out of curiosity closed in after the naked runners had whizzed by and blocked any would-be pursuers. A few Monolith employees who had staked out positions before the advance team arrived took pictures of the show and posted them on the company's Web site to prove it had happened. Nobody got hurt. Although police showed up ten minutes after the streaking, nobody ran afoul of the law.

The same, alas, could not be said at Microsoft, which was gearing for the biggest legal battle in its twenty-three-year existence.

About a week after St. John's streak party, Microsoft officially responded to the Justice Department, claiming that the browser was an integrated part of the operating system. As such, the company could require computer manufacturers to include it. The DOJ had noted that Microsoft used to distribute the browser separately from the operating system and accused the company of bundling the two only as a means to torpedo Netscape and other Internet competitors. But Microsoft countered in its response on November 10 that integration of the two products had been in the works for years. In fact, Gates said the company had decided to bundle the products at a meeting on April 5, 1994—two days before Netscape became an official company.

Nonetheless, presiding U.S. district court judge Thomas Penfield Jackson, the same judge who had signed the famous 1995 consent decree, dealt Microsoft a blow on December 11 when he issued a preliminary injunction ordering the company to stop, at least temporarily, forcing computer makers to install the Internet Explorer browser with Windows 95. Not only did the judge assume the role of software engineer, he played a zealous one—at that time, the government hadn't even requested the injunction.

Jackson tabled the government's request to impose a daily $1 million fine, but assigned a "special master" to the case, Harvard Law School professor Lawrence Lessig. The professor was supposed to act as an impartial reviewer of technical issues and render an opinion on the merits of the government's case by the end of May 1998.

Jackson wanted Microsoft to remove IE from Windows, but the wording of his ruling left his meaning open to interpretation. Microsoft responded literally to Jackson's orders by ripping out all of IE and underlying code from the operating system. Instead of merely removing the logo from the desktop screen, Microsoft offered computer makers browser-less Windows 95 operating systems in two unpalatable flavors: a two-year-old version or one that didn't work. Microsoft had been warning the government that removing the browser would disable the operating system as it was then configured.

"The court ordered us to build a car without an engine," opined Microsoft spokesman John Pinette.

Microsoft, of course, still offered computer makers the choice of installing Windows 95 with IE 4 and argued in court that it had a right to imbue its operating system with any features it saw fit, including "a ham sandwich."

DOJ's Klein was indignant and accused the company of mocking the judge's orders. He petitioned the court to declare Microsoft in contempt and renewed his call to slap on a $1-million-a-day fine. Furthermore—to the astonishment of Microsoft friends and foes alike—he wanted the court to require the company to submit any future operating-system upgrades or browsers to the government for approval thirty days before release.

What, one wonders, would Klein have made of Chrome had he known about it?

"If the U.S. government is going to decide what features go into software," Nathan Myhrvold, Microsoft's technological seer, was quoted, "it means the end of the software business. What's the point of us doing this if we can't put the features in?"

Later that month, Microsoft also challenged special master Lessig † as biased, noting that he had once likened downloading Internet Explorer to "dealing with the devil."

An irate Jackson had little sympathy. On December 19 he had a court technician use Windows' add/remove function to "uninstall" IE 3.02. The demonstration removed the IE icon from the desktop without breaking Windows—a feat that took less than two minutes. The judge wanted Microsoft's IE logo off of Windows. A defiant Microsoft declared that the add/remove function left IE's code inside the operating system, and while it disabled IE, it didn't remove it, as the judge had ordered.

As the fireworks exploded between the government and the world's largest software company, Engstrom was dealing with explosions of his own. Morris Beton, general manager at Microsoft's Developer Relations Group, continued to balk at evangelizing Chrome, in part because the superfast computers needed to handle the new technology weren't even on the market. Moreover, word had it that Developer Relations suspected Engstrom was dragging his feet on finishing enhancements to DirectX in retaliation for not getting evangelist support for Chrome. The suspicion was unfounded, but nonetheless posed another unnecessary internal political hassle and continued the pattern of friction Engstrom had had with others at Microsoft.

In addition, another company reorganization was in the works, driven this time by savage top-level infighting and by a need to shelter against the brewing antitrust storm. Jim Allchin, the senior executive in charge of Windows NT, was in position to finish off rival Brad Silverberg, the man who once oversaw Windows 95 and the company's first Internet group. While Silverberg was on leave of absence, Allchin moved to consolidate Internet development under the Windows group.

It was well known that Microsoft planned to eventually replace Windows 95 and 98 with consumer versions of Windows NT, the operating system initially targeting businesses. Allchin had made a convincing case that he should be the one to guide the Windows migration. Now that Microsoft was making good on its threat to fuse a browser to Windows—the very tactic that had triggered the antitrust stir—the company decided it was a convenient time to align the two divisions. Microsoft couldn't credibly argue that the two technologies were the same if the two were under different administrations.

Allchin's argument that the two technologies needed to be under one command, namely his, carried the day. While Silverberg vacationed, Allchin took control. He was now lord over the company's operating-systems and Internet groups.

Silverberg announced he would extend his hiatus to spend more time with his family, or, as word had it, until a suitable job opened. Allchin's coup also had far-reaching consequences for Engstrom.

Silverberg had given the green light to DirectX at a time when others inside Microsoft wanted to derail the project, and he had supported the purchase of Dimension X when Engstrom wanted it. The dethroning of Silverberg would leave Engstrom with one less crucial executive ally.

"Brad is someone I have tremendous respect for," says Engstrom. "I would like to be a cookie-cutter version of him."

Silverberg would not be the only ally lost to this latest reshuffle. David Cole would replace John Ludwig as vice president for Microsoft's Web Client and Consumer Experience Division. Cole would be responsible for consumer-oriented Windows and multimedia development. Ludwig would move to Microsoft's Interactive Media Group to work on combining the Microsoft Network, Outlook Express E-mail software, and Microsoft's home page. Eisler, sensing an opportunity to move out from Engstrom's shadow and work on Internet-related technology—among the marquee assignments at Microsoft—decided to follow Ludwig. Eisler, whose office was next door to Engstrom's, later relocated from Building 30, off the main drag at Microsoft, to digs inside Building 9, amid the cluster of X-shaped buildings at the campus's epicenter and near Gates's lair.

With Ludwig's imminent departure, Chrome's future became cloudy.

"There was a big discussion about the future of Chrome when it was learned John would be leaving," says McCartney. "We were losing a guardian vice president in John."

To top it off, Engstrom's back was killing him. Two ruptured spinal disks had ended his weight lifting at the Pro Club months ago. But a fear of doctors had deterred him from seeking treatment. So, he endured the pain of a cross-country flight to the Internet World '97 conference in New York for the debut of his DirectAnimation API, the technology that allowed programmers to time sound and animation to mouse clicks and other user events. It was a dismal December day in the city, and the packaged excitement inside the Jacob K. Javits Center did little to lift Engstrom's spirits.

Tech trade shows, like bad rock concerts, are far too loud and go on far too long. Inside the Javits Center blared the incessant drone of techno noise, with software and hardware companies clawing for notice and a sale.

Noticeably absent on the trade show floor, however, was Netscape. The company would announce layoffs and report losses for 1997 of more than $115 million, far more grim than what analysts had predicted. Netscape blamed Microsoft, of course. But it also acknowledged that longer time-to-market cycles with its new line of corporate-enterprise software as well as competition from others had slowed expected sales. It costs money to establish a presence at major trade shows, and by December '97, Netscape's budget had no money for trade-show per diems and related expenses.

Engstrom could care less. His Chrome developers were in revolt. He had been battling with McCartney and Heddle over DirectAnimation before he left for New York. Engstrom wanted to use DirectAnimation in Chrome and establish the new technology as a standard in Windows—a strategy that fit into his larger mission of improving Windows' ability to play back multimedia and thus compete against Apple's QuickTime.

But using DirectAnimation for Chrome was more complicated and time-consuming. McCartney wanted to use the simpler, more established, and better performing Direct3D Retained Mode. The benefits associated with DirectAnimation, in McCartney's estimation, were not worth the complexity of implementing it. In the end McCartney had to spend countless hours coding DirectAnimation for Chrome, delaying the project and creating residual tension between Engstrom and his team.

"DirectAnimation was more theoretical rather than practical," McCartney says. "DirectAnimation is basically a language. Nobody wants to learn a new language. Eric wanted and still wants a single multimedia runtime on Windows that everybody uses, not just for games, but for all multimedia. Our mission was Chrome, not this larger mission to make DirectAnimation the single multimedia runtime and attack QuickTime."

Engstrom would acknowledge that he wanted Apple to help build a single DirectX-based solution to play back multimedia on Windows and that QuickTime duplicated a lot of Microsoft's efforts. But he would insist that he wasn't trying to "attack" QuickTime or "knife the baby." He reiterated that he wanted to erase technical incompatibilities, which hurt the playback of multimedia on Windows and frustrated consumers.

This message of putting the consumer first reflected some of the changes Engstrom had undergone in graduating from Beastie Boy program manager to general manager of multimedia. He no longer wrote specs and oversaw development of one project, but now was in charge of many, including Chrome and aspects of the Windows Media Player. The mentoring sessions with Ludwig, coupled with greater responsibilities and having to answer more directly to senior executives, compelled Engstrom to sharpen his diplomatic skills—to a degree. Once, while Bill Gates was en route to look over an early Chrome demo, one of Engstrom's worker bees tapped the wrong sequence of keys, causing a crash and forcing her to reboot the computer and reinstall the demo—a delay that consumed twenty minutes.

Fortunately, Gates was late, minimizing the agony of the reboot. Instead of screaming, Engstrom told her it was his fault for entrusting her with the task and stepped outside to bang his head against the wall.

But Engstrom's mellowing and desire for a single, unified approach to running multimedia on Windows weren't major concerns for McCartney.

"Our reviews and stock allocations and money were going to be based on if Chrome was a success. I didn't see DirectAnimation helping that," McCartney adds. "Developers don't want to be told what to use. They just want to make the most efficient technology."

Engstrom now calls his decision to force Chrome to be built on DirectAnimation "the greatest mistake" of his career.

"I should have let Colin and Bob pick the best technological solution for the immediate mission," he says. "I was worried about the chess game too many moves in advance. I chose to follow my orders to the letter, rather than stopping at a results-based interpretation of them [as] I have always used in the past."

At any rate, Engstrom, who earlier that year couldn't convince Apple to swap codecs, was now having trouble convincing his own team to use DirectAnimation. Coupled with his aching back and with the government's now wanting sign-off approval of any forthcoming operating-system upgrade and browser technologies—Chrome classified under both—Engstrom was thus in little mood to schmooze yet another day and play booster at an annoyingly loud trade show. His return flight to Seattle could not depart soon enough. Engstrom had been discussing Chrome with Paul Scholz, the Web designer from Dayton, and another potential Chrome partner when he glanced at his watch and decided it was time to go. One of those with whom he had been holding court said he'd like to arrange a meeting and would E-mail to iron out logistics. Engstrom hauled himself to his feet and pushed his thin-wire glasses to his round face.

"Sounds good," he said. Then he wagged his finger in gentle admonishment. "But I, uh, don't like a lot of data in my E-mail."

12

THIS IS NOT YOUR MOTHER'S BROWSER

John Sculley, the former chief executive officer of Apple, prowled the indoor courtyard of Bellevue's Embassy Suites, as shards of Pacific Northwest light lanced the vaulted glass ceiling. Once the sworn enemy of Bill Gates and an international icon who held court with movie stars and presidents, Sculley now drew little notice from the crowd of Web developers, programmers, and corporate representatives gathered here at the invite-only request of Microsoft and Intel. It was the week before Super Bowl XXXII, and the two companies were hosting the first technical design review of Chrome.

"Who's the old dude?" someone asked. Many of those grabbing free Danishes and coffee were too young to know or care that they were in the presence of a fallen king, a man who for ten years presided over a company that had revolutionized the personal-computer industry. That was fine with Sculley. Anonymity has its own incalculable comfort. Sculley, a corporate turnaround artist and former president of Pepsi-Cola Co., made history in 1985 when he tossed out the very man who had hired him—none other than Steve Jobs. Sculley's karma materialized in the summer of 1993 at Apple headquarters, when the Apple board met in a conference room a few doors away from his office and scripted his humiliating overthrow. Sculley had been at the helm when Apple filed its famous "look-and-feel" lawsuit against Microsoft. Once a pesky thorn in Gates's side, Sculley was now a quiet ally.

Half a decade removed from those torturous days at Apple, when revenues were plunging swifter than the knives to his back, the fifty-eight-year-old Sculley appeared at ease in his light wool sweater and hunter-green corduroys. Gray streaked his hair, but his darting eyes showed that his mind still raced. Like a gaunt professor making his rounds at a liberal arts college, Sculley walked from group to group of young people huddled in the hotel's riparian lobby, diving into and out of conversations. He was representing his company, LivePicture Inc., a Web-based photo and imaging service, and was serving as mentor to two other high-tech start-ups invited to the design review. Some members of his team were programmers he had handpicked while on a talent safari in Israel—high-IQ techies he had nurtured for this very occasion. Unlike some who strolled into the Embassy Suites that morning, Sculley was confident about Chrome, not only as a technology, but also as a business-model component. Having battled Microsoft for years, Sculley had switched allegiance and was playing ball with Chairman Bill's team.

"I've been doing a lot of the work under the radar screen for the last two years betting that Microsoft would do something like Chrome," Sculley confided the first day of the design review. "We knew that the only way multimedia would happen on the Internet is that Microsoft and Intel would have to decide it was important. The platform can only be developed by those who can get out to the tens of millions, and no start-up can do that."

Sculley's feelings for Microsoft had clearly softened. He was willing to work with his former foe and eagerly embraced its Web strategy. The same could not be said of the government and Judge Jackson, who were growing increasingly annoyed with the crew from Redmond. At a hearing just days prior to the Chrome design review, Jackson rejected Microsoft's claim that the court's "special master," Professor Lessig, was biased and should be removed. Microsoft, recall, had questioned Lessig's credibility because of E-mail correspondence he had had with

Netscape, including one where he had likened using Internet Explorer to selling his soul to the devil.

Jackson called Microsoft's accusations "both trivial and altogether nonprobative."

"They are, therefore, defamatory and the court finds that they were not made in good faith," he said. "Had [the accusations] been made in a more formal manner, [Microsoft] might well have incurred sanctions."

Moreover, the judge was enraged by the way Microsoft had handled his order to temporarily unbundle IE from the operating system and grilled David Cole, Engstrom's soon-to-be boss and Microsoft's vice president of Consumer Platforms Business.

"It seemed absolutely clear to you that I entered an order that required that you distribute a product that would not work. That's what you're telling me?" Jackson asked Cole.

"In plain English, yes," Cole replied. "We followed that order. It wasn't my place to consider the consequences of that."

Cole showed that the add/remove procedure the court had demonstrated earlier only removed twenty-six files that access Internet Explorer, leaving the browser's basic program files intact within Windows 95.

Microsoft's tough stance did little to help its image. Letter writers, columnists, and even employees were questioning the company's hard-line position.

Microsoft's rank and file had always been aware of industry hostility; competitors had been firing barbs at Microsoft virtually since its inception in 1975. Yet antitrust battles with the Federal Trade Commission and the Justice Department earlier in the 1990s occurred without the general public taking much notice. During all those earlier battles, Microsoft had told its employees to just make software and not to worry about government probes. Gates himself dismissed the investigations as by-products of complaints from competitors who had failed in the marketplace and ran to the government for help. Ironically, Microsoft's conduct in the market had compelled competitors in

Silicon Valley and elsewhere to play the political lobbying game—a game Microsoft had stayed out of until the attacks began drawing corporate blood.

By 1998 the public's computer consciousness had expanded with the growth of the Internet and society's increasing dependence on software, hardware, and the bits and bytes that were once the cloistered province of geeks. Microsoft commercials regularly aired on television. Nine out of ten personal computers in the world now ran Windows. Microsoft the brand had become as well known as Coca-Cola, and now the U.S. government was telling the people that Microsoft was bad for them. The message started to resonate in the press and the public.

America traditionally celebrates the up-and-comer or the underdog, only to turn on it when it becomes successful, particularly if the successful fail to demonstrate the requisite humility. Politicians, celebrities, and sports figures endure this American rite—now it was Microsoft's turn, and the magnitude of the criticism caught some employees off guard.

"It's like I don't even want to tell people where I work anymore," said one Microsoft contract worker.

Microsoft executives found themselves alternately apologizing and defending the company's response to Judge Jackson's order. Two days before the Chrome design review, Brad Chase, Microsoft's vice president of Developer Relations Group and Marketing, appeared on National Public Radio's *Talk of the Nation*. If Chase was hoping to score a public-relations grand slam, he struck out. He seemed outflanked by hostile callers and guests Jamie Love, director of Ralph Nader's Consumer Project on Technology, and Paul Gillen, editor in chief of *ComputerWorld* magazine.

"Customers . . . are not all convinced that the browser is part of the operating system," Gillen remarked.

An unapologetic Chase toed the company line.

"The reason we're being firm is that [there's] a very important principle here. And that principle is our ability to integrate new features in the operating system."

Trouble brewed overseas as well. About the same time Chase was on the air, Japan's Fair Trade Commission raided Microsoft's offices in Tokyo and searched more than six hours for evidence that Microsoft was violating Japanese antitrust laws, mirroring the company's problems with U.S. regulators. The Japanese were looking into whether Microsoft was violating the Japanese Antimonopoly Act by integrating the Internet Explorer browser into Windows 95. Moreover, it was probing to find if the software giant was pressuring computer makers into bundling Microsoft applications, including Word and Excel.

Although Microsoft was having tough going inside Judge Jackson's courtroom as well as in the court of public opinion, Engstrom was smiling for the first time in weeks. His bad back was feeling a little better. And just two days before the design review, he and Morris Beton, the manager at Developer Relations Group, had reached a truce. In a savvy political move, Engstrom had forwarded to Beton mail from Gates, Myhrvold, and Group Vice President of Platforms and Applications Paul Maritz, who all gave Chrome the thumbs-up. Faced with these all-powerful endorsements, Beton relented and said he would evangelize Chrome.

Still, the two-day technical design review would prove to be a crucial litmus test for the project. Defeating rivals inside Microsoft was one thing. Recruiting external allies to support the cause was another. Microsoft was asking Web designers to build sites that would only be viewable with a Microsoft browser on computers running Intel processors, and high-speed ones at that. This was where Engstrom and, to a lesser extent, Eisler—who was by now just orbiting the periphery of the project in preparation to join Ludwig and didn't attend the design review—would gauge potential market success. If the programmers and corporate representatives at the review didn't at least embrace the concept of Chrome, there was little hope it would gain momentum, let alone commercial success.

Engstrom had stayed up most of the night preparing his PowerPoint slides and organizing his keynote talk for the next morning. At 9 A.M. Monday, January 19, some 130 people, all under tight-lipped nondisclosure agreements, picked up their silver binders—the words "Chrome Microsoft CONFIDENTIAL" emblazoned on the covers—and filed into the Diplomat and Ambassador conference rooms. Diplomat. Ambassador. Two words normally not associated with Engstrom, who struggled to live down his well-earned reputation for being one of the most cantankerous people on Bill Gates's payroll.

"Eric can be extremely charming and he has extraordinary social skills," says Chris Phillips, Engstrom's business manager. "But he's more known for blowing up at people."

Engstrom was on his best behavior at the design review. At the time it was the largest group ever assembled to preview Chrome and hear Microsoft's plans for the technology. Some of those queued under palm trees near the Embassy's indoor river had heard whispers about Chrome's troubles with Developer Relations Group. (Executives at Monolith, aware of the rift, took pains to shield their Web developers from knowing the truth for fear of what it would do to troop morale.) Some also wondered if the world really cared about 3-D on the Web, or Microsoft's flavor of it. Still others remarked that Chrome might just be a cynical way to lure people into buying Intel-based computers, that the technology was a contrivance to justify the production and marketing of expensive home and office PCs.

If Engstrom was nervous, he didn't show it.

A picture of a biplane flew across an overhead screen, and in bold red letters—shadowed to appear in 3-D—scrolled the words, "This Is Not Your Mother's Browser." With the spotlight glaring off his glasses and absorbed in the fibers of his black shirt, the Dark Prince of Chrome began by asking the audience to "dream a little bit." Chrome was still in its alpha stage, just an infant and a temperamental one at that. Its performance was buggy. Programmers were still writing code. While Chrome could render some 3-D objects well, the technology had a long way to go and Engstrom reminded everyone of that.

Perhaps reflecting the "new Eric," Engstrom's presentation was part motivational speaker, part counselor, part vintage evangelist. He told the audience Chrome was tooled for high-end computers that didn't yet exist, but that Intel and computer makers intended to have them in the stores for back-to-school and Christmas '98. Later that morning, an Intel representative would outline the product schedule. The new computers would start at about $1,500 and run at 350 MHz or better, about half again as fast as most high-end PCs on the market in December '97. The Intel rep also revealed that by the first half of '99—or sooner—the world would see the rollout of the company's new superpowerful Pentium III processors, code-named Katmai after the Alaskan coastal wilderness.

The Katmai would be installed in machines costing about $2,000 and come loaded with standard sixty-four megabytes of RAM and eight gigabyte hard drives. These super-PCs of the time would initially be targeted at corporate purchasers and an upscale demographic. Guys, mostly, with lots of disposable income to spend on themselves. People much like Engstrom.

Chrome's strategy, then, was risky, since according to Computer Intelligence, a research firm in La Jolla, California, personal computers costing less than $1,000 accounted for nearly 40 percent of sales during the 1997 buying season.

Engstrom softened portions of his message by making those in the room feel they were part of Microsoft's team—part of Bill's family, and by inference, entitled to a portion of the imperial treasure.

"The whole point of this is to show you where we're going over the next three to four years . . . so you can provide feedback and help us with our vision," Engstrom said. "We can't make this successful without your help."

His overview included Intel's role in Chrome's development. Chrome would advance in concert with production of Intel's more powerful microprocessing chips, the brains under a computer's hood. Not since deployment of the Windows operating system had the symbiosis between these two companies been so pronounced. Chrome needed fast computers. Intel needed a reason to make fast computer chips. Chrome satisfied both interests.

Microsoft knew that initially only a relatively small number of consumers would be able to afford computers equipped with Chrome. Yet Engstrom argued that was one of Chrome's greatest assets, because Web developers could target an identifiable niche. Moreover, Moore's Law dictated that prices of fast computers would drop, meaning more people would eventually be able to afford Chrome-capable machines. According to Engstrom's game plan, as those machines became more ubiquitous, developers would increasingly author Chrome sites because the 3-D enhancements would generate more traffic and, thus, boost revenue. Engstrom quoted International Data Corp. figures estimating that by year 2000 there would be 2.5 billion Web sites, more than five times the estimated 351 million in existence as of January 1, 1998.

"Making your Web pages stand out is going to be a big challenge," he said.

Most everyone in the room missed the irony. Engstrom did not surf the Web. In fact, he knew remarkably little about the Net. For years he had thought the Internet's independent standards-setting body, the World Wide Web Consortium, was property of Microsoft.

Would that Gates could make it so.

"I hate browsing the Internet," Engstrom has confessed before, yet here he was, talking about improving the Web experience using game-foundation technology he had helped conceive and develop.

"The Web is an extremely limited place for delivering high-quality multimedia," he told the audience. "It does a great job for text, simple images, and animated GIFs. But *Monday Night Football* graphics would almost be impossible."

Endowing the Web with television-like graphics was alluring for many of those seated before him. Heads nodded at the idea of shattering screen transitions, or navigation bars that swung back to reveal ads or to expose more screen real estate. The possibilities were as endless as they were novel. Already, New Jersey–based KaTrix Millennium RUSH was developing a little 3-D cartoon man similar to one of the characters in the movie *Toy Story*. The figure would almost have intelligence. He'd be able to talk to users, lead them around

Web sites, and react to mouse movements. If you hit him with your cursor, the character could complain and tell you to watch it. Hit him one too many times, he'd walk around the Web page with a limp. This sort of interactivity, if perfected and well marketed, would be popular with any demographic. Computer-illiterate housewives and family members of the Chrome team who saw a demo of this character in early 1998 said they wanted Chrome-enabled computers.

Better still was that Chrome didn't penalize those who didn't have Chrome-enabled machines or browsers. If someone using a Mac with a Netscape browser, say, hit upon a Chrome-plated Web site, the browser could ignore the Chrome instructions and display an alternative, conventional static page.

More impressive for those at the design review, however, was Engstrom's announcement that Microsoft was going to ship Chrome aboard Windows 98 machines. Except for minor improvements and tighter integration with the Internet Explorer browser, Windows 98 didn't have a lot to differentiate itself from its ubiquitous predecessor, Windows 95. This was a major reason why Developer Relations Group didn't want to evangelize Windows 98. Chrome changed all that. Engstrom was positioning Chrome to be one of the star features in the new operating system.

That Microsoft promised to ship Chrome with Windows 98, and later Windows NT 5, was enough to persuade many at the design review to embrace the technology. (Windows NT 5, renamed Windows 2000 before its launch, marked Microsoft's phaseout of Windows 95 and 98 operating systems. Eventually, Microsoft planned to ship nothing but annual or biannual versions of the NT-based operating system.) Engstrom indicated there might even be a Macintosh version of Chrome at some point.

"There's no doubt anymore that it will ship," Engstrom said when asked about the reality of Chrome's run to market. "That wasn't true two months ago or one month ago. All I had was a videotape."

In fact, approval to integrate Chrome with Windows 98 wasn't official until two days before the design review, something Engstrom didn't see the need to share.

"Like all new products at Microsoft, there's always a certain risk. But I have E-mail from Bill, from Nathan, from Paul [Maritz]. The only thing I'm worried about is that it won't ship when I said it would, and that carries a certain amount of risk, too.

"It may be the last thing I do here," he added, "but it will ship."

As reassuring as his words were now, Engstrom had earlier expressed a thought that could feed the cynical. True, Chrome promised a new world of possibilities and functionality on the Web. But, the computer industry "is also running out of reasons for end users to upgrade their systems," Engstrom said. "Because the faster computers become, at some point they're as fast as you need them."

Jim Hoffman, chief executive officer of Bigfoot, a New York–based E-mail directory service, didn't think Engstrom was confessing a dark computer-industry secret.

"He's being honest," says Hoffman, who had dispatched one of his employees to the design review at the urging of friend Paul Scholz, the Dayton Web designer. "Three-D and voice recognition are the last frontiers of processing speeds. The computer industry is down to the last couple of things that can make you jump up to the next level."

Like a pitchman selling juicers on late-night TV, Engstrom was making a convincing case. He cited demographic studies showing who would buy the new Chrome-equipped computers, outlined shipping schedules, and demonstrated some of its uses. Then he got to one of his favorite if not more ethereal aspects of Chrome—the "knowledge browser." Engstrom envisioned a day when people would draw 3-D pictures instead of words to communicate. "I don't know quite how to get there . . . ," he admitted. "But we believe pictures work better at removing ambiguity from the description of how something works." It was late in his talk, and as he explained how much easier it would be to draw an illustration of an apogee rather than describe one in writing, the crowd's interest seemed to wane. Hands went up as people sensed an opportunity to ask questions.

Later, while an Intel representative outlined rollout schedules for the upcoming crop of superfast computers, Engstrom sat under the canopy of indoor palms and elaborated on his notion of a knowledge browser.

Engstrom's greatest aspiration for Chrome was ultimately based on the theory of the origin of language—that we started talking to one another for survival, to let our fellow knuckle-draggers know where to dig for the plumpest grubs or how to pursue and slay woolly mammoths.

"Like, 'The beast is a little to the left,' instead of 'Ugghh,'" Engstrom said. "Maybe we wouldn't have invented language if we realized how miserable it is to talk to each other sometimes."

While everyone broke for lunch, he continued his discussion without fortifying himself at the buffet table.

"Sixty percent of your cerebrum is devoted to the visualization of things—throw a rock and hit a target—that's what kept you alive. We've been talking for very little time. If you were to redesign the brain, you'd put in another twenty percent just to deal with text. But we don't have that, so we should modify the text into something we can deal with more easily, which is images and audio.

"Chrome is like—I don't know how to say this without sounding a little green—but it's almost an attempt to go back to what's more comfortable for the ape without throwing away polyester. You can make [the computer] draw pictures for you instead of writing all this text. The future will prove one way or another who was right about this."

He stopped there to let the impact of his words sink in. He had spoken nonstop for about half an hour, his voice rising above the din of clanging dishes and lunchroom chatter. The cacophony was dimming as the programmers filed back into the conference rooms. What were all these people thinking? Would they and the companies they represented nurture Chrome and procreate the seed Engstrom, Eisler, and St. John had so fiercely germinated?

"You don't know how these things go over until the second day," Engstrom said. "People tell me I can melt walls, but when I leave the room, the walls come back. It takes a little while . . ."

Paul Scholz had been in a slow smolder, circling for a chance to snatch Engstrom's attention. The flashCast president was irked because Engstrom had not used any flashCast demo pages during Chrome's inaugural presentation. Microsoft had sent Scholz typically terse but flattering E-mail a few weeks before, saying that flashCast's demos were some of the best produced to date. flashCast was one of the smallest companies represented at the design review. Having its demo pages featured during Engstrom's opening remarks would have been an invaluable networking and marketing entrée. Scholz and his four-man crew from Dayton had sat in the back row during Monday morning's briefing, giddy with expectation.

"When's he gonna show our stuff, man?" Scholz had groused. His pride suffered further injury when Engstrom ran through demos from Monolith, the blood-and-guts game firm from nearby Kirkland. A rivalry of sorts had developed between Monolith and flashCast. Each was feverishly curious and critical of the other's work. Scholz referred to Monolith's 3-D robots as "little cartoons." Monolith's lead Chrome man, Spencer Maiers, irreverently called Scholz "Johnny flashCast."

Engstrom, in his new role as diplomat, consoled Scholz on a bridge spanning the lobby's river. He explained that he meant no slight and that he had grabbed a handful of demos from his digital filing cabinet and stuck them in his presentation without malicious intent.

"I'm not very good with names or whose demos I should show," Engstrom said while holding court with the men from flashCast later that afternoon. It was the first time Scholz's band—including Inky, the absentminded but bright Web artist—had ever met Engstrom. It was then Marc Kuperstein, the former Lexis-Nexis programmer who had helped Scholz produce Chrome demos, walked over. Kuperstein had just been hired at Developer Relations Group, and Scholz introduced him to Engstrom. Kuperstein found himself in a socially awkward situation. Just two days before he was saying how Engstrom was "screwing himself by failing to deliver what's owed," namely the latest enhancements to DirectX. Kuperstein, echoing earlier suspicions from Developer Relations Group, was convinced Engstrom had retaliated against DRG by diverting manpower and money to Chrome from other already scheduled and evangelized projects.

While it was true Engstrom had pulled resources from DirectX, his motivation had far less to do with retaliation than with survival. Microsoft's previous reorganization had threatened the existence not only of Chrome but of Engstrom's team. Chrome was in peril and required Engstrom's immediate attention. Engstrom had delegated authority over DirectX to competent lieutenants and forged off to battle the imminent threat. Kuperstein did not know that the very day he had predicted that Engstrom's days were numbered, managers at Developer Relations Group had spun an about-face and decided to evangelize Chrome.

Scholz showed Engstrom a doodle Inky had drawn on a paper napkin that morning depicting the Internet Explorer *e* logo squashing Netscape's Godzilla mascot. Engstrom, allowing himself a moment of levity, put on a small show of bravado for the flashCast crew and Kuperstein.

"I would have invited Netscape here," Engstrom boasted. "I have nothing to fear. But I wouldn't have invited [founder and vice president of technology Marc] Andreessen. He's an asshole. I'm the test when it comes to assholes. It's hard to be a bigger asshole than me and he just blows right past me."

Engstrom excused himself a short time later. His smiling face concealed a certain anxiety. He was thinking about how well he had sold Chrome this day. He could take comfort that some, like Sculley, already believed Chrome was worth the investment.

"Someone who thinks out carefully what this additional processing power and eventual bandwidth can be used for and gets the architecture right back in 1998 has a huge advantage," Sculley said during a break in the design review. "[Chrome] has huge implications for electronic commerce, entertainment, on games, all kinds of services that can be offered over the next four or five years. If you get that stuff wrong, trying to fix it four or five years later is horrendously difficult as Microsoft found out with DOS."

Sculley applauded Microsoft's modest initial goals for the technology, such as the flapping navigation bar and the relatively simple-to-use 3-D animation.

"When it gets better, as the processors get bigger and the software gets more robust and more people are doing things with content, it will probably be one of the biggest areas down the road in entertainment and E-commerce," he said.

That night Intel hosted dinner and drinks at Jillian's, a former downtown-Seattle warehouse converted into a yuppie pool hall—ferns, lacquered white oak, the works. Intel issued everyone two red, rafflelike tickets, redeemable at the bar for well drinks and tap beer, which didn't satisfy everyone. "If Microsoft had been putting this on, it would have been an open bar," grumbled one Microsoftie. But there was nothing stopping people from running up their own tabs, and most surpassed the two-drink minimum. Just to be sure those invited to the design review made it for day two, Intel also sprang for a fleet of shuttles to ferry people to the Embassy Suites.

Computers hate smoke, and as it so happens, so do many young techies. As a consequence Jillian's was a pool hall largely bereft of cigarette haze. Pearl Jam tunes cranked over the crack of billiard balls. Engstrom, still dressed in his black CHROME—FAST AND FLASHY T-shirt, was among a group shooting trick shots. The winners got little Intel "Bunny Man" dolls, miniatures of the neon-space-suit-clad disco dancers popularized in the Pentium II television commercials. The buzz around some of the pool tables was that Chrome was cool technology. Was it just pints of Red Hook talking?

"We didn't know if there would be a market for Chrome and we were skeptical about 450-plus megahertz machines," said Kevin Guyton, a twentysomething founding partner of CyberDesign, an Internet firm in Orchard Park, New York. "But to hear Eric Engstrom say it will ship with Internet Explorer, that's what sold me." Little beads of sweat clung to his nose. "We see where people will buy the hardware. Chrome will define the modern Internet."

Some offered cautious, if not more sober, assessments in the days and weeks following the design review.

"It's very clear we don't know what we're going to do with

Chrome," said Joel Truher, vice president of Wired Ventures Inc., the parent of *Wired* magazine and the Wired.com Web site. Truher, like many others, was intrigued by Chrome's potential, in the things it would be able to do later in its development. Wired was particularly interested in being able to pump big pictures quickly over the Internet to personal computers with relatively slow modems. But in January 1998, Chrome was just too young. As far as the public knew, it didn't even exist, so there wasn't even a market. Moreover, Truher remembered all too well how his company had blundered into early experimentation with Internet Explorer 4.0. Wired had sunk untold numbers of man-hours and cash on prerelease versions of IE 4 in 1997. Like flashCast and a couple hundred other companies, Wired received early versions of IE 4, giving the company a sneak peek and enabling it to build Web sites for the new browser. But Truher said Wired spent an inordinate amount of time chasing down bugs that Microsoft discovered and fixed on its own anyway.

Yes, Wired got the jump on some competitors by building Web sites that took advantage of the browser's greater functionality. But the experience playing with the new browser also proved to be a colossal waste of money for Wired. Truher said the company was gun-shy of pouring more resources into an unproven, albeit cool, technology.

"We worked on IE 4 without any cost-benefit analysis," Truher said. "We're in a situation now where we'd like to make some money."

Eric Rudolph, a video producer at Asymetrix Learning Systems Inc., an on-line education firm in Bellevue, Washington, was typical of many fence-sitters. Asymetrix would use Chrome in doses at first— slick transitions and fades between pages and the like—but it wasn't yet betting the future of the company on Microsoft's new technology. Rudolph noted that VRML, the 3-D virtual reality modeling language, had failed to take the Internet by storm. He also questioned Chrome's supposed ease of use, which required developers to master a new set of authoring tags and tools.

"All the Web authors I know are just learning [Dynamic HTML], and not getting it, frankly," he said. "This whole mishmash of

DirectAnimation and tags seems like too many ways to get things done. It seems pretty complex."

Still, Chrome's immediate payoff was faster download time for animated graphics. And anything that delivered faster downloads "would be a hit," Rudolph said.

Other developers would evoke the chicken-or-the-egg dilemma. Which comes first—Chrome content or Chrome-enabled computers? Without content, computer makers would be loath to pay for and install Chrome technology in their PCs. But without Chrome-capable machines, why would developers spend time and money making Chrome-plated Web sites no one could see?

"People don't need to upgrade appliances, unless you're a techie geek," said Bigfoot's Hoffman.

According to Hoffman, Bigfoot would wait out early incarnations of Chrome 1.0 and see what the market dictated. Hoffman recalled the day in 1985 at the Plaza Hotel in New York when Gates unveiled Windows 1.0. It was a weak operating system. Or, as Hoffman observed, "It didn't do a fuck of a lot." But Hoffman figured that's where the market would eventually migrate and he wanted to be in position to take advantage of it.

"Microsoft nearly always gets things right, but usually not the first time," he said, overlooking instant market flops such as Microsoft BOB, the cartoonish user interface that was supposed to make computers easier to use. Shadowboxing, Hoffman called his strategy—"I want to see where the moves are." His company would likely deploy a version of Chrome to give people a different way to view search results on his service. But not for a while. He didn't have the manpower to spare in early 1998 to, as he emphasized, "play" with the technology.

Moreover, he disliked how Chrome could be used to take advantage of lag time or network latency to slip ads between new Web pages. When users click a hyperlink to a new Web page, there's always a delay as the next page loads. Chrome could be used to insert messages from Madison Avenue.

"Aren't we supposed to be delivering pages really quickly?" he asked. "This interstitial advertising concerns me. We'd be doing clever things that change the user experience, but not in a positive way."

The danger of Chrome, and many emerging technologies, as Hoffman saw it, was that it could be masturbatory—a plaything to please the digital desires of closeted techies, rather than a useful product to satisfy consumers.

Bob Heddle, Chrome's lead program manager, bluntly tackled this issue as the second day of the design review drew to a close.

"We're out to make money," Heddle said. "Microsoft makes money when people go out and buy computers. Intel makes a lot of money, too. That's how we make money here, by pushing sales of new computers."

And Microsoft believed people would buy these new computers if they understood that, for the first time in history, high-end machines would be capable of displaying Web sites better than low-end machines. Up until now, the Web was the great equalizer. Your mom's 486 PC running Windows 3.1 could view, say, the Porsche Web site as well as the computer that sat on Bill Gates's desk. But Chrome is "not your mother's browser." Chrome gave you speedy downloads and animated, 3-D graphics much better than anything ever before seen on the Web. To use an automotive analogy, you no longer had to drive your dad's Cutlass Supreme, you could drive Engstrom's Turbo 911.

And if you didn't have a Chrome-enabled machine and called up a Chrome-plated Web page, so what? Animations could appear as still images, just like on a conventional site.

But as the design review came to a close on the second day, it was clear Chrome would have to overcome timidity in the developer community.

Microsoft and its mercenaries had tried to evangelize a roomful of Web developers, and it was clear Chrome's message had received mixed reviews. Paul Scholz had delivered a presentation earlier that afternoon demonstrating real-world business applications of Chrome—3-D probability distribution graphs, collapsing navigation bars, and multiple Web pages mapped to spheres, cubes, and other shapes. Using his own business as an example, he admonished his contemporaries that they would achieve a significant competitive advantage if they were among the first to work with this new technology.

But Scholz was followed to the podium by the boys from Monolith, whose presentation, while visually interesting, was a bit too laden with *um*s and *ah*s and not up to toastmaster standards. Moreover, the two Monolith presenters gave in to the impulse to exhaustively promote their Web site and games, a protocol lapse that elicited muffled groans from those in the back rows.

Chris Gibbin, a partner with DNA Studio, a Los Angeles–based Web firm that builds sites for the likes of Sony and Paramount, found himself put on the spot in the waning moments of the session. One of Engstrom's men wrapped up the meeting by singling out Gibbin in the back of the room and asking his thoughts. Gibbin candidly, if somewhat reluctantly, questioned if the new *über* computers would sell. He also wondered if the market would embrace Chrome. Java, for example, had much more momentum at the time, and Gibbin still couldn't convince customers to buy fully enabled Java sites. Moreover, half his clientele used Macintosh computers. Not only was Chrome elitist technology built for the high-end demographic, it was divisive because it would only run on Intel-based computers running Windows 98 or Windows NT. Chrome was unproven technology. Although he didn't say so publicly, Gibbin and others had joked that Chrome could make the personal Web site get a whole lot uglier. They evoked the scenario of college sophomores mapping their faces and other body parts onto 3-D spheres. Rather than revolutionary, Chrome "could be dangerous," some wryly said.

Gibbin's company would initially walk the middle of the road. Sure, Chrome as a concept was exciting. And he was flattered that the Empire had invited his small, nine-man company to play with emerging technology. But he had a monthly $50,000 payroll to meet. He had more doubt than desire. There were no guarantees with Chrome.

The subtext of his remarks was, "If the market moves to it, we'll embrace it."

Scholz, who had swiveled in his front-row chair to listen, nodded as if in agreement, then issued a challenge:

"The Germans have a saying that I think applies here. *'Keine Hoden, kein Eisenkreuz,'* which means, 'No balls, no Iron Cross.'"

13

SQUEEZE PLAYS

Schoolgirls touring the nation's Capitol squealed when they caught sight of computerdom's emperor and his courtiers of handlers and home-state politicians. On Tuesday, March 3, 1998, Bill Gates had returned to the same building where he had once served as a page and took his rightful place in the Senate Judiciary Committee's hot seat. History was in the making. Even Patrick Leahy, the esteemed senator from Vermont and ranking Democrat on the committee, felt compelled to take snapshots of Gates and an unprecedented gathering of high tech's most powerful figures.

Senator Orrin Hatch finally had his prey inside the colonial-brown lair of political power—Room 216 of the Hart Senate Office Building. The room was one of the few places on earth where Gates and all his billions seemed strangely impotent, despite the fact his company had belatedly doubled its lobbying efforts. Hatch had met with Gates for more than an hour the day before to reassure him that the hearing would be impartial. Yet the proceeding, dubbed "Market Power and Structural Change in the Software Industry," signaled that the beltway was fitting a noose for the Redmond giant. Indeed, many saw the hearing as mortar for a larger antitrust lawsuit under construction at the Justice Department—a case that would eventually rope a Beastie Boy.

Hatch said the inquiry was necessary to determine whether Microsoft was exploiting its hegemony in the PC operating-system market to control the Internet and other markets. The senator repeated that failure to corral an unchecked monopolist could later lead to the more unsavory prospect of establishing an Internet governing committee—anathema to the libertarian spirit of the Web.

It would prove to be an exhausting, futile day for Gates, who found himself seated before hostile senators and flanked by bitter rivals Scott McNealy, the toothy CEO of Sun Microsystems, and James Barksdale, the CEO of Netscape and the industry's poster child of market abuse at the hands of Microsoft.

Gates fended off accusations he lorded over a monopoly and stressed that Microsoft had done more than its part to supply the computer revolution and the masses with affordable, innovative software. Yet his rhetorical swordsmanship was no match for the big guns of government and the theatrics of Barksdale.

At one point, Barksdale stood with his back to the standing-room-only crowd.

"I'd like a show of hands," Barksdale said. "How many people in this audience use PCs? Not Macintoshes, now; that's only about three percent of the shipments. How many of you use Intel-based PCs in this audience?"

Nearly all raised their hands.

"Of that group who use PCs, how many of you use a PC without Microsoft's operating system?"

Everyone who had been holding his hand aloft dropped it. Without turning around, Barksdale delivered his punch line:

"Gentlemen, that's a monopoly."

Hatch needed no such demonstration. "There is enough indication here that there is a monopoly, and the monopoly is being used and it may be being used in violation of the law," the senator said after the proceedings.

Gates never lost his cool before the senators. Never flashed his famous temper. But he was clearly weary of the hearing and looked forward to boarding his jet home—the world's richest man had long since stopped flying coach aboard commercial airliners.

Even as this moment of dread for Gates was ending, another was beginning for one of his most ambitious soldiers—Eric Engstrom.

Engstrom missed the televised proceedings. His mind and body were literally thousands of miles away, aboard a plane returning to Seattle. In fact, he had arrived just hours before Gates. Engstrom had been sailing off the British Virgin Islands, fittingly vacationing in the very waters once plied by pirates. Engstrom had been buoyed by the upbeat feedback he had heard from the design review in January and by the Developer Relations Group's agreement to bang the pots for his pet project. He had felt confident enough in Chrome's progress to leave it on autopilot.

"When I left everything was fine," Engstrom recalls. "Marketing and development was brought in. We had a plan. All the senior management said, 'We're set.' "

Engstrom flew to the Caribbean with assurances Project Chrome was alive and well. His optimism was misplaced. When he returned, his project lay prone on a gurney.

"They're canceling Chrome," Heddle told Engstrom.

David Cole, the man who had helped pilot Windows 95 to completion and had replaced John Ludwig—Chrome's guardian vice president—had taken the opportunity of Engstrom's absence to place Chrome in a holding cell, where imprisoned technologies at Microsoft typically await execution. Members of the Internet Explorer team and others hostile to Chrome were lobbying Cole, who reportedly now deemed Chrome an "unacceptable risk" to Windows 98 as well as the launch schedule of IE 5—a spurious argument given that IE 5's rollout date was a fleeing target somewhere in the future. Cole said he was pushing back Chrome's release from June to at least August.

Chrome would only be available through computer makers, who would assure that the technology was loaded on the proper types of machines. Chrome needed the fastest computers, equipped with at least sixty-four megabytes of random access memory (RAM), the best

3-D graphics cards of the time, and the newest advanced graphics ports (AGPs). Releasing Chrome through computer makers had become a quality-control decision. By keeping Chrome off store shelves and unavailable for download via the Web, Microsoft eliminated the chance someone would load the technology on a lesser PC, reducing the likelihood of problems and thus keeping costly tech-support calls to a minimum. To get a technology loaded on machines and deployed throughout the market takes about six weeks. Shipping Chrome in August meant it would miss the threshold for back-to-school sales. Further delays would mean Chrome would miss the more lucrative Christmas season.

"Cole said 'unacceptable risk,' but I'm telling you it was political," one Chrome member says.

Rivals inside the Internet Explorer team had pushed for Chrome's derailment. The IE team was enraged that Chrome was slated to piggyback on a modified version of IE 4 and feared that the new technology would cause computers to freeze or break. IE's engineers didn't want their proven product adulterated with unproven technology. Bitter mail flew between the Chrome and IE camps.

"They didn't want another team releasing HTML technology that was at the core of the browser," says McCartney, Chrome's Scottish bulwark. "It could break God knows how many machines. They were concerned about our timetable for release. They didn't believe we could ship on time. Many of these were legitimate concerns, but maybe not expressed in the most cooperative fashion."

Some of the IE team's wrath was territorial.

"People on [the IE team] whose code we were enhancing just can't deal with it," Engstrom said at the time. "They just can't accept it, which to me I find really funny. The highest compliment is if somebody takes something I make and does something else with it. To me that's what an engineer should live for."

Engstrom was a man of contradictions. Here he was shown embracing the utilitarian philosophy of a Linus Torvalds, inventor of the free and open operating system known as Linux, a system where the world's programmers were invited to help add and refine. Yet

Engstrom jealously guarded his own technology and attacked projects he believed to be threats—internal Microsoft initiatives WinG, Surround Video, and iHammer, among others, had all been on Engstrom's hit list at one time.

Before leaving on vacation, Engstrom had made a tactical retreat and settled on shipping Chrome with IE 5 instead of a modified version of IE 4. It was a gesture of compromise. Now Engstrom felt angry and betrayed. The Thursday after returning from the Virgin Islands, Engstrom stormed into Cole's office, telling him that failure to ship Chrome in conjunction with the rollout of Windows 98 in June was a mistake. The conversation went something like this:

"It's bad for Windows 98 and useless for Chrome in August because it's too late for the Christmas machines," Engstrom argued.

"You're overreacting," Cole said.

"I'm just telling you what my team's telling me. It's up to you to save Chrome. All the people who are trying to kill it work for you now."

Cole scheduled another meeting with Engstrom the following morning. Engstrom should have stayed in bed.

"I think you should go look for another job now," Cole began. Engstrom's days at Microsoft's Building 30, it appeared, were numbered.

Engstrom's office was next to Eisler's, who had dubbed his the Hostility Suite. On the small window that faced the hallway Eisler had taped a doctored photo from that week's Senate hearing. In it Gates was glancing at McNealy and Barksdale and muses about having the two CEOs killed, while McNealy and Barksdale plot to roll Bill for his billions.

McNealy: "You grab him. I'll grab the 40 billion . . ."

Barksdale: "He keeps it on him??"

Engstrom sought counsel with Eisler, who was himself leaving Building 30 under entirely different circumstances. While Engstrom was momentarily down, Eisler was on the rise. He would be moving to Building 9 soon, literally a stone's throw to Building 8, Gates's executive office. After earning nearly a dozen patents and years of toiling as an unsung hero in Microsoft's multimedia arena, Eisler was being lofted to general manager of NetShow. Eisler would be in charge of the server side of the technology, the pitching software that pumped streaming video and audio to PCs via the Web— a neat match to Engstrom, who was working on the client side of what was now called Windows Media Player.

Eisler had more good news. He had fallen in love and was engaged to be married to Kathryn Kaufman, a leggy Malibu blonde known as KT. As upset as Engstrom was over his professional setback, he said at the time he was elated with Eisler's newfound personal happiness and professional success.

During the previous reorganization, when Allchin had displaced Silverberg and consolidated his control over Internet and Windows development, Eisler was handed the opportunity of working with either the operating-system group or the Internet team. He readily chose to follow John Ludwig to work on Web essentials, such as Microsoft's home page, E-mail software, and other related technologies.

Eisler had labored with Windows technology in one way or another for most of the decade. Extenders, editors, hardware abstraction layers, drivers, you name it, when it came to Windows, Eisler had done just about all. He felt no challenge in standing sentry over an established technology. Now was a time for something new. The Internet, an emerging and vast new frontier, was an obvious choice for someone who savored seizing new ground. When the position for general manager—a rung below vice president— opened for NetShow (now Windows Media). Eisler jumped at it, despite the fact he knew next to nothing about server and streaming Web technology. Conquering the unknown, however, was what a Beastie Boy did.

NetShow provided new ground to take and, better still, an established, dominant competitor—Rob Glaser's RealNetworks. What Apple had been to multimedia, RealNetworks was to streaming audio and video. RealNetworks owned almost all the streaming video and audio player market share, and its technology set the standard. Since

Glaser was an ex-Microsoft executive with licensing agreements with the Redmond firm—Glaser's player would ship as part of Windows 98—many on Eisler's team wondered how they could effectively compete. Eisler discovered that his new NetShow team was suffering from an inferiority complex, and he intended to cure it.

"Yeah, RealNetworks owned market share," Eisler recalls. "Glaser's a very smart man, and we were shipping his player in Windows 98. It created angst for my team.

"One of the things I instilled in this group was that they not treat Rob as this holy demon avenger who's so smart we can't compete."

One of the things Eisler also didn't want his new team to do was compete where the enemy was strong. Among other things, Eisler was training his team's energy on creating NetShow Theater, code-named Tiger, a video-on-demand technology that was later folded into Windows Media. The company envisioned the technology being deployed in airplanes, airports, homes, or wherever people found themselves cooped up for hours at a stretch.

Despite Eisler's growing banquet of responsibilities, he carved time for Engstrom when his friend's back was against the wall. The regular mentoring sessions with Ludwig had paid dividends. Like Engstrom, Eisler had matured and had learned a little about corporate diplomacy. For Engstrom's sake and for that of his team, Eisler counseled his friend to try to work things out with Cole.

The next night Engstrom met with St. John, the fallen Beastie Boy. His advice was the same as it had been since he left Microsoft. St. John said it's better on the outside. Evoking Mel Gibson's dying cry in *Braveheart,* St. John boomed, "Freedom! *Freedom!*"

Engstrom found himself alone with his troubled thoughts on Sunday. He grabbed a frozen pizza from the downstairs fridge and popped it in the microwave. Despite his computer engineering prowess, he still struggled occasionally to achieve the right cooking time and temperature for one of his ever-present packaged frozen entrées. Engstrom was a big-picture guy who eschewed details. In fact, Eisler taught him how to program his VCR to stop flashing "12:00."

With the single-serve pizza cooked and consumed, Engstrom

snatched a cigar from his wood humidor, poured himself two fingers of Macallan single-malt Scotch, and strolled the boat dock of his Holmes Point house on the shores of Lake Washington. Save for the piles of goose feces, the dock stretching into the steel-blue water was an ideal peninsula of solitude. He talked bleakly of his future at Microsoft and that of Chrome.

"I believe when I leave, they'll reorg in such a way Chrome no longer will have an identity as a distinct product," he said. "They'll break it apart. The XML part will go to the IE team, and the underlying multimedia part of it will join the foundation team, and the tools will go to [Microsoft] Office."

The prospect of Chrome's being ripped apart was too cruel a thought for Engstrom. This was his dream project, a stand-alone Internet product that he and the Beastie Boys had hoped millions would use.

Alternating between self-pity and resolve to stay, Engstrom lamented the loss of Chrome's "vision," his idea of turning a Web browser into a means of communicating with others in real time using a blend of text and 3-D pictures.

"There are two people on the planet who understand the vision, and those two people are now not working on it, assuming I'm off it on Monday," he said. "That's kind of funny. What it means is you build something that everyone loves in the executive staff, and you get in this argument with your boss about when to ship it, and he decides he doesn't want you working on it anymore. The birthing process is so amazingly fragile."

However, Engstrom's spirits lightened as he mused about Chrome's first press leak, which appeared March 18 in *Feed*, an on-line magazine. Mark Pesce, one of the fathers of virtual reality modeling language or VRML, had written an alarmist article about Chrome, claiming it was a threat to Internet standards, not to mention his beloved VRML. He argued that Microsoft and others in the industry were delivering too many proprietary means to author for and read content on the Internet. Chrome, which could only be used on a fast

Intel-based computer running Windows with an Internet Explorer browser, was bad because it didn't march in step with his egalitarian, homogenous notions of cyberspace.

"Just as Europe has suffered through two thousand years of language-driven conflicts, we're about to see Balkanization of the Web, as it breaks into the parts that you can read versus the parts I can," Pesce wrote. "Soon enough, you'll launch into a Web site and find nothing—no text, no images, no sound—and not just because you're using Netscape Communicator when you should be using Internet Explorer (or vice versa); but rather because your browser simply doesn't know how to translate the forty or fifty new and unintelligible XML tags it's encountered into anything it can render visibly."

Engstrom smiled. He was far less concerned about the press leak than his squad of marketing people, who monitored the Web and print world daily for "unauthorized" reports.

"Mark's a hoot," Engstrom said, pulling the adjective deep from his country-boy roots. "Here's one of those things I'm just not smart enough to figure out. You read an article that says that Microsoft is the huge company with too much market share and that's the reason they don't innovate.

"Then we come up with Chrome and they say, 'They're innovating! Those fuckers!' People always say Microsoft doesn't want to innovate. Well, we may be bad at it, but the desire to innovate is in every fiber of our existence."

Engstrom was scheduled to talk about Chrome before thousands at the annual three-day Windows Hardware Engineering Conference at the Orange County Convention Center in Orlando, Florida, later that month. Programs had been printed. Schedules were locked in. Engstrom's face and biography even appeared on the list of speakers. Despite the impending implosion of Chrome, the show had to go on.

In the end, after weighing the advice of his two friends and his lone inner voice, Engstrom resolved to see Chrome through, to force Microsoft to either keep him or fire him.

"I like this project enough that I'm going to try to stay," he said.

"Which disturbs me because it's so much like begging and that's just not me. But I've got to consider the people who've been killing themselves on this. So I will go beg.

"I'll know on Monday if I'm looking for another job."

That week proved pivotal for Chrome and Engstrom. He had told his team that he might well be removed and that Chrome might be sent to the morgue by Friday. He asked members of his team if they still wanted to remain with the project. After long discussions and soul-searching, to a man and woman all agreed to stay.

"We had made significant progress on Chrome at that point," says Colin McCartney. "We felt we should just see it through. And we kind of believed in the project, too."

That was testament to Engstrom's leadership. While Heddle and others sometimes argued with Engstrom—indeed, Heddle and Engstrom were not on speaking terms for much of 1998—they all respected him. Engstrom had by now amassed a force of some 250 people, a little more than 100 of whom were working on Chrome, or at least thought they were. Chrome was Engstrom's top priority. To keep morale aloft, he told some of his crew they were helping with Chrome when they were in fact working on lower-priority missions.

"I wanted them to feel they were part of [Chrome]," Engstrom says. "It was the coolest project at Microsoft. I didn't want my people to feel alienated."

It worked. They clung to Chrome out of loyalty to the project.

Others under Engstrom's command had been with him during the chaotic and heady days of DirectX and were willing to stick by him now.

"It seemed like Chrome was getting canceled daily," recalls Chris Phillips, Engstrom's business manager at the time. "I remember having to convince the team that Eric was happy and things were okay.

"It was always like that. There's never been any major support for multimedia at Microsoft, at least that's how it seemed. Yet there always have been groups that have gunned for our technology," Phillips adds. "I was in meetings where people have said, 'I will control DirectX.'

"I'd say, 'Yeah? Does Eric know?' They'd back off."

Engstrom was as loyal to his employees as he was to his technology. "They were extremely loyal in return," Phillips adds.

Engstrom received words of encouragement via E-mail. But from Engstrom's perspective, things still seemed bleak.

From: Eric Engstrom
Sent: Tuesday, March 10, 1998 10:02 AM
To: Paul Scholz
Cc: Craig Eisler
Subject: RE: Keep your chin up

I am going skiing from Friday 1pm on. I will be back Sunday night. Have you ever read Fountainhead by Ayn Rand, Paul? If so, I am feeling very much like Howard Roarke at the moment.

From: Paul Scholz
Sent: Tuesday, March 10, 1998 12:48 PM
To: Eric Engstrom
Cc: Craig Eisler
Subject: RE: Keep your chin up

Let's get together on Monday. I never did read the Fountainhead . . . saw part of the movie. Howard, as I recall, wanted to build a building *his* way, and no other, so if he couldn't build it his way, he chose to build nothing at all. I hope you haven't decided to give up building cool stuff . . . that would be a mistake.

Paul

As Engstrom girded for an uphill battle with his new boss, reinforcements stormed in from outside the company. Intel representatives, tipped to the fact Microsoft was deemphasizing Chrome for possible phaseout, raised a loud protest. Intel wanted to know why the project was being delayed. Intel explained that the company had invested time, personnel, and money into the new technology. In fact, Intel had written the portions of code for Chrome that handled some of the TV-like page transitions, such as shattering effects, pond ripples, and waves.

Chrome was to be one of the key selling points for Intel's faster line of Pentium II and new Pentium III microprocessors. Computer makers had been sold on the idea. Promises had been made. Contracts had been signed. Derailing Chrome was not in Intel's—therefore Microsoft's—best interest, Intel argued. Although it's unclear who at Microsoft alerted Intel—and Engstrom refuses to discuss the issue in detail—it's clear that Engstrom's early partnership with the world's leading chipmaker triggered an unintended reward. Cole relented and agreed to keep Chrome afloat. Microsoft would tell the public the technology would roll out the first half of 1999, but in reality Engstrom's team was shooting for a late-July or early-August release to computer makers. That would be too late for back-to-school sales, but still in time for Christmas.

Cole and Engstrom also worked to patch up their shaky relationship. With the release date of Chrome settled, Engstrom and Cole could talk about how to get along. The two discovered they had more in common than either had originally thought—both were ultra-intelligent, type A corporate warriors who knew well the rush of going in for the kill and delivering industry-changing technology. Cole appreciated Engstrom's passion for making technology. Engstrom identified with Cole's aggressiveness. Engstrom would later say Cole was shaping up to be "one of the best bosses I ever had." That sentiment would be short-lived.

Yet the Chrome team was not about to rest after its eleventh-hour rescue by Intel nor its recently healed relationship with Cole. Concerned that Chrome's message had been drowned out amid the conflict with Cole, the chaos to ship Windows 98, and the ongoing legal battles with the U.S. government, Engstrom and the Chrome team decided to do a little internal evangelizing and embarked on a technology tour of Microsoft vice presidents. Engstrom and his team demonstrated Chrome for Nathan Myhrvold, Paul Maritz, Jim Allchin, and other higher-ups and reiterated the ideas that set this technology apart from so many others in development at the company.

"This was for Chrome's survival," McCartney recalls. "To get upper management on our side to ensure Chrome would not be killed."

The team knocked out "some pretty cool demos pretty damn fast," McCartney says. Myhrvold was the first stop on the VP tour.

"This is the kind of stuff we should be doing more of," Myhrvold said, according to McCartney. "We don't want to shit on international standards, but we want to make Windows the best for viewing Web content. Nothing wrong with that."

The rest of the presentations to other executives went just as well. Senior managers and others were particularly impressed that Chrome could download images three to a thousand times faster than conventional graphics formats. After a near-death experience, Chrome was up and on its feet again.

Shortly after, Engstrom and other general managers met with David Cole to review head-count status and requests. Head count is the true barometer of executive opinion. If a veep doesn't like your project, you won't get more personnel. Engstrom watched as Cole rejected the requests of other general managers.

"You don't need that many," Cole would say. "You can get by with two less."

Then he got to Engstrom's numbers. Cole noticed Engstrom had cut thirteen software testers from his team and swapped them for developers to rush Chrome to completion.

"You don't have enough testers," Cole said.

"I know," Engstrom replied. "I cut my number because I needed more developers. I can always find a way to test it."

"You put the thirteen testers back in there. I'll go get them all for you."

Engstrom smiled. He knew what the next GM in line was thinking: "You just got all my people."

Chrome's resurrection showcased the Darwinian nature of software development at Microsoft, where opportunistic predators and competitors often kill or kidnap sick or newborn technologies. Survival of the fittest is systemic to the Redmond organism. Although it's doubtful Gates designed this matrix on a white board, he's the one responsible for creating a corporate culture of conflict. It was Gates, after all, who demanded that Microsoft hire only the brightest and most competitive. Far from creating a utopian climate where all these bright minds harmonically competed toward common goals, hiring hypercompetitive people with high IQs led naturally to the formation of competitive groups that often battled one another as fiercely as they did outside foes. Internecine backstabbing did not evaporate in the presence of great intelligence and wealth, it became more brutal. Engstrom demonstrated Gatesian bloodlust when he lunged to kill iHammer, Tod Nielsen's attempt at marrying multimedia special effects with the browser—a potential threat to Chrome. That kind of ruthlessness could be found at all levels of Microsoft, one of the most visible examples being Jim Allchin's consolidation of operating systems and Internet technologies while Brad Silverberg was on vacation. (Silverberg returned in 1999 as a part-time consultant.)

So, too, the practice of culling weak ideas began with Gates and became a technique most Microsoft managers employed. Gates has always challenged ideas, often with "That's the stupidest thing I've ever heard," if for no other reason than to see if the presenter could articulate and debate a proposed technology's merits. Those who sputtered got to leave the room, taking their stillborn technologies with them. As in nature, those who could defend themselves—and Engstrom was a master at defense—were generally allowed to propagate. For if your technology could survive inside the cutthroat world of Microsoft, chances were it could survive in the equally cutthroat high-tech market.

14

"THE OPERATING SYSTEM THE GOVERNMENT DOESN'T WANT YOU TO HAVE"

Blue smoke lifted from the platform stage as an army of three thousand media geeks and technology freaks stormed the dark confines of Hall D inside Orlando's oversize Orange County Convention Center. Eager Japanese writers and photographers clustered near the stage like mantis, oblivious to the green laser-beam daggers slicing overhead. Van Halen's "Running with the Devil" blared from the digital sound system, a curious prelude to the arrival of the master of ceremonies, Bill Gates.

This was March 26, the second day of WinHEC, the annual Windows Hardware Engineering Conference, and Gates was to deliver that morning's keynote—"Beyond a Computer on Every Desk." WinHEC was all about "advancing the platform," and in this case *platform* meant Intel-compatible PCs running Windows, and some of the biggest names in semiconductor and computer hardware were on hand—Intel, Digital Equipment Corp., Hewlett-Packard, Texas Instruments—all the usual suspects.

Nearly a half hour late, Gates, clad in a red, short-sleeve shirt and khaki Dockers, strode onstage to a rock star's welcome. Eschewing any talk about the company's growing legal woes, Gates played to the computer-hardware makers and chipmakers in the audience, saying consumers and the industry needed all the memory storage and processing speed that innovation could deliver. That message resonated with Engstrom, who was waiting in the wings. Chrome, at least initially, would require the fastest PCs money could buy. Gates also spoke about the problems of delivering affordable, high-speed Internet access, a theme he juxtaposed with the promise of delivering via the Web digital TV and video broadcasts that could be modified by consumers. In short, he discussed his vision of the "Web lifestyle," where the Internet would mature into a mainstream way of communicating and become as ubiquitous as the telephone.

While Gates told the audience that the world needed bigger, faster, better PCs, it was Engstrom and his sidekick Bob Heddle who showed why. This was the largest crowd to date to see a demo of Chrome. Although Jim Allchin, Microsoft's powerful vice president in charge of Windows and Internet development, had mentioned Chrome during his keynote the day before, it was Engstrom and Heddle who would take the technology out for a real spin.

The demo would be tame compared with the type of extravaganzas St. John had schemed up in the past. Chrome's marketing people—those on Engstrom's staff in charge of enticing software and Web-site developers to build plug-ins and Chrome-plated sites—lacked the chutzpah of St. John. Moreover, Engstrom was flying solo since St. John, adrift from the Empire, was dabbling with day trading on the stock market, while Eisler, the former DirectX code monkey, was piloting NetShow. Even if the whole crew had been aboard for this show, the three would have found themselves confined. Engstrom was sharing the event's billing with Microsoft's top executives. There was no place for the vomitoria, vagina monsters, and faux-alien spaceships that had served as props to boost DirectX. In this arena, Engstrom had to behave more like a good corporate soldier, and the rules called for him to stand on a stage and preside over a high-tech, albeit staid, slide show.

Like Gates and his minions, Engstrom and Heddle wore identical red, short-sleeve shirts and khaki Dockers, a symbol of unity that was just this side of disingenuous. Engstrom and Heddle were still barely on speaking terms. Heddle, still irked that Engstrom had forced the Chrome team to use DirectAnimation instead of the simpler Direct3D Retain Mode, believed the Beastie Boy was a meddling micromanager.

Despite the rift, Engstrom took pains to inform the audience that Heddle and Colin McCartney, who was back in Redmond, were the workhorses behind this new technology. Engstrom rewarded loyalty, differences with his team leaders notwithstanding.

Heddle handled most of the hour-long general session, demonstrating what were by now to him familiar examples of Chrome— 3-D fish swimming in a Windows screen "aquarium"; a hot-air balloon touring across a sample Web page; a cube mapped with multiple Web sites; and a flashCast-made mock news site that hurled the viewer inside a granite sphere.

Engstrom and Heddle exchanged scripted banter: "So, you can author Chrome using Notepad?" Engstrom inquired, referring to the stripped-down word processor that's standard issue with Windows.

"That's right, Eric, because we've found that thirty-eight percent of people actually use Notepad to author their Web pages."

Engstrom soon took over and said Chrome's initial goals were modest—"to make normal Web browsing faster." This would be done by using an entirely new species of digital information for the Web. That this new class of information needed faster computers played well to the partisan crowd, which was looking to their counterparts in the software industry to give consumers reasons to upgrade PCs. Chrome would target the upcoming line of 350-megahertz computers and continue to aim for faster computers as they rolled out through the new millennium.

This was possible only because Chrome sat on top of and took advantage of DirectX, which was being fitted to Windows 98 and upcoming Windows NT operating systems, to be renamed Windows

RENEGADES OF THE EMPIRE

2000. DirectX, the once parasitic technology, was now endemic to the Windows organism.

Engstrom used the podium to share his vision of Chrome's future, where Chrome would change the look and feel of Windows, bringing 3-D not only to the Web but to Microsoft's long line of software applications. He also seized the opportunity to share his vision of the "knowledge browser," where people used Chrome-enabled browsers to communicate in 3-D images in real time from anywhere in the world.

Delusional? Not nearly as much as Jay Torborg, Engstrom's multimedia nemesis who had proceeded him onstage that day. Torborg still entertained ideas about resurrecting Talisman, the 3-D chip venture that had collapsed months before.

"Talisman wasn't even supposed to be up there," Engstrom said after his presentation, referring to one of Torborg's slides.

Although Engstrom and Heddle received loud applause before the crowd broke for lunch, a few were skeptical of, even cynical about, Engstrom's plan.

"That technology demo was embarrassing," said computer-industry writer Jerry Pournelle, author of *Byte* magazine's popular column "Chaos Manor." "Obviously this is the first step toward putting 3-D into [Microsoft] Office, which is what I've been saying Microsoft was up to for a long time.

"But I think it's rather chilling that Engstrom said we could read less and read less often," Pournelle said. "I'm sorry, I'm a writer. What's this whole business about authoring in pictures? I thought we wrote."

Pournelle likened Chrome to "hiding a nailed fist inside the velvet glove," because as cool as Chrome might be, Engstrom had said the technology would only run on the yet-to-be-released Windows 98 and Windows 2000 operating systems equipped with Internet Explorer 5.

"I think it's great they're trying to push things forward, don't get me wrong on that," Pournelle said before heading off for lunch. "But it creates more fear and uncertainty and doubt. You must upgrade or die. You will be assimilated."

Which is exactly what the government and Microsoft competitors feared.

The very day Engstrom talked about his brave new vision of communicating through 3-D images, Senator Hatch and others on the Senate Judiciary Committee wrote Gates requesting that Microsoft allow its business partners to release contract documents. Netscape and Sun Microsystems had already told the committee they would allow their partners to let government snoopers have a look at their respective contracts. The senators wanted to examine how Microsoft dealt with computer makers and Internet service and content providers. The request was a companion to a larger antitrust case simmering at the Justice Department.

Microsoft began taking fire from all directions. Throughout the ensuing seven weeks, speculation mounted as to when—not if—Attorney General Janet Reno and her antitrust warriors would launch the broader antitrust attack. The DOJ was already taking depositions from computer makers and others in the industry. Ammunition also arrived via Microsoft competitors. In late March, Netscape stated in its annual 10-K report to the Securities and Exchange Commission that Microsoft was using its market-share muscle to strong-arm major Web content developers to build sites only viewable with Internet Explorer browsers.

"Netscape believes that Microsoft may be using co-marketing funds and other inducements to have Web sites developed exclusively for Internet Explorer or using technology that may only be accessed by Internet Explorer," the company wrote. "Such actions may materially adversely affect Netscape's business, operating results, or financial condition."

Rumors of war began in earnest the first week of April, when the *Wall Street Journal* quoted unnamed sources as saying the government wanted to file a broad lawsuit before May 15—the day Microsoft was scheduled to ship Windows 98 to computer makers. The paper said the government believed it had enough evidence to prove Microsoft illegally maintained and extended its monopoly with Windows and had violated the 1995 consent decree by bundling its browser with the operating system.

The article was among the first of what would be many to quote damaging internal Microsoft memos outlining ways to kill competition and leverage the market share of Windows. The *Journal* piece lifted segments from a confidential 1996 strategic plan, which directed managers to gain exclusive licensing deals for the IE browser with the nation's five largest Internet service providers, including America Online.

"You should be able to break most of Netscape's licensing deals and return them to our advantage because our browsers are free," the plan stated. "We should have absolutely dominant browser share in the corporate space."

Microsoft said it was unfazed by the Department of Justice probe and would ship Windows 98 on schedule.

Nonetheless, Microsoft's latent political lobbying cranked into gear. Democratic senator Patty Murray, the once-celebrated Seattle "mom in tennis shoes," publicly denounced the DOJ for leaking documents and trying the case in the media. The euphoria of Murray's victory during the so-called year of the woman in 1992 contrasted with her anemic senatorial record. She had authored no major pieces of legislation to date during her term and was largely quiet on contemporary controversies and issues affecting her home state, including trade imbalance with other nations and salmon protection. Yet attacks on Microsoft stirred her maternal ire.

"It is inappropriate for the Department [of Justice] to leak information regarding this investigation and to prosecute in the press one of America's most inventive and creative companies," Murray said.

The leaks could, however, have come from any number of holes. Twenty state attorneys general were lining up with the Justice Department, sharing and subpoenaing company documents in a move that mirrored the successful multifront attack on the tobacco industry. California, Texas, New York, and Massachusetts were technology-rich states interested in diving into Bill Gates's wallet. Even states on the periphery of the software industry were climbing over the transom. Chris Davey, a spokesman for Ohio attorney general Betty Montgomery, said in early April, "We don't have plans at this time to take any antitrust action in Ohio against Microsoft."

Ohio did an about-face in a matter of days.

Multistate antitrust and consumer cases can potentially pay huge rewards in the form of damages. Moreover, there was little political risk in piling on Microsoft. This combination proved too irresistible for many attorneys general, many of whom lusted for reelection or higher office. There is a reason, after all, wags refer to the attorneys general national organization as the National Association of Aspiring Governors.

The noose was tightening. Hoping to avoid a lawsuit, Microsoft met for three hours with DOJ's antitrust chief, Joel Klein, on Friday, April 10. Yet any credibility Microsoft had going into the meeting was undermined that very day when the *Los Angeles Times* reported that the company was poised to launch a "grassroots" letter-writing campaign to influence state antitrust investigations.

Microsoft planned to pay freelance writers to pen letters of support, then plant these "spontaneous" testimonials in major newspapers and magazines. Microsoft's PR firm Edelman Public Relations was in on the scheme. As if that weren't embarrassing enough, Microsoft spokesman Greg Shaw denied any knowledge about the so-called Astroturf campaign, but reversed himself when confronted with the fact his name appeared in confidential documents detailing the plan.

State attorneys general were not amused.

"When it comes to knowledge of computer technology, I take my hat off to Mr. Gates," one attorney general was quoted. "But if he wants to enter the field of political intrigue, I say welcome to my world, Mr. Gates, I'm ready to do battle."

As it had in the days before the Senate Judiciary Committee in March, Microsoft dropped contract provisions with some of its partners before meeting with Joel Klein and other DOJ officials. The company freed more than two dozen national and international Web content providers from requirements that they promote and distribute the Internet Explorer browser exclusively. But Microsoft was unwilling to give more ground and the DOJ was not satisfied. Talks between the two sides continued after that first meeting to no avail.

Meanwhile, the Software Publishers Association—of which Microsoft was a proud member—fired off a letter to Klein suggesting "remedies" to fix the Redmond company. The association wanted the government to split up Gates's Empire much as it had the old Ma Bell phone monopoly, with Microsoft's operating-system group forming one company and its applications division forming another. The association also wanted the government to prohibit Microsoft from giving away products as part of the Windows operating system.

As if all that weren't enough, Microsoft even found itself under attack overseas. Brazil opened an investigation into Microsoft's South American subsidiary, pursuing allegations the company unfairly bundled Microsoft Money—a financial management program—with an application called Microsoft for Small Businesses.

Despite the foreign and domestic skirmishes and speculation that the Justice Department might seek an injunction to delay the launch of Windows 98, Gates told his employees not to be distracted by all the legal noise, that the new operating-system upgrade would roll out on schedule. It was full steam ahead. The Chrome team took the message to heart.

"From a developer's point of view, the government probes didn't affect us," recalls Colin McCartney.

Indeed, despite having an antitrust target painted on their backs, Microsoft and Engstrom continued their aggressive march for market share. In early April, Engstrom phoned Apple and left a message for CEO Steve Jobs. Microsoft and seven other companies were promoting a new multimedia streaming file format called Advanced Authoring Format (AAF) to be announced at the National Association of Broadcasters trade show in Las Vegas the first week of April. But Microsoft had received panicked calls from Avid, a software company that had helped develop AAF, requesting the announcement be delayed. It seems Apple, tearing a page from Gates's playbook, had threatened to cut off Avid's supply of Macintosh computers if Avid supported the AAF initiative. Avid received high-end Macs from Apple and resold them after installing authoring software and hardware products. An Apple embargo could cripple Avid. With just days before the scheduled AAF announcement, Engstrom called Jobs to see what he was up to and persuade Apple to join the AAF cause. Jobs asked Phil Schiller, Apple's vice president of worldwide product marketing, to deal with Engstrom.

While having lunch with business manager Chris Phillips, Engstrom got a page from Schiller. The Beastie Boy excused himself from the table and stepped outside to return the call. After a brief discussion about how the two companies could work together, Schiller says Engstrom issued another stark warning urging Apple to keep its multimedia playback technology away from Windows.

"I don't want you to misunderstand," Schiller recalls Engstrom saying. "We're going to compete fiercely on multimedia playback, and we don't let anybody have playback in Windows. We consider that part of the operating system, so you're going to have to give up multimedia playback on Windows."

But if Apple was unwilling, Microsoft could throw more than a hundred developers at improving DirectX multimedia authoring software for Windows—software that might not be compatible with Apple's QuickTime for Windows and thus potentially bad for developers creating content for QuickTime and consumers who tried to use Apple's playback technology.

Engstrom doesn't remember the discussion quite that way. He says he reiterated that Microsoft was willing to work jointly with Apple to incorporate elements of QuickTime into an enhanced-version multimedia playback based on DirectX.

If Apple was offended by Engstrom's tone, the company didn't tip its hand. Its true feelings, however, would be inscribed in the public record in but a few short months.

Meanwhile, Engstrom swiveled his attention back to Chrome. It was business as usual on April 15 at San Francisco's Palace of Fine Arts, where Intel officially unveiled its long-awaited 350- and 400-MHz Pentium II processors, the very chips that would enable the first version of Chrome to run. Microsoft and its Chrome-content partners such as Monolith and flashCast had for months been using prototype computers equipped with the superfast chips. Now it was the world's turn. Microsoft vice president Paul Maritz and Engstrom appeared in a video together shown at the event and trumpeted the need for faster PCs. Intel and Microsoft marketers, of course, obligingly demonstrated Chrome later that morning.

The Chrome demo elicited more oohs and aahs. The same could not be said of a demo Bill Gates put on for Windows 98 less than a week later. At the Comdex computer trade show in Chicago, a machine running Windows 98 collapsed when an unfortunate Microsoft employee plugged in a scanner. A red-faced Gates moved to another computer to complete his demonstration.

"I guess we still have some bugs to work out," he said. "That must be why we're not shipping Windows 98 yet."

The same day Gates's demo fizzled, former Supreme Court nominee Robert Bork, former U.S. senator Bob Dole, and an assortment of Microsoft competitors formed an unlikely anti-Gates lobbying alliance called the Project to Promote Competition and Innovation in the Digital Age. Bork, a self-described free-marketer, said he joined the alliance because he believed Microsoft was violating Section 2 of the Sherman Antitrust Act. As it so happened, he also was on Netscape's legal-team payroll.

"Microsoft has . . . overwhelming market share, and it imposes conditions on those with whom it deals that exclude rivals without any apparent justification on the grounds of efficiency," Bork wrote in letters to newspapers and magazines. "There are many documents in the public domain that make clear that Microsoft specifically intended to crush competition."

Bork complained Microsoft prohibited original equipment manufacturers—computer makers—from altering the first display screen of Windows and forbade service providers to "advertise or promote any non-Microsoft Web browser or even mention that such a browser is available."

But the Sherman Act of 1890, and its cousin the Clayton Act of 1914, which bans anticompetitive mergers and some predatory tactics such as discriminatory pricing contracts, targeted the railroad and oil barons of the smokestack age. Regulators historically hunted the dominant company or companies that conspired to raise prices— the telltale sign of an abusive monopoly. But most software and computer prices had plummeted or remained stable even as technology advanced. How then could regulators apply the nation's nineteenth-century antitrust laws to the information age?

If Microsoft and antitrust observers were hoping for an answer to that question at a federal Appeals Court hearing April 21, they were disappointed. The hearing was to determine Microsoft's request to permanently remove Professor Lawrence Lessig as special master in the case the Justice Department had filed in October. The company also sought to overturn Judge Thomas Penfield Jackson's ruling that Microsoft provide PC makers a version of Windows 95 without the Internet Explorer browser. The Appeals Court, however, failed to reach a decision on the Lessig and browser issues that day and put off ruling until June.

More fruitless talks between Microsoft and Assistant U.S. Attorney General Joel Klein ensued amid more scandalous reports of alleged Microsoft misdeeds. The DOJ confirmed it was investigating a June 1995 meeting between Bill Gates and Netscape executives Marc Andreessen and James Barksdale, where Gates allegedly suggested the two companies carve up the browser market. Andreessen and Barksdale claimed Gates suggested Netscape stop making a browser for Windows, and in return Microsoft—which had not yet released its own browser—would grant the California company special access to certain application programming interfaces in Windows to develop other technologies.

Andreessen and Barksdale refused.

"It was like a visit by Don Corleone," Andreessen said about the meeting. "I expected to find a bloody computer monitor in my bed the next day."

Microsoft called the accusation unfounded and would later counter-punch with damaging documents of its own.

Nonetheless, the claim echoed those of Apple executives, who privately accused Beastie Boy Engstrom of trying to muscle that company out of enhancing QuickTime in the Internet multimedia market. Those accusations, like the Netscape meeting, would become key weapons in the Justice Department's escalating war against Microsoft.

At the same time Apple and Netscape were grumbling about Microsoft's business practices, former Apple CEO John Sculley was defending his former Northwest nemesis. In interviews prior to addressing the Washington Software and Digital Media Alliance's Online Advantage '98 conference, Sculley called the government's case against Microsoft "absurd" and predicted the Redmond company would prevail. This coming from the man who once accused Gates of stealing the point-and-click graphical user interface idea from Apple and who authorized that company's pricey, time-consuming, and ill-fated "look-and-feel" lawsuit against Microsoft.

Sculley, who had a lot riding on Chrome and, hence, Windows 98, said any antitrust action by state attorneys general would be "political harassment."

He cited America Online and Intuit, maker of the personal financial management software Quicken, as two companies that had pummeled Microsoft when it had tried to compete with them.

"What the government is trying to do is completely unjustified," Sculley said. "Just because Microsoft is brilliant in one part of the market doesn't mean they'll be able to dominate in another part. . . . Microsoft won't always be the winner."

The next day, May 5, Gates took the offensive. He and an invited group of about fifty computer-industry executives said at an hour-long news conference that the government could cripple the national economy if it blocked or delayed rollout of Windows 98. The new operating-system upgrade tightly integrated browser technology—the two would be inseparable—and the Justice Department waffled as to how or if it should force the software company to modify Windows 98. Gates argued that integration was the mother of innovation.

"In America, innovation is progress and progress means economic growth for the PC industry, for consumers, and for the nation," Gates declared at the midtown-Manhattan news conference. "Holding up the release of a major software innovation like Windows 98 would be like telling General Motors they can't come out with new cars this fall or telling Paramount they can't come out with any new movies on July Fourth."

Technology was the tonic fueling 25 percent of economic growth, Gates said, adding that the computer industry employed millions and was growing faster than any other segment of the economy. Pull the plug on Windows 98, he argued, and the government could "retard" innovation and create profound unemployment and economic catastrophe across America.

Critics, including the newly formed Project to Promote Competition and Innovation, derided the conference as merely a "public relations extravaganza" and an elaborate plug for Windows 98. In stark contrast to the trainloads of money dumped into hyping Windows 95, Microsoft had spent next to nothing promoting its new operating-system upgrade, which was not all that innovative, despite Gates's pronouncements to the contrary.

The favorable paradox, from Microsoft's vantage, was that Redmond's heretofore low-key rollout of Windows 98 led to speculation as to what the DOJ might do and generated news stories—a free source of advertising.

Even fallen Beastie Boy Alex St. John, who took a decidedly jaundiced view of Gates's "song and dance," fed the hype.

"There's nothing like the opportunity afforded by a captive audience expecting real news about the DOJ to use as a forum to promote Windows 98," St. John wrote in a posting on the *Boot* magazine Web site. "I think it was also an effort to set up the stock market for a little high-tech crash if/when lawsuits are announced. When people's portfolios take a hit because the government opened up on Microsoft, they'll be less inclined to be supportive of their representatives persecuting the empire."

St. John, a hyperactive day trader at the time, knew all about suffering portfolios. He had tried to profit on Gates's Manhattan performance by hoarding Microsoft stock during a momentary downturn and selling on an upswing. Although St. John had a love/hate relationship with Microsoft, he had no such equivocations or qualms about making money off his former employer. And had it not been for an overly conscientious broker, he would have made a killing that day.

From his Kirkland, Washington, home St. John predicted that Microsoft's share price would drop as Wall Street fretted about what Gates would say, but that the price would rebound in short order. He padded into his corner office, where dragon and gargoyle figurines stood sentinel in a wood bookcase, and fired up his computer, giddy with the certainty he was about to become a wealthier man. As expected, Microsoft stock dipped in the moments before Gates's news conference. St. John watched as the price seemingly bottomed. He raced to the keyboard and ordered Charles Schwab & Company to buy 100,000 options of Microsoft—valued at about $300,000 and the largest order he had ever placed. St. John had bought low and would sell high when the market regained its senses and pushed up Microsoft's stock.

Sure enough, as Gates spoke, Microsoft's price crawled up and St. John again pulled the trigger, this time instructing Schwab to sell for a tidy profit the shares he just purchased.

As is often the case in a yo-yoing market, Microsoft's stock price started dropping south again. But St. John had already sold . . . or so he thought. As he counted dollar signs, the phone rang. On the other end was a concerned broker from Schwab calling to confirm the large sell order. St. John was stunned. Precious moments were lapsing. The share price was dropping and his order was still in limbo.

"Just sell, you idiot! Sell!" St. John screamed into the receiver. It was too late. By the time Schwab sold the order, Microsoft stock had dipped to below what St. John had paid. Instead of pocketing millions, he lost more than $70,000, all within the narrow span of ten minutes.

On Friday, May 15, Microsoft was ready to ship Windows 98 to computer makers. The new operating system would be available for consumers June 25. But Gates and Klein agreed to huddle for eleventh-hour talks to stem antitrust action against the company. Klein and his DOJ colleagues were expecting Microsoft to make major concessions, such as selling a browserless version of Windows 98 at a cheaper price or including Netscape's competing browser as well as IE 4 with the new operating system. Those expectations, in retrospect, were astoundingly naive. Microsoft's position was that the browser had become an integral feature of the operating system. Selling a browserless operating system contradicted the company's position. Moreover, Microsoft would never voluntarily bundle a competing product with Windows without licensing payments.

So, it's not surprising that the talks collapsed before they really began. Microsoft shipped Windows 98 to computer makers on Monday, May 18.

That very day the U.S. Department of Justice and twenty states—poised for weeks to strike—filed lawsuits against Microsoft, setting up what would become one of the most riveting antitrust trials of the century. The feds and the states accused Microsoft of illegally tying a separate product—a browser—to its dominant Windows operating system to gain control of the Internet. The governments also charged the company of illegally colluding with partners and strong-arming weaker competitors. The cornerstone of these allegations was the infamous June 1995 meeting Gates had had with Netscape as well as the meetings Engstrom and other Microsoft officials had had with Apple regarding QuickTime. Finally, the federal and state governments accused Microsoft of maintaining and growing its monopoly by coercing partners and competitors to sign exclusive licensing deals and prohibiting computer makers from altering the Windows start-up screen—important because a company that controlled what viewers saw could influence where on-line viewers "traveled" or made purchases in cyberspace.

The feds and the states argued that unless steps were taken to level the digital playing field, consumers would ultimately suffer because Microsoft would gain control of the Internet—a place where society increasingly did everything from post pornography to buy cars and theater tickets.

Microsoft, the governments were saying, must be stopped now before Gates seized a chokehold on the Internet.

Gates called the lawsuits "a step backward for America, consumers, and for the personal computer industry that is leading our nation's economy into the twenty-first century."

Yet all that free publicity kept feeding interest about Windows 98, which was the topic of business talk shows and the featured attraction on the front pages of daily newspapers and business publications. Consumers seemed convinced that Win98 was a must-have product. Retailers reported an unexpectedly huge number of advance orders for the new operating system.

"The government has created more demand for Windows 98 than could ever have been generated by a marketing program," declared Lawrence Mondry, an executive vice president of CompUSA, America's largest chain of computer stores.

Justice Department officials could only shrug.

"We told you we wouldn't wreck the U.S. economy," quipped one DOJ official when asked about the inadvertent marketing bonanza.

Rob Enderle, an analyst with Giga Information Group, predicted Windows 98 had a "huge opportunity" to set sales records because of the lawsuit hoopla. "I suggested that Microsoft market the product as, 'This is the operating system the government doesn't want you to have.' "

15

SISYPHUS ON A ROLL

Judge Thomas Penfield Jackson wanted to prove he could move at the speed of software development. Within a week of the antitrust fusillade, the judge set a trial date for September 8, 1998. He would clear his docket that month for the Microsoft case, which he estimated would take but three weeks or so. Microsoft pleaded for a seven-month delay. No dice, said Jackson, who was already on record as not trusting the eclectic collection of Microsoft attorneys, including John Warden, a stout and commanding Southern orator; Michael Lacovara, a smooth shark in a handsome suit; and William Neukom, Microsoft's chief in-house counsel and maybe the only fellow in the company to wear bow ties.

This case, Jackson said in effect, would not be a replay of the ill-fated, thirteen-year government inquisition of IBM. That case, which focused on IBM's alleged monopoly in the mainframe computer market, ended in a stalemate when the personal computer industry—led, ironically enough, by Microsoft—took off in the late eighties.

The Microsoft case underscored the futility of Gates's belated political palm-greasing. The $1.3 million Microsoft handed out in 1997 and 1998—two-thirds of it to Republicans—was three times what the company had given in the previous election cycle. All, it appears, to no avail.

Gates conceded that the company should have done as good a job pleasing the beltway as it had done pleasing Wall Street.

"I'll admit, there was a naïveté here about spending time talking to the politicians in D.C. about the PC industry and the benefits it's creating," Gates told *Fortune* magazine. "We think of ourselves as having to move very fast, and that we can just focus on the products; at some point we got to a level of success where that was a little naive, and we're paying the price."

While Gates was distracted with his mounting legal and political woes, Eric Engstrom was trying to move Project Chrome full steam ahead. He and his DirectX team had released some sort of new or updated product every Christmas for four years running. They didn't want to break that string of successes. His marketing people had been telling the press that Chrome would be available for high-end machines by mid-1999. In fact, Engstrom and lead developers Bob Heddle and Colin McCartney were busy jettisoning features, trimming Chrome's capability in hopes of hitting the market by Christmas '98. One of the abandoned features was Spice, the primitive Chrome authoring tool formerly dubbed Caffeine.

The first version of Chrome would merely offer quick downloads of cool 3-D graphics. Succeeding incarnations of the technology would be able to offer data visualization for business applications and would eventually carry Engstrom's promise of a "knowledge browser" that enabled people to communicate on the Web via interactive 3-D objects.

To get there, however, Engstrom needed updated Chrome demos to show to Microsoft managers, marketers, and trade show audiences. McCartney and other developers were constantly refining Chrome's coding—necessary to advance the technology. But the inevitable effect was that previous Chrome-plated demo pages wouldn't work with the updated coding. Faced with the contradictory forces of constantly changing code and a fixed deadline, Engstrom agreed that Paul Scholz should relocate Dayton-based flashCast to Redmond.

Now a six-person operation, flashCast had become a de facto Chrome shop. In fact, the company had produced more prototype Chrome content than any other independent content provider under Engstrom's command. Microsoft had tapped Scholz to produce high-profile demos for the likes of Porsche and top Microsoft executives, including Gates. One of flashCast's more impressive efforts was the *Lost in Space* motion-picture demonstration site created for New Line Cinema. Engstrom's marketing team believed Chrome and motion-picture Web sites made for a natural pairing. Microsoft, with the help of flashCast, Chrome-plated sites based on a studio's own motion pictures, in essence trying to sell Hollywood its own familiar bill of goods.

But the selection of *Lost in Space* was particularly intriguing and carried a buried germ of irony. The movie, starring William Hurt, Gary Oldman, and Mimi Rogers, flopped with critics and at the box office. But the computerized special effects were eye-popping. Those effects were created on SGI workstation computers using OpenGL, the 3-D rendering engine fallen Beastie Boy Alex St. John had battled because it competed with DirectX in the PC game market. SGI received a plug in the opening act. A commercial voice-over says that the Robinson family's Jupiter Mission to Alpha Prime was made possible by the army and SGI. "SGI," the announcer intones. "Saving the future."

At times Microsoft put flashCast's future in peril. While Scholz and his band pumped out Chrome-plated Web sites at a dizzying pace, Microsoft's accounting department sat on invoices. Scholz sent plaintive E-mails.

> **From:** Paul Scholz
> **Date:** Monday, May 11, 1998 5:18 PM
> **To:** 'Eric Engstrom'
> **Cc:** 'Craig Eisler'; 'chromearchive@flashcast.com'
> **Subject:** Ammo Report
>
> We have enough ammunition to sustain offensive operations through the end of next week, after which I must turn my

RENEGADES OF THE EMPIRE

time and attention to the problem of keeping my troops fed and housed without re-supply from your headquarters.

Our stocks have dwindled from our pre-Chrome hoard of $40k to about $6k. After our next invoice to you, the total amount due will stand at well over $100k. I estimate that we will require at least $20k to meet the double threat of mid-month payroll and end-of-quarter/year tax obligations.

Paul Scholz
Commander, Microsoft Mercenary Forces
North American Theatre of Operations

Once, while Microsoft's accounting machine slowly turned, Engstrom quietly mailed a personal check to Scholz for $25,000. The gesture further cemented Scholz's loyalty to Engstrom and the Chrome cause. Scholz easily decided to trade his windowless office on Dayton's run-down Wayne Avenue for three third-story, windowless offices at Microsoft's Building 30. Scholz would be closer to Chrome developers and, more important, business contacts inside Gates's kingdom.

"We're like the Visigoths," Scholz said, referring to the first barbarian tribespeople to loot the Western Roman Empire. "Eric's going to point us to where the gold is."

It didn't take Scholz and his young charges long to establish themselves in the Seattle area and inside Fortress Microsoft. He and his five employees were provided orange badges, standard issue for all visiting contract workers. The badges opened the card-activated locks throughout the Empire and allowed visitors to move freely through the hallways, very much like away teams on *Star Trek* can stroll unmolested aboard enemy Borg ships.

Within weeks Scholz was speaking his mind about performance problems plaguing Chrome. flashCast was building Chrome demo pages for the Windows 98 launch scheduled for June 25, and Scholz was nervous. By now Chrome had problems even rendering text. The Chrome browser was displaying aliased or jagged-edged letters, unacceptable even in the most primitive of graphics and word-processing applications. Chrome also had significant problems with drivers, the software that told the hardware—in this case hardware accelerator cards—what to do. Hardware accelerators were primarily designed to enhance computer games, not to speed the download of Web content.

"We're using drivers for something they weren't designed to do," explained Engstrom.

Scholz understood the problem, but the stress of building a demo for Gates, and for a "major" product launch such as Windows 98 no less, caused Scholz's blood pressure to boil. "Performance still sucks big time," he wrote Engstrom. "I could not, in all truth, recommend to any commercial customer that they expend funds to build stuff with Chrome.

"Take what you've got, pare it down to the bare essentials, and make it perfect," Scholz added. "Otherwise, you risk going down in flames amongst commercial designers. You are trying to accomplish way too much for Chrome 1, and quality is suffering as a result."

Scholz wasn't acclimated to the Microsoft ethos, where it's acceptable to release primitive and less-than-perfect software with the understanding that performance will usually evolve by the third generation. He wasn't rewarded for his candor, but he wasn't punished for it either.

"Paul has never been through a design-one release before," Engstrom would explain. "We won't be perfect this release, but you can do some pretty cool things."

Scholz's angst echoed that found on Microsoft's Chrome beta newsgroup, where would-be Chrome Web designers initially fumed about lack of technical support and the dearth of documentation for the new technology. Developers were having a hard time getting Microsoft to answer questions.

"Hellloooo," read one repeated posting. "Is anybody there?"

The unresponsiveness was due in large part to the lack of resources Microsoft allocated to Chrome.

Despite the success of mainstreaming DirectX into Windows,

Microsoft decision makers largely paid lip service to multimedia, according to those in Engstrom's camp. And despite Microsoft Developer Relations Group's pledge to Chrome, that support failed to materialize.

"Multimedia has never been a high priority with Microsoft executives," muttered Chris Phillips, Engstrom's trusted business manager.

Phillips likened Engstrom to Sisyphus, the mythological Greek king who offended Zeus and was punished by being forced to roll an enormous boulder up a steep hill for eternity. Every time the boulder reached the top, the rock would roll back down and Sisyphus would have to restart his futile task.

"We launched DirectX and it became this huge success," Phillips said. "And now we had Chrome and everyone was saying how cool it was, but it was terribly hard getting support.

"Like Eric always says, 'No good deed shall go unpunished.' "

Chrome was temperamental technology, requiring the latest computers configured in just the right way. One Microsoft Developer Relations Group evangelist criticized Chrome because it was only animating objects at the glacier pace of one frame per second. DRG complained that Chrome was too raw. But the evangelist had failed to turn on his computer's hardware accelerator and didn't allocate enough memory to the browser.

User foul-ups easily hampered Chrome's performance, which was a primary reason Engstrom wanted Chrome deployed only through computer makers who could ensure the technology rode on the right types of machines.

In addition, Windows 98 also needed some modifications to accommodate Chrome and make it perform more smoothly, Engstrom knew. Fortunately, his relationship had improved with those in the Windows operating-system group and was much better than the one he endured with the Internet Explorer team. In fact, relations with the IE group—already strained—soured again when Engstrom persuaded Cole that Chrome should ship with a modified version of Internet Explorer 4, instead of waiting until the release of

IE 5. Plumbing Chrome with IE 4 would position the technology for the Christmas '98 retail season.

Performance and internal political problems notwithstanding, Chrome was making headway on other fronts, particularly with third-party vendor support. Chrome product managers Leslie Evans and Audra Gaines-Mulkern—a former administrative assistant for Bill Gates—lured more than a dozen multimedia and Web-development companies to embrace Chrome. These companies were building plug-ins and other software tools for Chrome. Plug-ins, the condiments of the software buffet, add special effects or enhancements to programs. MetaCreations Corporation, for instance, a major player in computer-imaging software, was making Chrome transition effects, such as Web pages that drained away like water in a toilet or curled up and rolled away like a scroll.

Chrome's architecture allowed other companies to set up shop inside the technology, thereby tying more vendors to yet another Microsoft product—an aspect that Gates's technology sorcerer Nathan Myhrvold and other executives found particularly delicious. Looking for other ways to deploy Chrome and pressed by Microsoft executives to again persuade Apple to agree to a deal in the multimedia playback market, Engstrom, Phillips, and DirectX veteran Cristiano Pierry arranged a meeting with Apple's top brass for June 15.

Apple had insisted that a ranking Microsoft executive also make an appearance. Vice President David Cole initially agreed to join the discussion, but pulled out at the last minute. Instead of canceling, Apple said the meeting could take place anyway.

On hand from Apple were Avadis "Avie" Tevanian Jr., the senior vice president of software engineering; Phil Schiller, vice president of worldwide product marketing; and Steve Jobs, the long-term interim CEO. QuickTime executives Tim Schaaff and Peter Hoddie also were present.

Jobs kept Engstrom and his entourage sitting in the executive conference room for forty-five minutes while Schaaff and Hoddie made small talk. The meeting was scheduled for only an hour, and

Engstrom grew frustrated that his time had been eroded. But he shouldn't have been sitting there at all. This was a doomed mission from the start. Schaaff and Hoddie had already finked to the Department of Justice.

Weeks before, they had told investigators Engstrom was trying to strong-arm Apple to abandon QuickTime for Windows. Moreover, they suggested that Microsoft had put coding into Windows that disabled or sabotaged the Apple multimedia player. Schaaff also recounted conversations about the antitrust case he had had with Phillips, who said most at Microsoft believed that technological changes and realignments in the industry would outpace litigation and render the case moot.

"I was sort of surprised at the open expression of this kind of cynicism about the process and arrogance that Microsoft would be able to get away with these things," Schaaff told the government.

Schaaff also said Phillips confided it was common practice inside Microsoft to destroy E-mails because "those create a paper trail that can be used against you in many of these cases, and that was a lesson he had learned early on in his time at Microsoft."

Hoddie had also spilled his guts to the DOJ, stating that Engstrom "was bent on killing QuickTime."

Again, the Microsoft trio reportedly didn't descend upon Cupertino on June 15 with just happy thoughts of selling Apple on Chrome. Apple executives would later contend that this—like the previous meetings—was another attempt by Microsoft to compel Apple to cease deploying QuickTime on Windows and to clear the way for NetShow or Windows Media Player, the streaming audio and video technology where Beastie Boys Engstrom and Eisler were at the helm.

Recall that unlike Microsoft's Windows Media Player, Apple's QuickTime ran on Macs as well as Intel-based computers. So could media players from market leader RealNetworks. Moreover, the International Standards Organization had recently adopted a QuickTime file format as the industry standard for pumping sound and video over the Internet. Microsoft now had to fret about two competitors when it came to delivering audio and video—Quick-Time and RealNetworks. So Apple believed Engstrom's visit was another attempt by Redmond to derail QuickTime development on the Internet and carpet the Web wall to wall with proprietary Microsoft technology.

Although Engstrom says his mission was to discuss ways to make sure the QuickTime and Windows media players were compatible, Apple again didn't see it that way. They say Engstrom proposed that the two companies combine DirectX and QuickTime and that Microsoft would control multimedia playback for Windows, while Apple could have the meager Macintosh and editing-tools markets.

Apple executives say Engstrom outlined a four-point "deal": Apple and Microsoft would cross-license and collaborate on all future codecs; Apple would adopt Microsoft's DirectX technology for Windows; Apple would adopt Microsoft's proprietary streaming technology; and finally, Apple would adopt the new Advanced Authoring Format that Microsoft and a half dozen other companies were advocating. Apple thought Microsoft's technology was inferior and was not about to abandon QuickTime, one of the company's most popular products.

Engstrom says he offered to share source code, modify file formats for the Windows Media Player, and acknowledged that he encouraged Apple to work with Microsoft to make a media player based on DirectX. He offered to have such a Windows Media Player display the QuickTime logo whenever a video file played. Engstrom also wanted the two companies to set up a Web site called Codec Central, where users could download new codecs from either company.

Yet Apple had already knifed Engstrom in the back. It wasn't about to cut a deal with him. Moreover, Apple's deeply held suspicions made Engstrom's other task—to sell Apple on Chrome—all but impossible.

In late 1997, the Cupertino company had unveiled its new super-fast G3 microprocessors, chips designed by Motorola and IBM. The third-generation chips—thus the name G3—were nearly twice as fast as their predecessors, the PowerPC 603e processors. The G3 targeted the publishing industry and gave Intel's fastest chips a run for their money. The chips were directly responsible for Apple's amazing turn-around. The company, which had lost more than $2 billion over the past two years, was now posting profits. Once-despondent Apple stockholders were watching their fortunes rise. Alex St. John was not among them. Since leaving Microsoft he had hitched a ride on Wall Street's then-strong bull-market run. He spent mornings lifting weights in his downstairs gym, day-trading technology stocks while watching the market's play-by-play on CNBC. As a self-described expert on Apple, one of his investment strategies was to "short" Apple stock—essentially wager that the company's stock price would drop. Given Apple's dismal performance and eroding market share, it was a sound game plan . . . until the G3 surfaced. St. John lost tens of thousands of dollars in January after Apple announced its surprise '97 fourth-quarter results. He would continue to bet against Apple and lose still more. St. John simply underestimated the new G3 chip's market potential.

Engstrom did not want to make the same mistake. Although Macintosh operating systems did not house DirectX and could not immediately utilize Chrome, Engstrom believed a Mac version of Chrome was possible with the new G3 chips—if Apple adopted DirectX.

The meeting with Jobs and his lieutenants lasted about an hour and a half. Engstrom put on his best show, trying to convince Apple's cofounder that (a) the world needed a "codec détente" and (b) it wanted to see the Web in 3-D.

Jobs had played ball with Gates the year before—taken Microsoft's $150 million, dropped Apple's "look-and-feel" lawsuit, agreed to make Internet Explorer the default browser on all Macs and to deploy Microsoft's version of the Java programming language. But Jobs had seen his company's fortunes change for the better since the previous summer's historic deal. For the first time in years the com-pany was now turning a profit, fueled by the hot sales of Macs with new, speedy G3 processors. Jobs drew the line with Chrome. He believed it competed too closely with QuickTime.

"It's not interesting," Jobs said of Chrome. "Not interesting."

Jobs also countered that not only should Microsoft abandon the AAF file format initiative, but scrap DirectX in favor of QuickTime. That was never going to happen.

With that, Engstrom and his two comrades left, ushered out by a smiling Schaaff, who said Jobs must have found the meeting constructive because it was the first time he had seen his brooding CEO sit through an entire presentation.

But Schaaff's smile was as bogus as the preceding meeting. The Beastie Boy had struck out.

By June, Apple had begun advertising its upcoming iMac, an all-in-one multimedia-capable, Internet-ready computer (that's what the *i* stands for) that looked nothing like any personal computer ever before built. The art-piece computer and monitor were housed in a cream-and-translucent-teal casing shaped kind of like the new Volkswagen Beetles unveiled earlier that year. In fact, Jobs likened the two products and complimented VW designers for "getting it right."

Despite the iMac's technological shortcomings—it lacked a floppy-disk drive, a DVD drive, had underpowered speakers, and came equipped with an inferior CD-ROM drive—the iMac, which later came in different colors, was destined to sell well.

But while Jobs had a cute little teal VW, Engstrom would have a big nasty chrome Harley.

Engstrom had grown increasingly frustrated by the lack of marketing for Chrome. Microsoft's own Developer Relations Group had slinked out of boosting this new technology, and St. John was no longer at DRG to siphon funds to benefit his friends. Moreover, many of St. John's DRG allies had scattered after Brad Chase and Tod Nielsen had moved in. In many ways, Engstrom had only himself to blame. He made no secret that he thought DRG had changed for the worse. As a result, Chase wanted nothing to do with supporting any multimedia marketing efforts associated with this Beastie Boy.

Unlike Eisler, Engstrom still maintained close contact with St. John on the outside. The former games evangelist enjoyed spending time at Engstrom's waterfront home, which was constantly in disrepair. Engstrom fancied himself a carpenter and was forever remodeling the interior. Exposed wires clung to ceilings; duct tape slapped on the floors mapped the location of a future spiral staircase; and computer parts, tools, and other metal flotsam spilled from tabletops and lined the walls. From the looks of the place, one might have thought an amphetamine addict, not a Microsoft millionaire, lived here. St. John was amused by the way Engstrom would cock his head back, sip expensive Scotch, and imperially sweep his hand to gesture where the marble staircase and exquisite banisters would go, all the while his voice was echoing off exposed concrete floors and bare walls.

Conversations invariably turned to his troubles at Microsoft, and he told St. John he was casting for a quick recipe to generate more press about Chrome.

"Let's see," St. John mused during one discussion. "Chrome is big, fat, slow, it's American made . . . You know, Eric, Chrome is a Harley."

Alex St. John may have been removed from Microsoft, but at his core he was still a renegade evangelist. He suggested Engstrom chrome-plate his 1997 Harley-Davidson Springer Softail. But not just chrome-plate a few pieces here and there. St. John told him to virtually dip the entire cycle in chrome—chrome-plate it from stem to stern. Like a crazed Laslo counseling Hunter "Gonzo" Thompson, St. John advised Engstrom that everything that was rubber or didn't have to be black metal for heat transfer should be chrome-plated.

That's not all. The cycle should be souped up somehow and, above all else, should be able to shoot flames . . . twenty feet, at least.

This would be no ordinary cycle. This would be the ultimate, potent symbol for Project Chrome—the testosterone machine that embodied "fast, flashy, and functional." Engstrom could ride it onstage at various events, delighting press and public alike.

Yes, Engstrom agreed. This was a good idea.

At Engstrom's behest, a Seattle detail shop chrome-plated virtually every surface of the bike. Mechanics turbocharged the cycle to 168 horsepower and fitted the machine with two nitrous-oxide booster tanks on the rear fender. The shop also equipped the machine with a butane igniter on the exhaust so it could shoot flames and, for a final elegant touch, wired the cycle's undercarriage with blue neon lights to give it an ethereal glow at night.

Engstrom's custom cycle, including purchase price, cost him $50,000. The final piece of the scheme—as St. John envisioned it— was for Microsoft to sponsor a contest where Engstrom would give away the cycle as first prize to the developer who built the best Chrome-plated Web site.

A contest featuring the giveaway of a one-of-a-kind Harley would generate the type of hype sorely lacking at this stage of Chrome's development. Engstrom claimed to have at least three major computer makers signed up to install Chrome on new PCs—partially solving one part of the chicken/egg equation. He had hoped to have Chrome in the hands of computer makers by May, but David Cole's decision and subsequent reversal, not to mention the technology's immaturity, had made that schedule untenable. The next target was July 15, which Engstrom conceded would be impossible. He was now gunning for early August.

"August fifteenth is the drop-dead week [to get Chrome] to OEMs," Engstrom declared.

Yet while Engstrom was confident computer makers would have Chrome in time for the Christmas season, the other part of the chicken/egg equation was to convince developers to build Chrome-plated Web pages. The easiest solution would have been to simply pay Web firms to build Chrome pages in hopes the new technology would generate enough critical mass, but Microsoft was not backing Chrome with the truckload of marketing money Engstrom had hoped for. Other than flashCast and a few others, hardly any developers were building Chrome-plated sites.

One bit of good news, from Engstrom's perspective, was that DRG head Brad Chase removed Bellevue-based Waggener Edstrom from marketing Chrome and handed the responsibility to DirectX product manager Leslie Evans, who would work in concert with Portland, Oregon–based MacKenzie Kesselring Inc. Waggener Edstrom is Microsoft's longtime public-relations firm, credited with helping orchestrate the massive hype for Windows 95 and refining the image of Bill Gates. But Engstrom said the company had trouble understanding Chrome and couldn't articulate a compelling sales story.

"Wag-Ed didn't have a clue about Chrome," Engstrom said at the time. "I'm getting used to that."

But Engstrom had a bigger problem. His relationship with Intel collapsed when the chipmaker refused his request to put up $10 million for a Chrome marketing campaign. Intel, which had ridden to Chrome's rescue when Cole had put a gun to the project's head earlier that year, was now unwilling to infuse Chrome with marketing cash. Intel viewed that as Microsoft's job. The issue underscored the quiet but widening rift between two high-tech titans dating back to 1995, when Gates allegedly pressured Intel to back off on developing the multimedia project known as Native Signal Processing and Java-based software—accusations Microsoft strongly denies.

Moreover, Intel had its own antitrust troubles stewing. Earlier in June the Federal Trade Commission had filed a lawsuit accusing the chipmaker of abusing its market dominance to punish competitors and customers—an allegation mirroring one of those against Microsoft. The FTC cited Intel's admission that it had erected "speed bumps" for its competitors by denying them access to technical information about its chips. Like Microsoft, Intel initially responded aggressively. It didn't deny it withheld information from competitors, but maintained it never broke the law.

Engstrom argued that Chrome was in Intel's best interest because it gave consumers a real reason to buy faster, more expensive computers. Despite assurances that it was backing Chrome, Engstrom maintains Intel hadn't delivered on its promise to post or fund development of Chrome-related Web pages.

"They kept talking about how they were going to and going to, but nothing happened," Engstrom recalled. "They said these things take time. I said, 'Well, you don't have time. Show me one page that your remarkable PR has produced. You can't, can you. You can't show me one stinking page.'

"About the third time going around I said forget it," Engstrom added, shaking his head. "You have to meet some of these people."

Although Intel and Microsoft would tell the public that they were working together on Chrome, Engstrom and his business team had privately begun courting Intel's rival chipmaker, Advanced Micro Devices, for its K6 microprocessors. The K6 was cheaper and technologically comparable to Intel's faster Pentium II chip. AMD was grateful for the chance to split the so-called Wintel alliance.

As Chrome's marketing woes festered, Engstrom increasingly turned to St. John for advice and support. As a result, St. John started to regain influence with Engstrom and with Chrome. Engstrom conceded that he would never have chrome-plated his Harley for a publicity stunt had St. John not suggested it.

The year away from Microsoft had been good for St. John. Despite his setbacks with underestimating the performance of Apple stock and that one mishap with day-trading Microsoft, he was making money on the market. He was savoring the notoriety of his *Boot* column. And as it turned out, he was hearing wedding bells again.

St. John had met Jeaneane Falkler, a freckled, fair-skinned, twenty-four-year-old Seattle University law student, at a ballroom dance class earlier that year. Although he still carried extra girth and she was as slender as a pipe cleaner, the two shared an abiding adoration for his ego.

"He comes off as better than other people," she said. "But it's justified."

On their first date he brought her an edition of *Boot* magazine, the one featuring him on the cover. The magazine was still in its shrink-wrap.

"I think he thought it would be a topic of conversation," she recalled. "I thought it was obnoxious."

Still, she was taken with his sense of daring and the two were making wedding plans for August—the same month fellow Beastie Boy Craig Eisler was scheduled to walk down the aisle with Kathryn "KT" Kaufman.

"I'm going to beat him to the altar," St. John said that summer.

St. John's competitive fires were, evidently, burning again.

Even as St. John and Engstrom nurtured their friendship, they became more distant from Eisler. Neither St. John nor Engstrom would be attending Eisler's wedding, for instance. St. John and Engstrom felt that one thing coming between them was Eisler's involvement with the Landmark Education Corporation's programs. They didn't understand the seminars or Eisler's invitation to join him. Additionally, since St. John and KT had never liked each other, he'd been scratched from the invitation list long ago.

16

THE WHITE-PAPER TRAIL

Eric Engstrom needed an author to write the definitive Chrome "white paper," an industry term for a print or on-line document used to explain a certain technology and why it's important. Engstrom's hunt began in his own living room. From where he was sitting, the best man for the job was his best friend, Alex St. John.

Chrome would have its official coming-out party at Siggraph '98, the international conference on computer graphics and interactive techniques, July 19–24. Once again the setting would be the massive Orange County Convention Center in Orlando. Engstrom wouldn't be standing onstage talking to a faceless sea of people about Chrome. This time he would be holding court with software developers, the media, and potential partners face-to-face on the exhibition floor. More than a dozen independent software vendors who had created tools and related Chrome technology would be on hand. There would be demonstrations, free CD-ROMs containing Chrome still-screen shots, and of course, the chrome-plated Harley.

St. John would be paid more than $20,000 for writing the twenty-page white paper, to be issued to the press and prospective developers and posted on Microsoft's new Chrome Web site. Engstrom insisted that selecting his close friend and fellow Beastie Boy to write the white paper had nothing to do with patronage.

"He's a good writer and nobody knows more about Chrome than he does," Engstrom said.

It had been more than a year since St. John had blown out of Microsoft. He now found himself reentering the Empire's powerful orbit. He appreciated the irony. His payment for the white paper marked the first time Microsoft had cut him a check since he'd crashed and burned trying to insulate Chrome the year before. St. John took the assignment seriously—after all, twenty grand was on the line. But he also took the opportunity to have a little fun. The paper included screen shots of sample Chrome-plated Web pages. One of the icons in one of the screen shots had a curious file name, nhojtsxela.by—which read "by.alexstjohn" backward.

Embedding hidden identifiers or secret programs inside applications or documents is as old as the software industry. Some hidden routines are useful, such as so-called trapdoors, which allow original programmers special access into a system. Others, such as "Easter eggs," are undocumented goodies programmers slip inside programs only to be discovered by accident or word of mouth. Easter eggs usually contain the names of the people who worked on the program and are in effect the software industry's equivalent of a byline or movie credit. Some eggs are simple to crack; most are complex. To open the Easter egg in Windows 98, for instance, you have to double-click the clock in the bottom right corner of the task bar. Choose the Time Zone Tab. Press CTRL-ALT-SHIFT. While holding down the Key Combo, click and drag from Cairo, Egypt, to Memphis, Tennessee. After dragging, let go of the Key Combo. Reclick CTRL-ALT-SHIFT. This time drag from Memphis to Bellevue, Washington. All that just to find out who wrote the program.

St. John's core message was simpler than cracking an Easter egg: Chrome would be easy to use and provide a rich, almost TV-like experience over the Web using low-speed Internet hookups.

"In the time it takes to consume this traditional compilation of text and images, the same information could have been conveyed in under ninety seconds if it had been presented in a single page of content enhanced with . . . [Chrome]," St. John's white paper began.

He had a flair for hyperbole, a quality not all at Microsoft appreciated—particularly marketers who were in charge of monitoring press coverage.

The public relations firm MacKenzie Kesselring by now was compiling weekly "Chrome Coverage Reports" about the nascent technology and posting them on a cork board near Engstrom's office. While these reports provided Engstrom and his team convenient summaries and full texts of what the press was writing about Chrome, they also reflected the inherent paranoia of PR people.

The reports contained a "rating system" on a scale from one to five: one being "very negative mention of Chrome," five being "Chrome prominently covered in [a] feature story." Chrome was receiving primarily positive reviews in the press—earning mostly ratings of four from Mackenzie Kesselring. Yet even praise of Chrome sometimes triggered alarm bells.

St. John was quoted in a June *Boot* article as saying, "If Chrome authoring is widely adopted, it will mean a dramatic transformation in the way the Web is viewed, as well as a huge advantage for Microsoft in its ongoing effort to dominate the 'Net."

MacKenzie Kesselring reacted with predictable anxiety.

"A very positive article," the press coverage report stated in the clip summary. "Except quotes in the body of the article position Chrome as a technology that will 'take over the 'Net.' This published observation, while positive in that it recognizes Chrome as a solid technology, does not represent the real purpose of Chrome."

With an antitrust case staring it in the face, the last thing Microsoft wanted to read was some uncontrollable ally talking about the Empire's "ongoing effort to dominate the 'Net."

Indeed, even as St. John was talking about Microsoft's desire for World Wide Web domination, the Department of Justice and twenty states were building a case to prove exactly that.

Now that a court date had been set, the government was playing hardball. It petitioned the court to unseal internal documents Microsoft submitted for the case. Microsoft, of course, objected on the grounds that it wanted to protect trade secrets. Unlike in any previous antitrust case, company E-mail would become a key weapon in the government's arsenal—E-mail in which Gates and other executives had seemingly plotted to kill competition to preserve and extend a monopoly.

In one correspondence, Senior Vice President Paul Maritz said the company planned to fuse the Internet Explorer browser into Windows as a means to "cut off Netscape's air supply."

The incriminating E-mail chatter that emerged before and during the trial prompted Microsoft lawyers to accuse the government of conducting "a trial by snippets." Wags in the press would wear buttons reading, "Free the Snippets!"

Indeed, at one point the release of documents became almost comical. In June the DOJ possessed what it considered a damning document penned by Jeffrey Raikes, Microsoft group vice president for Sales and Marketing. In it, Raikes talked about "Windows paradise" being under siege and that "Netscape pollution must be eradicated."

But the document was part of a script in a gag video that parodied hip-hop star Coolio's "Gangsta Paradise." It was one of the annual motivational videos Raikes produced for his sales force.

It was a prank, but one humorless DOJ official said, "It does not appear on its face to be a joke."

Microsoft responded to the government's dour disposition by unleashing its most forceful pretrial counterattack, a three-page essay written by Bill Gates.

Calling the antitrust case "the government's lawsuit on behalf of Netscape," Gates wrote in *The Economist* magazine: "We are defending the legal right of every company to decide which features go into its own products. . . . America's antitrust laws do not provide any basis for government regulators to attempt to design software products."

Others in the industry took potshots at Microsoft.

Larry Ellison, the *GQ*-esque CEO of Oracle and longtime enemy of Gates, publicly called for all registered voters to file their own antitrust lawsuits against Microsoft, claiming the company was a plagiarist, not an innovator.

"If an innovative piece of software comes along, Microsoft copies it and adds it to Windows," Ellison said. "Bill calls this innovation. It's the end of innovation."

Fortunately for Microsoft, Ellison wasn't one of the three U.S. Circuit Court of Appeals judges reviewing district court judge Thomas Penfield Jackson's earlier injunction requiring Microsoft to offer a browserless version of Windows 95.

On June 23, just as Microsoft was about to roll out its preview or test version of Internet Explorer 5 to developers, the Appeals Court handed the software giant a major victory.

The court ruled 2–1 that Microsoft could bundle a browser with Windows. Furthermore, the Appeals Court removed Lawrence Lessig, the special master Judge Jackson had appointed to review technical matters in the case. The three-judge panel was "inclined to conclude" that the combined operating system and browser was a "genuine integration" permitted under the 1995 consent decree at the heart of that case.

"The limited competence of courts to evaluate high-tech product designs and the high cost of error should make them wary of second-guessing the claimed benefits of a particular design decision," wrote U.S. Circuit Court of Appeals for the District of Columbia judge Stephen Williams.

The ruling shot Microsoft shares to an all-time high of $100.75, accounting for stock splits.

The panel seemed to be echoing the admonishment of the famous Judge Learned Hand, who declared long ago that "the successful competitor, having been urged to compete, must not be turned upon when he wins."

The ruling also fueled consumer interest in Windows 98, launched just two days after the appeals victory. Unlike the marketing orgy surrounding Windows 95, the release of Windows 98 was a ho-hum affair. Analysts estimated Microsoft spent about $10 million, compared with the reported $30 million to $100 million for the Windows 95 launch. Yet the release of Windows 98 was considered the biggest software rollout since Windows 95. The company said the new operating system contained more than three thousand upgrades. Others also noted that Win98 crashed less often than its predecessor and, of course, was more tightly integrated with the Internet Explorer browser.

The release put a spotlight on San Francisco, the main site for the coming out of Windows 98. The theme of the launch was "Route 98—another milestone on the computing highway."

The Chrome team had been giddy.

Chrome was to be featured in the Windows 98 coming-out party. The day before, Chrome marketing wonk Brent Ethington sent mail to the team, congratulating Paul Scholz for the demo he pulled together for Brad Chase.

"This is just the first of many activities over the coming months that the marketing team is driving that will result in visibility for Chrome," Ethington wrote.

True, Chrome got its shining minute of fame when Brad Chase demonstrated Chrome while the world's press cameras were rolling.

But another internal Microsoft storm was brewing into which Chrome would be swept. As so often is the case at Microsoft, this storm began innocuously enough. David Cole, the man who had guided Windows 95 out the door a few years prior, was taking a three-month vacation. Cole had verbally jousted with Judge Thomas Penfield Jackson at a grueling hearing in January. Cole had faced the wrath of Intel when he virtually canceled Chrome in March, only to emerge as the technology's second guardian vice president. He felt he needed the rest. But departing meant he would leave his territory unguarded. And in the Darwinian battlefield inside Microsoft, opportunists are quick to seize undefended terrain.

17

PHONE CALL IN ORLANDO

Alex St. John lit dozens of fuses and watched more than $1,000 turn to ash. He had spent lavishly for a Fourth of July party Eric Engstrom was hosting at his lakeshore house. Good thing there was a large body of water nearby. While others drank spirits, wine, and ale, a sober St. John went wild, igniting Chinese-made fireworks in a pyrotechnic frenzy. A pinwheel he had mounted to a patio support beam failed to spin, torching the beam. St. John raced to a hose to douse the flames climbing up Engstrom's house.

Engstrom had a good laugh and offered St. John's fiancée, Jeaneane, a celebratory cigar snatched from his mahogany humidor. St. John turned serious, then furious, as Engstrom helped Jeaneane light the stogie. St. John, just moments before the mirthmaker, yelled at Engstrom for pushing "poison" on his bride-to-be. Then he turned on Jeaneane, reminding her she had quit smoking just five months before and accused her of polluting her body. Unable to get her to stop, St. John stomped to his car and drove off in a huff. Jeaneane enjoyed her cigar and after a while took a taxi home.

A few days later, when the incident had blown over, Engstrom met with another fiery near-disaster. Gasoline shot into his crotch as he gunned his custom Harley-Davidson along Seattle's State Route 520 Bridge, that floating ribbon of asphalt linking the Emerald City and the Redmond Mothership. The bridge was constipated with its usual traffic jam that sweltering July afternoon when a fuel-hose connection broke on the big hog and forced Engstrom to stop. Rubbernecking commuters were treated to a rare sight. Aside from witnessing a fuming man in gas-soaked jeans, those inching along SR-520 were among the first to lay eyes on Engstrom's 1997 turbocharged Harley Springer—the only Harley on the planet covered from stem to stern with forty pounds of chrome plating, equipped with two, five-pound nitrous oxide booster tanks on the rear fender, and butane exhaust capable of shooting twenty-foot flames.

The Seattle-area shop that had customized the cycle had missed deadlines and rung up cost overruns. As Engstrom dialed his ever-present mobile phone for roadside assistance, he grew enraged at the mechanics, who had in his mind deceived and now nearly killed him.

All that anger was in Engstrom's rearview mirror on Tuesday, July 21, opening exhibition day at the Siggraph '98 conference in Orlando—Chrome's actual debut. No longer just a demo up on a stage, Chrome was now floor-show technology ready for public scrutiny. Only it wasn't called Chrome anymore. Microsoft was unable to secure international rights to the trademark, so two weeks before the conference Chrome was renamed Chromeffects. No one really liked the name and even marketers had trouble remembering to call the technology by its new moniker.

Still, the next day there was a palpable buzz at the Chromeffects booth, which generated heavy foot traffic and interest in this new "fast, flashy, and functional" technology. A keg of Thomas Kemper root beer bobbed in a tub of melting ice. Blue lights swirled above the chrome-plated Harley, as a French television crew interviewed Engstrom sitting on the big beast.

The Harley was now merely a prop, rather than a grand prize. Although Engstrom's own skeletal marketing staff had loved the contest idea, Microsoft's legal department dubbed the cycle a "God machine"—you ride it and the next stop is the afterlife—and put the kibosh on Engstrom's plan to give it away. Already burdened with a massive antitrust suit, the last thing company lawyers wanted to take on was liability in the form of a turbocharged chopper.

But Engstrom resisted the notion that legal whining could stop him. St. John had been kicking around the idea of starting a Web-development company built around Chrome. Although this venture was just in the white-board stage, Engstrom was thinking ahead to the day when St. John's independent company might be able to get away with sponsoring a Chrome Harley contest.

"It's just a piece of art," Engstrom said of the cycle, noting that it was far more powerful than a production-model Harley. "I'm going to find a way to give it away to the company that builds the best Chrome Web site. As cool as the bike is, I want someone else to have it. I like that story."

Meanwhile, Engstrom's business manager, Chris Phillips, was talking with the press in an interview closet.

"But isn't Chromeffects another Microsoft attempt to bifurcate the Web?" asked one superserious pressman.

Bifurcate and *balkanize* were buzzwords Microsoft critics used to describe Redmond's plot to take over the Web. Some viewed Chromeffects as part of Microsoft's strategy to introduce proprietary Internet programming languages and technologies that worked better or only on Windows, the world's dominate PC platform. This would force developers to write Web software for Windows, thereby maintaining and extending Microsoft's hegemony, or so the theory went.

Phillips didn't like this particular journalist, who had disingenuously prefaced his remarks by stating, "Now, I'm not a Microsoft basher . . ." Moreover, Phillips didn't like being confronted with the accusation that Microsoft was megalomaniacal.

"So, what you are telling me is just because everything else on the Web sucks, we should suck, too?" Phillips barked.

The attending media handler from MacKenzie Kesselring flinched at the outburst, but Phillips managed to remain civil throughout the rest of the interview.

Phillips emerged from the interrogation booth and made a bee-line to Engstrom.

"I'm the master manipulator," he said, beaming at Engstrom, who cautioned him to keep his voice down.

"There's press here," Engstrom said.

About a dozen independent software partner companies, including MetaCreations, Katrix, and John Sculley's Live Picture, flanked the perimeter of Engstrom's corner lot on the expansive exhibition floor.

PR people handed out testimonials or "case studies" from companies such as SkyMall, the upscale in-flight catalog retailer, which had Chrome-plated its site.

"It's going to make Web sites much more appealing to shoppers and to viewers," a SkyMall adviser stated. "I'm very excited about what it's doing for us today as well as where we see the technology headed."

Stepping aside for a few moments of quiet before his next interview, Engstrom swept his hand around his temporary kingdom.

"Something like fourteen companies are here that changed their course to endorse our product," he said. "I hope it works."

This is how Microsoft launches most products. The Empire clusters a few partners around the periphery of a Microsoft booth, while a cadre of smooth-talking marketing reps extol the virtues of the technology and play some videotaped testimonials. One-on-one interviews are conducted in makeshift pressrooms, and sheaves of literature and CD-ROMs are passed out.

Yet Engstrom lamented that Microsoft was not throwing more marketing money at his project.

"Getting developers to use Chromeffects is going to be a hard problem," Engstrom said, careful to use the new name for his technology. "We originally wanted to bootstrap it to some cash. We don't have that cash. But Chromeffects is easy enough and the results are cool enough and the download story is so smooth, plus there's my bike giveaway. Things like that will help sell it. I think the game developers especially will start using it."

Again, his fallout with Intel hurt. And without Developer Relations

Group's support, it was nearly impossible for Engstrom to swing more marketing money behind Chrome. He was forced to carve out funds from other projects he oversaw. As it turned out, he was well on his way to overshooting his Chrome budget by more than $2 million. His big spending was a throwback to the cowboy days of DirectX, when the Beastie Boys, aided by St. John's easy access to DRG's cash hoard, burned through resources without authorization. But Microsoft bean counters would take a decidedly dimmer view of Engstrom's spending on Chrome, which unlike DirectX lacked a targeted install base and widespread developer support.

As disappointed as he was about the lack of marketing cash, he was pleased with his marketing team's ingenuity. Leslie Evans of Microsoft and Olivia Riley of MacKenzie Kesselring, the two women in charge of banging the pots for Chromeffects, had dreamed up novel parting gifts—a pair of chrome balls set inside a purple velvet box. To get their hands on the jingly chrome balls, Siggraph participants had to collect at least six Chromeffects coupon cards, available by visiting the booths of Chromeffects partners and sitting through their demonstrations. Requiring patronage at partner booths in exchange for little trinkets is a standard trade-show tactic. However, the gifts are usually T-shirts or baseball caps, not chrome-plated balls.

Engstrom appreciated the symbolism. "My only contribution was requesting that the balls not come in leather bags," he joked.

His grin was infectious. Microsoft product managers were nearly trembling with relief and excitement.

"Can you believe it's finally out?" Audra Gaines-Mulkern said. "It's been such a roller coaster."

But everyone knew the ride wasn't over. Yes, Chrome was now on public display and refinements had improved the technology. It now could render quality text in the browser, a feat not feasible just two weeks before Siggraph. And Chrome could now run on a 300 MHz computer, instead of a 350 MHz machine—important because it meant the technology could be fused to cheaper PCs, which could generate more sales of Chrome-enabled computers.

Computer makers such as Gateway, Compaq, and Dell were scheduled to begin installing Chromeffects before the end of August, Microsoft confided. Meanwhile, a Chromeffects software development kit, which would enable developers to build Chrome sites, would be available for download August 17.

Despite the looming antitrust case, things were looking up for Chrome and the company.

In the days and weeks before Siggraph, industry analysts had reported Microsoft had narrowed the gap in browser market share. Netscape had slipped to 52 percent, while Microsoft had jumped to more than 45 percent.

On the antitrust front, three prominent Republican senators unexpectedly rushed to Microsoft's defense and accused the Justice Department of feeding confidential information about Microsoft to foreign governments. Senators Jeff Sessions of Alabama, Spencer Abraham of Michigan, and Jon Kyl of Arizona said the DOJ was helping other governments with their own antitrust investigations. The DOJ denied the allegation.

Later, the twenty states that had joined in the antitrust lawsuit scaled back their attack and dropped accusations dealing with the alleged illegal bundling of the Outlook Express E-mail program with Windows.

And the day before Engstrom took the wraps off Chromeffects, Microsoft announced fourth-quarter sales of $4 billion, with eye-popping annual revenue at more than $14 billion and no debt. Microsoft had officially surpassed IBM as the biggest software maker on the planet.

It was late afternoon. Engstrom and Phillips stood under the swirling blue lights on the exhibition floor, basking in the glory of their latest technological debut. Engstrom mused on Chrome's potential and his own future with the company.

"I think there's a decade of stuff to be done with it," Engstrom predicted. "After three years it will become clear what needs to be done, and then it will be just a matter of time. There will be three revs before they take it away from me."

There was no malice in his voice. He spoke in that same, satisfied imperial manner he assumed when he talked about how the duct tape on his floor was destined to be a marble spiral staircase. But unlike the staircase, Chrome actually existed. Engstrom had guided the project through Microsoft's potent political minefield and hauled it out of the grave at least once during its relatively long development stage. The technology had survived near-mutiny from Engstrom's developers and a frontal assault from Engstrom's upper management. His team had been able to persuade more than a dozen companies to develop Web sites and software for Chrome, as well as win a few major customers such as SkyMall. Although the Chrome launch lacked the grandeur of St. John's DirectX spectacles, Engstrom could still boast having the world's only chrome-plated Harley. He looked forward to the day in the near future when Chromeffects, née Chrome, would be hardwired to fast computers and in the hands of consumers.

The crowd was thinning toward late afternoon and Engstrom found himself fielding fewer questions about the big chrome Harley under the blue spinning lights. He and Phillips discussed how the day had gone and what was on tap for that night. Phillips said one of the press guys had asked about Fahrenheit, the Microsoft initiative to create a converged OpenGL and DirectX application programming interface. Engstrom chuckled and asked if anyone had inquired about Talisman, the dreaded 3-D chip design Jay Torborg had to date failed to produce. No one had.

Not long after, Phillips shrugged and said, "Well, you wanna go?" It was more of a prod than a question. Engstrom, satisfied with the launch and tired of playing trade-show host, agreed it was time to head back to the palatial Hyatt Regency Cypress Gardens. Engstrom was looking forward to romping around Disney World that evening with a lady friend. Phillips was debating whether to attend an Intel party in downtown Orlando. While making their way to the exit, Engstrom and Phillips privately mocked the neon red-and-green Japanese motorcycles other vendors were using as booth props. The two stepped out of the air-conditioned convention center and into the thick, bright Orlando afternoon. As Phillips lit a cigarette, Engstrom's mobile phone rang.

"You're kidding!" Engstrom said, waiting for a crosswalk light to turn green. "You've got to be joking."

It was Mark Murray, Microsoft's top spokesman. The *Wall Street Journal* was poised to run a story about Microsoft allegedly strong-arming Apple in an attempt to carve up the multimedia market. Apple's Tim Schaaf and Philip Schiller had told government investi-gators about Engstrom's field trips to the company's Cupertino head-quarters. Now Apple's version of those encounters was about to appear in the world's leading business daily. The timing might have been mere coincidence. Then again, given the history between the two companies, Apple more than likely timed its leak—a nice piece of evangelism, one could say—to the *Journal* to roughly coincide with the debut of Engstrom's new multimedia technology.

The story wouldn't mention Engstrom by name, but it would recount how Apple executives believed Microsoft was trying to force the smaller company out of the streaming media market. The story would also reveal that Apple suspected Microsoft of sabotaging QuickTime so it wouldn't work well on Windows.

The brief phone conversation had ended by the time Engstrom slipped inside Phillips's rented Buick Skylark.

"We were trying to be nice guys for a change," Engstrom said, struggling to finish his thought. "What I love is . . . is . . . God damn it! God damn it!"

"At least you'll get to talk to Bill," Phillips chuckled as he drove onto the freeway.

Engstrom dialed Christiano Pierry, who had been a party to the Apple visits. Engstrom instructed Pierry not to talk with *Wall Street Journal* reporter John Wilke.

"I wouldn't send any E-mail on this for obvious reasons," Engstrom added. "I think that you should just not respond to him. It's pretty clear where this whole pain in the butt came from. Probably the same person [at Apple] who sent you the E-mail. No good deed will ever go unpunished. Bye."

Engstrom speculated that he'd have to testify in the upcoming antitrust trial and said he relished the thought of sitting in the hot seat.

"I wish I could give those people a piece of my mind," Engstrom said as he clanked a pair of chrome balls in his thick hand.

Phillips, who didn't share his partner's enthusiasm, complained that the *Wall Street Journal* would run a story without first letting Microsoft officials give it a once-over.

Engstrom shook his head in disbelief as Phillips moved the car past the Hyatt Regency sentry and up the long driveway.

"What I find funny, of all the things in a long list of things I've done that actually caused somebody some pain because I won, I get nailed for this. For this!"

In Engstrom's mind, his talks with Apple were innocent excursions to discuss swapping technology, not intimidating market-carving sorties as described by Apple execs.

"I guess we all delete mail, huh?" Phillips joked.

"We can't," Engstrom quickly said. "That's destroying evidence."

On Thursday, July 23, the day after Engstrom fielded the cell phone call, the *Wall Street Journal* ran its story outlining Apple's complaint that Microsoft had tried to bully it out of the steaming multi-media market and, failing to do that, had altered Windows to disable QuickTime. That *same* day, Rob Glaser, the CEO of RealNetworks and former Microsoft executive, testified before the Senate Judiciary Committee that Microsoft deliberately wrote code into Windows to disable his company's competing streaming media player.

Engstrom, whose duties included developing Microsoft's Windows Media Player, would get his wish. He was now hurtling toward the front lines of one of the century's greatest antitrust battles.

18

GOD.COM

Within weeks of Chrome's unveiling, the buzz in the trade press was white-hot. The idea of transporting video-game-like animation to the heretofore static Web fueled the enthusiasm of tech writers and analysts.

"When there are 50 million Chromeffects-capable systems delivered (say a year from now), the technology will be the coolest reason to upgrade a PC," industry newsletter *The Peddie Report* opined.

Rob Enderle, a Microsoft-friendly analyst with Giga Group, likened Chrome to "a religious experience."

"I would call it revolutionary," Enderle said. "When I first looked at this, it was like discovering the Web for the first time."

Even *MacWeek*, the trade journal devoted to covering Apple, said, "After years of playing second fiddle to Apple's cross-platform QuickTime technology, Microsoft may have raised the stakes with its latest multimedia offering.

"It's cool software, and it's not often I say Microsoft has cool software," the article went on, quoting David Card, an analyst at New York–based Jupiter Communications. "Apple doesn't have anything comparable."

Riding this momentum was Alex St. John. The Beastie Boy who had helped dream the idea of Chrome was now prepared to put the technology to work for him. After knocking the idea around with Eric Engstrom, St. John formed his first company, appropriately named WildTangent Inc. Like flashCast, St. John's start-up would be a Chrome-plating shop that would build advanced, high-end Web sites. But St. John couldn't do it alone and embarked on a frenetic hiring spree. He searched across Puget Sound and around the world. He even recruited Cambridge mathematician Jeremy Kenyon, a programmer and former colleague St. John knew from his days at Harlequin Ltd. in England. Within weeks he had assembled a team of almost a dozen highly skilled employees eager to explore the potential of Chromeffects and make riches on Bill Gates's coattails.

Lacking a base of operations, St. John called in carpenters to convert his downstairs gym into a residential high-tech headquarters. Jeaneane, St. John's fiancée, who was now living at his Kirkland home, didn't mind that her husband-to-be was starting a new business just a few weeks before the nuptials.

"We're stress junkies," she would say, parroting one of his favorite phrases.

Microsoft program managers and others on Engstrom's team, however, weren't thrilled with having St. John linking his fortunes to the nascent technology. They remembered him as the loose cannon who couldn't get along with colleagues and delighted and profited in taking public potshots at Microsoft after he was cast out.

Their apprehension deepened when Engstrom arranged for St. John, the prodigal evangelist, to set up temporary shop inside four first-floor offices at Building 30.

"No one trusts him," several said.

"I don't think Eric's thinking wisely about this one," others lamented.

No one was more troubled by St. John's return to the Empire than Paul Scholz, the president of flashCast. Not only did St. John gain choice first-floor office space with windows, WildTangent would compete for a dwindling pool of development money—money that Engstrom was not authorized to spend but was spending nonetheless.

There was no lack of acrimony between Scholz and St. John. In fact, before he formed WildTangent, St. John had proposed that Scholz and he join forces. Actually, St. John had wanted to absorb flashCast in order to fast-track his new company. Engstrom and St. John had talked about leveraging flashCast's expertise with Chrome and coupling it with St. John's magnetic talent for marketing. St. John, of course, would be in charge, and Scholz would act as subservient vice president. They would make millions, St. John said. Engstrom, who admired Scholz's development skills, said Scholz would be an idiot to turn down this opportunity.

Scholz had pledged his unflinching fealty to Engstrom and struggled with what was now the biggest business decision of his life. Should he just fold the tent he had labored so hard to erect? Had he moved his entire company to Redmond only to relinquish it to Microsoft's most famous malcontent?

During the long summer nights, Scholz retreated to the rooftop of his floating house on the scalloped waters of Seattle's Lake Union. With the jeweled skyline twinkling to the south, he volleyed the pros and cons of handing the reins of flashCast to St. John.

"Eric tells me it's the smartest thing I could do," Scholz said. "But, fuck, you know? flashCast may be small and we may have these hokey Dayton values and everything, but we're the best at what we do and it's mine. I built it."

St. John had sensed Scholz's reluctance and suspected that "Paul may not have the stomach for what I propose to do." So he prepared a litmus test. St. John requested that Scholz register a half dozen Web site or domain names through Network Solutions' Internic service. Internic was the gatekeeper of Web-site names and charged a $119 fee for companies, organizations, and individuals to claim two-year, renewable rights to a certain domain with the *com, net,* and *org* suffixes. Among the names St. John requested Scholz secure was god.com. Although Scholz never proselytized, he acknowledged that he was a nonpracticing Christian and believed that Jesus was the world's savior. St. John, an avowed atheist, said he wanted to push Scholz's tolerance threshold.

"This is a little test," St. John said. "If Paul does what I ask him to do, he passes."

Scholz registered all the names but god.com, which he said had already been taken. But even if it hadn't, Scholz said he wouldn't have registered it, at least not for an atheist like St. John.

Theological issues aside, Scholz decided it was in his best interest not to go into business with St. John. He was too reckless, Scholz thought.

"Alex lacks the moral authority to lead troops into battle," Scholz told Engstrom, who, in turn, bluntly told Scholz he was being an idiot.

The rebuke confirmed for St. John what he had thought all along.

"Paul's a religious zealot, and zealots don't know how to win," St. John said.

Thus WildTangent was born and incubated inside the protective womb of Building 30.

St. John wasted no time getting up to speed on Chrome. Although he had never built a Web site, he believed Chrome was more like writing game code than writing HTML. Whatever, he and his team quickly managed to produce Chrome-plated Web sites that even Scholz was forced to admit "looked pretty damn cool."

Launching the start-up did not interrupt St. John's wedding plans. In fact, they would become part of a Chrome promotional event. The wedding would be a "traditional" Las Vegas wedding. Like Chrome, it promised to be "fast, flashy, and functional." St. John had invited *Boot* magazine to cover his wedding and arranged for the publication to interview Engstrom. Engstrom had been making inquiries on how to become an official pagan priest—he wanted to perform the wedding ceremony. He also wanted to bring his chrome-plated Harley. Unfortunately for history, Engstrom did neither of those things. He didn't have time to complete the steps necessary to become a bona fide pagan priest, and the bike still had some mechanical troubles.

However, Engstrom did attend the August 12 wedding and chatted with *Boot* magazine about Chrome.

Just two weeks later, the other Beastie Boy, Craig Eisler, married KT in a more conventional ceremony in her native Malibu, then jetted to Hawaii for their honeymoon. The couple appeared happy enough.

"All went REALLY well on our honeymoon and on our wedding day," he wrote in one E-mail. ". . . KT is the most beautiful and awesome bride that ever lived or ever will live!"

As a Microsoft executive, Eisler had grown more conservative. Perhaps it was KT's influence or his involvement with Landmark Education Forum. Or maybe it was the time spent away from Engstrom and St. John. For whatever reason, Eisler was not gambling with his career as general manager of NetShow. Yet given the nature of Microsoft, he could not escape controversy. Before his wedding, the company had announced that NetShow server software would be bundled free with Windows 2000, formerly Windows NT, saying the technology was part of the operating system. It was the same strategy Microsoft had used in integrating the browser with Windows 95 and Win98. Because Windows 2000 and succeeding versions of it would eventually replace Windows 95 and 98 in the consumer market, many wondered if it was just a matter of time before the government moved against Eisler's new domain.

Eisler, however, had learned how to advance up the corporate rungs by keeping a lower profile. Unlike Engstrom, Eisler had hung up his cowboy spurs. Eisler was not paying visits to Apple and other competitors. He was not about to go over budget and spend funds he was not authorized to blow. Moreover, he made sure to keep his distance from St. John, whose entreaties for lunch went unrequited.

While St. John's WildTangent plans proceeded on schedule, the looming antitrust case was delayed, first until September 23, then to October 19. The government had been broadening its attack against Microsoft's business practices. Although the court allowed each side just twelve witnesses, the Justice Department was taking longer than expected to conduct depositions from its key players. Microsoft would not call Gates to the stand and neither would the DOJ—it didn't want to waste one of its few witnesses with someone hostile to its cause. However, the government would use hours of Gates's video-taped deposition testimony.

Moreover, a half dozen media companies, citing the 1913 Publicity in Taking Evidence Act, petitioned the court to cover the depositions of top Microsoft officials, including Bill Gates.

Microsoft, contending the 1913 law was outdated and irrelevant, wanted the depositions to take place behind closed doors. The company filed a quick appeal. Even the government sided with Microsoft on this one. The media presence would be a distraction, DOJ officials said. But Judge Thomas Penfield Jackson said he was compelled by the archaic statute to open the depositions to the petitioning media outlets—the *New York Times,* the *Seattle Times;* computer trade publisher Ziff-Davis; and two news services, Reuters and Bloomberg News.

An appeals court said it would review the issue, yet in the meantime allowed depositions to take place in private. Because the trial was scheduled to start before the appeals court made a ruling, Microsoft essentially got its wish.

As the government was taking statements from its witnesses, the *Seattle Times* broke a story on September 20 that featured details of the meetings Microsoft had had with Apple. The article marked the first time Eric Engstrom and his business manager, Chris Phillips, were mentioned as participants in an alleged scheme to carve up the streaming multimedia market.

"A series of meetings between the summer of 1997 and April of this year has drawn the attention of government investigators who see the talks as another example of Microsoft crossing the line from cooperation to attempted collusion," the article stated.

It went on to detail the first 1997 encounter where Engstrom and Phillips met with Apple's Tim Schaaff, director of QuickTime engineering, and Peter Hoddie, senior QuickTime architect. Engstrom allegedly suggested Apple eliminate QuickTime from the Windows market.

"Are you suggesting that we knife the baby?" asked Hoddie, referring to QuickTime.

Phillips is said to have replied, "You'd have to knife the baby."

Phillips told coworkers at Building 30 that he had never said anything about knifing a baby. Few believed him.

"We all know how he talks," said one former Chrome worker. "He said it."

On September 28, eight days after the article appeared, Engstrom was in Washington, D.C., where Department of Justice investigators had subpoenaed him to testify in a closed-door deposition. It turned out to be an all-day affair. Engstrom was in agony. His back had deteriorated and he was scheduled for surgery in mid-October. Yet he put the physical pain behind him and focused on the battle at hand. He slurped a case of diet Coke as he defended himself and Microsoft. So animated and aggressive was Engstrom that the stenographer on several occasions asked him to slow down. Among the accusations the government pursued was that Microsoft had written code into Windows that sabotaged competing software, particularly Apple's QuickTime and RealNetworks' media players. Both companies accused Microsoft of deliberately rigging Windows to disable their players.

Engstrom said that was laughable. Windows not only broke competing software, it also broke Microsoft's own products, including programs offered in the top-selling Office suite.

In early October, the government revised its twelve-man witness list to include Apple executive Avie Tevanian and Sun Microsystems executive James Gosling. Tevanian would speak about the alleged strong-arm tactics by Engstrom and Phillips, while Gosling would claim that Microsoft had violated a licensing agreement by "polluting" the Java programming language to make it run better on Windows.

Microsoft, impressed with Engstrom's performance at the deposition, quickly responded and inserted him into its twelve-man lineup. Engstrom replaced Yusuf Mehdi, Microsoft's director of Windows marketing. Engstrom, the former hick from eastern Washington and arguably the beastliest of the Beastie Boys, would be among just twenty-four people to testify in person at arguably the most riveting antitrust case in modern history. He would share the witness stand with the biggest names at Microsoft—senior executives Paul Maritz, James Allchin, Brad Chase, and Cameron Myhrvold. Although he was not granting interviews, Engstrom's name began appearing in *USA Today,* the *New York Times,* and the *Wall Street Journal,* among countless other publications. He had matriculated from the trade papers to the mainstream press.

"Looks like Eric got his wish," St. John giggled. "He's going to be famous."

19

ONCE MORE INTO THE BREACH

The November issue of *Maximum PC,* formerly *Boot* magazine, hit newsstands in October. For the first time, Eric Engstrom found himself featured inside a glossy mag. The article was a question-and-answer piece on Chromeffects spanning six pages under the headline "MS Caches In," a play of words on *cache,* defined as a dedicated bank of high-speed memory used to improve computer performance.

The interview had taken place in Las Vegas when Engstrom was in town for St. John's August wedding. The article had a gambling theme and focused on Microsoft's risky gambit to bring a gamelike 3-D experience to the Web using low-bandwidth connections. Microsoft was betting that computer makers would pay a per-unit licensing fee to install Chrome on their high-end PCs. At the same time, the company was wagering that developers would build Chrome-plated Web sites for Chrome-enabled machines not yet on the market.

Engstrom, dressed in a stiff beige leisure suit and a loud polyester shirt open to expose a gold chain, was supposed to look like a professional cardsharp. But the consensus among those back at Building 30 was that Engstrom looked more like a cheesy car salesman or one of those guys who breaks fingers for a living—essentially someone you wouldn't trust with your money.

"Chromeffects is an attempt to turn multimedia into a billion-dollar industry," he had told the magazine, noting that the technology marked the first time Microsoft had built a product "that pushes the envelope of high-performance machines."

He said the company estimated that 60 million computers would be sold with Chromeffects in 1999. There was reason for his optimism. As recently as early September, Steve Ballmer, Microsoft's second-in-command, had declared that Chromeffects was "mainstream technology for the future." Even Bill Gates had publicly called Chrome a strategic way for developers to harness the power of the 3-D graphics capabilities of Windows and further Microsoft's Internet goals.

That summer Ballmer was promoted to president of Microsoft when Gates stepped aside to focus more on his first love—technology development. With an endorsement from Gates *and* Ballmer, who now gripped Microsoft's major administrative reins, the future of Chromeffects seemed secure.

"I don't have any fear that Chromeffects won't be a success," Engstrom predicted.

But that was in August, before the ill winds of October started blowing across Microsoft, the land where "no good deed shall go unpunished."

And so it happened that between early September, when Ballmer talked about Chromeffects as "mainstream technology," to just days before the antitrust trial, an extraordinary convergence of events conspired to doom Engstrom's plans to ride Chromeffects to greater glory inside the Empire. While Engstrom braced for his ascension to the witness stand, his career as a Microsoft innovator and renegade was in a tailspin.

Distractions closed in on Engstrom in early October. Foremost on his mind was excruciating pain. His spine had deteriorated and the agony literally brought him to his knees. Colleagues could hear his howls of torment from behind his closed second-floor door. As much as he hated the idea of retreating, he decided to stay home the second week of October. His surgery, scheduled the week the antitrust trial started, could not come soon enough.

Then there was the pain of preparing for the trial itself. Chris Phillips was now spending much of his time at Eric's house, reviewing their version of events and making sure Engstrom would deliver a message consistent with his pretrial deposition as well as testimony of other Microsoft executives. Engstrom and Phillips figured into the government's most serious antitrust charge against Microsoft—that the company intimidated competitors in order to illegally maintain and extend a monopoly. The government held up Netscape as its prime example, alleging that Microsoft, having failed at colluding with its smaller rival, set about to kill it by bundling a browser free with every copy of Windows sold. The allegations from Apple were reinforcements to buttress the case.

Government lawyers and Apple executives portrayed Engstrom and Phillips as henchmen, digital-age goons dispatched to enforce the will of Godfather Gates. It was all too inconceivable for Engstrom, who maintained he was just trying to compete in a ferociously competitive and often fickle industry.

Indeed, for all its reputation as a frontier for risk-taking, where pools of venture capital spawn start-ups and explosive initial public offerings, the computer industry can be as timid as a Miami pensioner when it comes to betting on new technology. Engstrom knew all too well that cooking up cool software was relatively easy. But not even mighty Microsoft could force-feed technology down the throats of the unwilling.

Despite all his efforts, by October Engstrom had been unable to convince computer makers to install Chromeffects on their faster PCs, which were now hitting store shelves. It wasn't a question of major computer makers not wanting Chrome. In fact they were eager and ready to wire the technology to their high-end, Windows 98 machines. But Engstrom was a victim of his own ambition and the industry's chicken/egg conundrum. Engstrom had overspent his budget to develop Chrome, and he ran out of money to pay Web-site developers to build Chrome-plated Web sites. Microsoft had promised computer makers that Chrome-plated sites would exist.

When Engstrom failed to deliver on that promise, computer makers didn't see a reason to install Chrome. This created a negative-feedback cycle. Engstrom's team discovered that without Chrome-enabled machines, it was virtually impossible to persuade Web developers to spend their own money to build Chrome-plated sites.

"The plan was to jump-start the process through marketing deals to encourage people to put Chrome content on their sites," explained Bob Heddle, Chrome's lead program manager. "But the sources of money dried up.

"We had no one making content," he added. "We went to OEMs and said there will be all these sites. There was a little bit of faith involved. In the end, there was some faith missing because some things that we said were going to happen didn't happen."

Still, Heddle and others didn't see that as terminal. After all, Microsoft was able to break the chicken/egg cycle with DirectX, the precursor technology that had invaded and conquered the PC-gaming industry. Microsoft gave DirectX away, generating enough critical mass for widespread market adoption. It was a formula that could work again.

"You have to break the cycle and that means giving [Chromeffects] to OEMs for free," Heddle said. "Or like what we did with DirectX—convince both the chicken and the egg that the problem was going to be solved."

Alex St. John suggested that Microsoft "get creative" with its OEM distribution. St. John had urgent reason to see Chrome succeed. His entire company was riding on Chrome. He had hired developers from near and far and brought them together with the promise they would be making cool technology and lots of money along the way. If Chrome collapsed, so would his business, or so it seemed.

Microsoft had never announced what it was going to charge computer makers for Chrome, but figures kicked around internally were between $3 and $5 per unit. St. John advised Engstrom to give Chromeffects to one OEM for free or at a reduced price and then start playing competing computer makers off each other. This was classic evangelism. The thinking was that once one OEM had Chrome—a technology that could lure consumers to buy or upgrade to more expensive high-end PCs—other computer makers would want it, too.

But Engstrom was not in control of Microsoft's OEM distribution strategy. Moreover, as a practical matter, it was too late for OEMs to install Chrome for Christmas '98. The holiday would have come and gone by the time computer makers received and configured Chrome-enabled machines, then shipped them to market.

Although OEMs were interested in the technology, by now they were hedging their bets. St. John said executives at chipmaker Advanced Micro Devices told him computer makers believed Microsoft would eventually bundle Chromeffects for free inside the operating system. After all, Microsoft was giving away its Internet Explorer browser and Windows Media Player. It was logical to assume that at some point Redmond would just incorporate Chrome as a standard function of Windows as well.

Engstrom wanted Chrome to be a premium add-on and a way for Windows to distinguish itself on the Internet by being able to display Web content better than any other type of operating system. Giving away Chrome was not part of Engstrom's grand plan.

"Chromeffects was not installed on OEM machines because I originally insisted on charging the OEMs for it," Engstrom says. "It was not because of lack of content. By the time I understood I had to give it away, it was impossible to push the 'free' price through [Microsoft's] OEM sales division."

As disappointing as a giveaway was, at least Engstrom, his team, and many in the industry believed Chrome would revolutionize the Web. But this was hardly the time for a revolution. Microsoft was insisting it wasn't trying to wrestle Netscape, Apple, and other competitors off the Internet. So having a Beastie Boy—the same Beastie Boy accused of strong-arming Apple—thundering around on a chrome-plated Harley and pounding his chest about a new breed of Internet technology ran afoul of Microsoft's interim strategy of taking a lower profile. Indeed, any hopes that Engstrom had of advancing his career on the wheels of Chrome were soon crushed under the weight of the Justice Department's antitrust suit and by yet another internal reorganization.

Debilitated by back pain and distracted by preparation for the antitrust case, Engstrom couldn't defend his territory when it was most vulnerable. Moreover, David Cole, Engstrom's overlord and the man who had almost killed Chrome only to resuscitate and champion it earlier that year, had been on a three-month leave. Engstrom's key guardian vice president had also left turf unguarded.

By early October it was rumored Chrome would be taken from Cole and Engstrom and handed to Deborah Black, the general manager of Windows presentation technologies and the woman with whom St. John had unsuccessfully sparred the previous year. Engstrom would be given the untenable option of working for Black, who knew nothing about Chrome. She did, however, know plenty about Engstrom.

"It's chaos over here right now," said one Chrome developer in the days before the reorg was officially announced.

Some blamed Cole for the reorg and installing Black over Engstrom.

"It was all David Cole all the time," said a couple of engineers.

St. John, however, had a different read. From his perspective, Jim Allchin, the cunning senior vice president in charge of Windows operating systems and Internet development, targeted multimedia and Chrome for himself in the reorg.

"They scavenge your pile when you're gone," said St. John. "I know. They did it to me when I was distracted with my divorce.

"This reorg and installing Deb Black was a consolidation of power under Jim Allchin. Cole was not defending his turf and Deb Black is a known quality who Allchin trusts to keep a hand on the rudder. Black is one of Allchin's lieutenants."

On Friday, October 16, three days before the antitrust trial, Black assembled the Chrome team to announce the reorg and declare that she was now in charge of Chromeffects. She also said Chrome would be delayed, indefinitely, while her new management team got up to speed on the technology. Those at the meeting described her as part den mother, part clipboard bureaucrat. She reportedly told the group that everyone's job was secure and that Chromeffects was just being reevaluated to strengthen its position in the market. As much as they wanted to believe it, few wanted to follow under her command.

"She was so mousy," said Paul Scholz, the president of flashCast. "It was like no one could buy her as someone who could lead troops. Say what you want about Eric, at least he's a leader."

Engstrom attended the meeting.

"I gave a little speech at the end asking them to give Deborah the same support they had given me," Engstrom says. "It was a futile act since she is incapable of leading people, but I did try."

It wasn't a pleasant day inside Building 30. St. John had sensed trouble days before Black called her meeting. He feared that invoices he had submitted weeks ago to Audra Gaines-Mulkern would face even longer delays amid the chaos of a reorg. Hoping to speed his invoices, St. John bought boxes of Godiva chocolates for all the key female administrative assistants. Program manager Linda Taylor received her box and on that fateful Friday dropped by St. John's offices on the first floor to thank him and ask what was the occasion. St. John told her about the invoices. Taylor marched off furiously to confront Gaines-Mulkern, who had just returned from a trade show. Taylor reportedly upbraided Gaines-Mulkern for letting the invoices lie fallow.

"There was a catfight," St. John said. "They started screaming at each other. Linda punched Audra, or at least slapped her in the face."

The Redmond police arrived. No arrests were made, but clearly the stress inside Building 30 had become unbearable.

Black's announcement of a reorg triggered a Chrome diaspora. Once it was clear Engstrom would no longer be holding the center, developers wasted no time fleeing. Colin McCartney, the Scotsman who had drafted the initial specs for Chrome and performed the bulk of the coding grunt work, left to join the DirectX Foundation team under Jay Torborg. Kip Olsen and Ajay Jindal, two other Chrome developers, shifted to work on the Windows Media Player.

Bob Heddle, Chrome's lead program manager, who had butted heads with Engstrom over the previous fourteen months, was unsure what he would do.

"I'm leaving," Heddle said. "I can't sit around here and watch it die painfully and slowly."

Engstrom was depressed that Microsoft had again stripped him of one of his creations and was unwilling to work for Black. The following Saturday he flew to St. Louis for his long-awaited back operation, which included removing two extra vertebrae at the end of his spine.

"I was born with an undeveloped tail," he would say. "I don't know where that puts me on the evolutionary tree."

Some joked that Engstrom was the missing link.

On Monday, October 19, the antitrust case against Microsoft began in U.S. District Court, Room 2—the same courthouse where Special Prosecutor Ken Starr had grilled former White House intern Monica Lewinsky just a few stormy weeks prior. Unlike President Clinton's lurid travails, the Microsoft case seemed far more sober and profound. More than just one man's reputation was at stake. Nothing less than the futures of Microsoft, the Internet, and how society accessed and used its digital treasures were on the line. In the crosshairs was Gates's Empire, America's wealthiest corporation. Not since the breakup of John D. Rockefeller's Standard Oil Trust in 1911 had the government targeted such a large and formidable prey. Like that turn-of-the-century case, the one against Microsoft would decide the fate of one of America's greatest companies and forever influence a vital portion of the nation's economic infrastructure. Back then it was about competition over access to oil and gas distribution. This case was about competition over access to something even more valuable—information. And whether he liked it or not, at some point Beastie Boy Eric Engstrom would be a part of it.

When Engstrom returned the next week from his back surgery, he showed the long scar that stretched from his posterior on up to his lower back.

"It looks like he has a two-foot ass crack," remarked one former colleague. "He should be a refrigerator repairman with a crack like that."

All mirth aside, Engstrom sought the counsel of group vice president Paul Maritz, then the third most powerful man at Microsoft, and told him he was having a miserable time coping with the collapse of Chromeffects. Maritz said he could arrange for the Beastie Boy to stay with Chromeffects on more favorable terms. But Engstrom wasn't interested in working on a fragmented, amorphous version of his creation with a crew of unseasoned developers, nor was he at all inclined to work with Deborah Black. Maritz then suggested Engstrom check with John Ludwig, Engstrom's former mentor, who was in charge of Microsoft Network, the company's troubled Internet service provider.

MSN was plagued with problems. It was slow and complicated compared to other Internet service providers, and as a result it was battling for customers. Engstrom agreed this was probably as good a place as any to restart. He could still draw a salary and watch as his vested stock options continued to make him wealthier.

"I need a job," he told Ludwig. "I'll do anything. I'll be a tester. I'll even clean your office. But I only have one request—I don't want to be second-guessed."

"In that case," Ludwig said, "I don't want you cleaning my office." However, he noted that he had "a real crisis" with MSN's Internet access and told Engstrom he could help fix the glitches to make it easier for customers to use.

After more than three years at Building 30, Engstrom packed up his office and moved to nearby MSN. He harbored no lasting ill will toward Microsoft. He knew the rules of engagement and was a willing warrior. While some speculated that he would lapse into "rest and vest mode" at MSN and sulk the way he once did at the company's Advanced Consumer Technology group, others thought differently. Programmers soon began submitting requests to become part of Engstrom's new team.

By November 12, Microsoft had quietly dismantled its elaborate Chromeffects Web page and replaced it with a vague outline describing the technology. "Chromeffects interactive media technology is an add-on feature coming soon to the Microsoft Windows 98 operating system," the document read.

The next day, Friday the thirteenth, Audra Gaines-Mulkern sent a memo to Chrome partners informing them that Chromeffects was being delayed—not killed. Chromeffects would still be revolutionary technology, but it wouldn't have its own brand name, its own distinct personality. Gaines-Mulkern said the technology would be threaded piecemeal into succeeding versions of the browser and operating systems. Like an organ donor, Chromeffects' vital components would be ripped out and stitched into the monster that "FrankenWindows" had become.

"We are stepping back and refactoring the Chromeffects technologies to better meet customer and your development needs," Gaines-Mulkern wrote. "Instead of releasing Chromeffects this Christmas, we will instead release Chromeffects technologies in multiple phases."

The memo stated that among other things Chromeffects 1.0 needed closer adherence to proposed Web-language standards, better authoring tool support, and "improved quality and performance of 3-D hardware device drivers."

The fifty-six extensible markup language or XML tags that formed the guts of Chrome would not ship until after Windows 2000 was released, meaning even if any developers wanted to use Chrome, they would have to use a thick chunk of Java programming to make it work—almost ensuring few would adopt the new technology.

Although the XML tags were the most open and easy to use for developers, many, including members of standards committees, applauded Microsoft's decision and agreed the steps would make a better product.

But St. John, who was now a Chrome Web-site developer, said it was all a smoke screen.

"The one good excuse for delaying Chrome is that it is slow," he said, noting that, for a virgin product, its performance wasn't all that bad. "But the rest of this stuff is just rationalization for disbanding enemy leaders."

Gaines-Mulkern concluded by stating, "We understand that this change in the release plans for Chromeffects represents a nontrivial change for you, our Chromeffects partners."

Indeed, companies from as far away as Tel Aviv were burned by the sudden flameout of Chromeffects. Even Intel was caught unaware, further straining the already unhappy marriage.

"Chromeffects was supposed to be released at the end of this year, and Microsoft hadn't bothered to tell Intel ahead of time," said Giga Information Group analyst Rob Enderle.

About a dozen companies had spent untold tens of thousands of dollars working on Chrome-related technology in hopes of seeing some return from Christmas sales. That wasn't going to happen in 1998. But not all Chrome partners were necessarily devastated. The software industry is unpredictable, at best. Product delays come with the terrain. And smart companies have contingency plans.

flashCast, the little Web firm that had relocated its Dayton, Ohio, office to Redmond, had started developing so-called Internet portal sites for the palm-sized computers that were becoming all the rage by late '98. A portal, like a virtual launchpad, is a Web site containing its own news, entertainment, software downloads, and other content as well as links to other sites. They were good starting points for exploring the Web, and Scholz and his band were working on ways to fuse the Web and palm-sized computers. Ironically, the implosion of the Chrome team helped flashCast. Chris Phillips, Engstrom's former business manager, left to become a business manager for Windows CE, the system software used in handhelds and palm-sized digital organizers.

"That can only be good for me," Scholz said in November. Microsoft would later pay Scholz more than $1 million to port the Windows Media Player to Windows CE and all non-Windows operating systems.

Vancouver, B.C.–based Vertigo Technology Inc. was another survivor.

"Sure we're disappointed," said company spokeswoman Barb Willans. "We would have liked to have seen this technology come to market [in 1998]. But has it stopped us in our tracks? No."

Hunt Interactive Inc., based near the epicenter of Chrome's development, suffered similar disappointment.

"We were going to be in the Microsoft booth at Comdex [in Las Vegas]," said John Hunt, company president. "We had plane tickets, hotel rooms, we were ready to go. Then the day before we're supposed to leave, we get that memo."

Hunt had built tools specifically targeting Chromeffects and was uncertain if the new, dismembered incarnation of the technology would be compatible with what his company had spent thousands and thousands of dollars building. Still, he remained philosophical.

"Nothing ships until it ships," he said, shrugging.

And what about St. John, who had recruited developers from as far away as England and whose WildTangent rode on the promise of Chrome? WildTangent's mission was to create Chrome-plated Web sites—sites that fewer than a dozen other companies could produce. It was supposed to be one of the first companies to use "mainstream technology for the future."

St. John sensed Chromeffects would survive in some fashion. It had to. Consumers expected their computers to deliver sound, images, animation, and even movie clips. Why would they expect anything less from the Internet, which was merely a vast network of computers? Multimedia on the Web was as inevitable as color was to television, he believed.

Even Engstrom, who held no ill will toward Microsoft, believed.

"Despite its faults, Microsoft is perhaps one of the only large great companies in the U.S. or the world, for that matter," Engstrom said a few weeks before his testimony. "The shit and lies that our competitors are stirring up only helps drive that home to me.

"The future will be fine. They will ship Chromeffects under someone else's flag in a couple of years, and in the end all that really matters for my personal goals at the 'Soft and the world is that it happens. You can't uninvent a good idea no matter how hard you try. All you can do is delay it a little bit."

There were signs for optimism. By Thanksgiving, Microsoft had reposted an edited version of St. John's white paper and other substantive material on a revamped Chromeffects Web site. Chromeffects, the site said, "would be coming soon."

Meanwhile, St. John and his team sat scratching their heads, figuring out their interim plan of attack. Then a strange thing happened. A stray synapse fired inside St. John's brain, triggering a long-forgotten memory. He recalled that at a Professional Developers Conference a few years prior, Paul Maritz had run an experimental version of Chrome when demonstrating the as-yet-released Internet Explorer 4 browser.

St. John recalled that in 1996, when he and fellow Beastie Boys Engstrom and Eisler were formulating Chrome, they had asked members of the Internet Explorer team to bury some prototype Chrome coding inside the then-nascent IE 4.0 browser. The prototype code allowed the browser access to DirectX multimedia capabilities.

Ironically, St. John and his WildTangent team were able to activate this long-dormant proto-Chrome capability by using a Java program. It was much harder to program for, but the buried function performed faster than the first version of Chrome 1.0 because it didn't have as many layers of coding to chew through. What's more, the technology already resided in IE 4, which was by that time installed inside millions of computers. And best of all, from WildTangent's point of view, it was undocumented and thus "utterly unknown in the universe."

Chrome lives!

St. John rubbed his hands and smiled when he saw the IE 4 browser jump to life, as a fast-animated 3-D star spun on the screen.

"All right, then," he said with a familiar devious grin. "Let's play again."

EPILOGUE

ALL MY BELOVED ENEMIES

Any confidence Eric Engstrom might have possessed walking into U.S. District Court that frigid February morning evaporated as he helplessly watched one of his own being devoured by the government's lead attorney, David Boies. It was a Friday, day fifty-seven of the antitrust trial, and this was Engstrom's first stroll into what had become for Microsoft a torture chamber. Roughly the dimensions of a giant shoe box, Room 2 of the E. Barrett Pettyman building was designed for discomfort. No windows broke the monotony of imposing wood paneling that reached two stories high. Ten rows of spartan, hardwood spectator benches made backsides throb. Some savvy veterans who had been attending, covering or participating in the trial, brought seat cushions. Recessed government fluorescent lighting cast milky illumination, but no shadows. And to the right of Judge Thomas Penfield Jackson sat Dan Rosen, Microsoft's meek general manager for new technology. The witness stand was shoved in the far corner and sat more than a few feet lower than the judge's chair, making the diminutive Rosen seem all that much smaller—and his lies all that much larger.

Rosen was Microsoft's key executive in dealing with Netscape during the crucial year of 1995, specifically at a June meeting when the government says the software giant tried to strong-arm Netscape out of the Windows browser business. E-mail after E-mail had shown that

Microsoft feared Netscape was becoming a threat to the Empire. Even Gates had stated so in his famous "Internet Tidal Wave" memo. Yet, incredulously, Rosen said he didn't see it that way. Pudgy, chinless, and a little ashen (was it the lighting?), Rosen said in his reed-thin voice, "[Netscape] said they wanted to be a partner, not a competitor— I believed them." Few, if anyone, believed Rosen—save for maybe his wife, who sat with hands clenched in the front row like a Little League mom watching her lil' slugger strike out, again and again and again.

Confronted with the fact that Gates himself had identified Netscape as a competitor, Rosen replied, "I thought I had a better perspective than Mr. Gates did on Netscape's intentions." Judge Jackson, who bears passing resemblance to the late House of Representatives Speaker Tip O'Neill, rolled his swollen eyes as a contingent of the world's media laughed aloud. Engstrom's broad shoulders slumped. Too depressed to watch Boies continue tearing the wings off Rosen, Engstrom did not return after the noon recess.

Bill Gates had set the tone of Microsoft's curious defense during his twenty hours of videotaped testimony filmed in August 1998. In the tape, Gates sat pouting in an oversize leather chair, quibbling with government attorneys over the definition of words such as *definition* and answering deposition questions with "I don't know," "I don't remember," or "I don't recall" more than two hundred times. When the trial began in October, Microsoft had promised that when it came time for its dozen witnesses to take the stand, the company would utterly destroy the government's case, which had so far been built on the damaging testimony of industry competitors and an unprecedented edifice of incriminating internal E-mail. But Microsoft sensed momentum would swing in its favor. America Online had since purchased Netscape in a $10 billion deal that Microsoft said proved there was abundant competition in the Internet market. The deal compelled South Carolina to withdraw from the case, leaving nineteen states and the federal government to continue the offensive.

But witness after Microsoft witness folded under Boies's relentless questioning. Vice President Paul Maritz was forced to explain his memo describing how Microsoft should bundle a browser with Windows to "cut off [Netscape's] air supply." Senior Vice President Jim Allchin fared no better. His testimony crumbled when a videotape that was supposed to prove Windows 98 performance suffered when uncoupled from the browser was shown to be doctored. Microsoft redid the video, but it failed to show that Windows 98 suffered any ill effects when the Internet Explorer browser was amputated from the operating system. Then there was Rosen, to date the worst of Microsoft's witnesses.

Engstrom skipped Monday's court session, which was a replay of Rosen trying to recast the meaning of words such as *browser* and *wrest* and *ownership*—in short, another disastrous day for Microsoft. But Engstrom returned Tuesday, February 23, day fifty-nine of the marathon trial. Engstrom and Microsoft's legal team marched into the courtroom, through the low-slung swinging doors separating spectators from litigants, and took their rightful places at a long wood table piled with legal briefs, black binders, and a computer running Windows with Internet Explorer—the same type of system the government was using to call up electronic copies of depositions and other evidence.

Microsoft's team sat at the same table where crack addicts wearing orange jail jumpsuits had been arraigned just moments before—a strange juxtaposition. There was Rosen again, hunched at the witness stand. It was Microsoft's turn to somehow undo the exquisite damage Boies had inflicted during the preceding days. "It's always inspiring to watch young people embark on heroic endeavors," Judge Jackson quipped as Microsoft attorney Michael Lacovara began the futile task of resuscitating Rosen's credibility.

Indeed, moments after Lacovara finished his gentle line of questioning, Engstrom and the rest of team Microsoft sat horrified as Boies, dressed in his signature rumpled blue suit and black Nikes, shredded Rosen.

During lunch the day before, in the courthouse's basement cafeteria, a writer for Ziff-Davis publishing accused Microsoft of con-structing a defense based on lies. "Not just little lies," the writer said. "But big, fuckin' eighteen-wheeler-sized lies."

Too bad for Microsoft that Rosen was still at the wheel. Under cross-examination, Rosen claimed that he hadn't even seen Netscape's browser before the infamous June '95 meeting with Netscape officials. How could Microsoft have thought the browser was a threat when he and other officials hadn't even seen the technology, Rosen was implying.

But Boies showed an E-mail Rosen had written in May that year in which Rosen asked for a copy of the Netscape browser from a col-league. Rosen explained that he had never got the copy and that at any rate it was a test version that didn't work. Yes, Rosen said, he was sure that's the way it was.

Boies looked over his half-rimmed glasses and paused for dramatic effect.

"You don't remember that, do you, sir? You're just making that up right now."

Microsoft attorneys leaned forward in unison, their jaws dropping.

"No, I remember it," Rosen said weakly.

Boies fed him some more hangman's rope. "You're sure it was May and not April?" Rosen said he was sure. Boies glanced at one of his assistants. Within seconds a one-sentence E-mail Rosen had written on April 27 appeared on courtroom computer screens and on the twin thirty-six-inch Mitsubishi TV monitors facing spectators.

"Do you remember who took the Netscape Win95 browser they gave us during our last meeting?" Rosen had written. "I'd like to get a copy."

Seventeen seconds elapsed. A clearly shaken Rosen could only reply, "I stand corrected," and admitted he had attended the meet-ing where the Netscape browser was handed out.

Now it was Engstrom's turn. He was Microsoft's tenth witness and was there to refute claims that he had tried to force Apple from mak-ing further advancements on QuickTime for Windows. Engstrom had been cooling his heels in D.C. for a week, during a bitter cold snap, awaiting his turn on the stand. His moment arrived at 2:08 P.M., when the avowed agnostic swore before God and country to tell the truth, the whole truth, and nothing but the truth.

Although Engstrom had chatted with an attractive courtroom sketch artist and appeared relaxed in the moments before taking the stand that afternoon, he was, in truth, terrified. The night before he had spent an hour doubled over a toilet in his Four Seasons hotel room, nauseous with anxiety. Men more powerful than he had tripped over the government's merciless line of questioning. Engstrom had practiced for this moment for months with Microsoft attorney Ted Edelman. The two had been paired because of their similarly blunt personalities. In fact, Edelman's office was intentionally located away from the rest of the legal team. Engstrom was told Edelman could sometimes be a little ruthless.

And so when Engstrom took the stand, the world got a refreshing change from the prevaricating, obfuscating executives who had come before. Engstrom didn't quibble over definitions. He didn't suffer from convenient amnesia. He didn't flinch from the fact that he enjoyed competing for market share.

For the first time in this trial, Boies would not be grilling a Microsoft witness. Confronting Engstrom was Phillip Malone, a sharp litigator who reportedly possessed a deep understanding of computers. Malone first asked about all the E-mail Engstrom had deleted from his computer's hard drive—why was all that E-mail missing? Engstrom said he routinely kills E-mail every two months because he uses an older machine with limited storage memory, mirroring computers presumably in use by people in the real world. Running software on older machines puts him in closer touch to customers, he explained.

(In fact, the trial had a chilling effect on the use of E-mail at Microsoft, so much so that it changed the culture in at least one profound way—employees were now holding more face-to-face meetings.)

Malone then sprang a surprise. Instead of focusing on Engstrom's sorties to Apple headquarters—which had been the subject of the government's deposition—Malone probed Engstrom's recollection on Intel's Native Signal Processing, that company's initiative to make a chip that would also handle multimedia and which duplicated DirectX functions. Malone called up internal Intel E-mail, indicating how upset Engstrom and Microsoft were over the NSP initiative. Malone wanted to know if Engstrom ever said Microsoft wanted complete control software drivers all the way "down to the iron."

Engstrom didn't blink. "That would not surprise me at all that I said that . . . I was quite full of myself at that point in my career." He explained that dependence on other companies to make drivers put Microsoft at the mercy of uncontrollable developers. At any rate, these drivers worked deep under the hood of a computer and end users were never exposed to them.

When Jackson called a late-afternoon break, Microsoft attorneys quickly huddled with Engstrom. They were concerned he was perhaps a "little too cocky." But this was not some absurd and doomed Willy Loman figure wasting the court's time. This was Engstrom, former yet still forever an evangelist, a jugular-mauling renegade and at heart a Beastie Boy.

When court resumed, Malone zeroed in on Engstrom's handling of the Dimension X acquisition, the San Francisco company known for its Java-based multimedia authoring software called Liquid Motion. Microsoft attorneys tried to voice objection to this line of questioning, saying it fell outside the scope of expected inquiry. The judge allowed Malone to continue.

Malone tried to snare Engstrom in his own E-mail, in which Engstrom talked about buying Dimension X to deprive Sun's JavaSoft division of tools it planned to share with Netscape. Malone made great issue of this paragraph:

"Given how important iHammer is to [Tod Nielsen], I would think derailing the iHammer equivalent for Netscape would be a HUGE thing. . . . We could achieve a big tactical win here by removing their key tool."

Again, Engstrom didn't blanch.

"The whole point of that paragraph is to vector [Tod Nielsen's] support for iHammer into the [Dimension X] acquisition," Engstrom said, giving a glimpse of the kind of internal warfare he engaged in at the company. "Quite frankly, iHammer was a project I wanted to kill at Microsoft, but I needed Tod Nielsen's support."

Nielsen, a fixture at the trial for weeks, squirmed in his seat cushion.

Malone didn't buy Engstrom's explanation and repeatedly rephrased questions trying to force Engstrom to admit an untruth—that the *only* reason Microsoft wanted Dimension X was to deny it for the competition.

"No," Engstrom said, his patience wearing thin. " 'Tod Nielsen will think this is a good thing,' that was the total sum of thought I put into that sentence. You are spending more time on this one sentence than I did writing it—by an order of magnitude. I wasn't prepared to have every word I wrote dissected."

Judge Jackson couldn't resist: "You've never been in court before."

It was one of the few times the judge laughed with a Microsoft witness, rather than at one. Court recessed for the day at 4:53 that afternoon.

Engstrom's performance was solid. Only Nielsen complained: "Did you have to use my name so many times?"

The next morning Engstrom entered the courtroom looking a little more cocksure. He was the only one wearing a bright yellow dress shirt. The court's congenial marshal shared an aside joke and Engstrom's laugh rumbled over the mumbled din of other conversations. Again Engstrom conversed with the courtroom sketch artist, requesting a copy of one of her drawings of him to hang in his still-unfinished house.

When the court came to order, Malone focused on the predictable—accusations that Engstrom had tried to shove Apple out of developing QuickTime for Windows and that Microsoft had inserted diabolical coding into the operating system to sabotage Apple's media player.

Engstrom said those meetings were benign codec-sharing missions and Apple never told him it felt that it was being muscled. Moreover, he pointed out, an independent testing laboratory concluded that it was bugs in QuickTime, not Windows, that were causing problems.

"Certainly I wanted them to use DirectX for video and audio playback on Windows," Engstrom acknowledged. "That was nonnegotiable."

But if Apple didn't cooperate, then Engstrom said he was prepared for battle.

"Understand," Engstrom added later, "I'm not going to sit down and watch television. I'm going to compete."

Engstrom recalled the infamous day in July at the Siggraph trade show in Orlando, noting that the day after he was told the *Wall Street Journal* was poised to run a piece containing allegations that Microsoft had sabotaged Apple's QuickTime, he had learned that Rob Glaser, the former Microsoft executive and founder of RealNetworks, had testified before the U.S. Senate that Microsoft had deliberately written code into Windows that broke the RealNetworks multimedia player.

Engstrom said he was called away from Siggraph, feeling betrayed by Apple and Glaser.

"I'm friends with Rob Glaser's wife," Engstrom told the court. "Understand my mind-set—this is not a good day for me."

Judge Jackson nodded. "I'm sympathetic to his bad day."

This happened to be a bad day for Malone and a singularly rare good day for Microsoft. Perhaps for the first time since Microsoft had begun hauling its handpicked witnesses to the stand, it had won a round. After a few anticlimactic redirect questions from Microsoft attorney Edelman, Engstrom was excused at 11:47 A.M. Microsoft would summon its two final witnesses before Friday, when the court would recess for an extended layover. Any good Engstrom had accomplished was quickly undone by the two executives who followed. German-born Joachim Kempin, Microsoft's senior executive in charge of managing the company's business relations with computer makers, left many with the impression he was using his less-than-perfect command of English to give deliberately confusing answers. Worse was Robert Muglia, Microsoft's last witness before the long break and the one executive in charge of Microsoft's Java efforts. Muglia tried to correct the judge that what Bill Gates *really* meant when he wrote "I am hard core about NOT supporting" a technology from Sun Microsystems was, in fact, just the opposite. As Muglia babbled some nonsense justification, Judge Jackson covered his face with one hand and thrust another at Muglia. *"No!"* Jackson yelled. "Stop!" Jackson stomped out of the courtroom for a ten-minute recess.

All of that would be of little concern to Engstrom. He had done his time inside the torture chamber. Now it was time to celebrate. He walked out of the courtroom and cinched his wool overcoat. Cristiano Pierry, the longtime DirectX veteran, patted Engstrom on the shoulder. "You did great, man." Pierry fished in his pocket and retrieved a little Nokia mobile phone with a Stars and Stripes faceplate. "Who should we call?" Before Engstrom could answer, Pierry was dialing Chris Phillips in Redmond, regaling him with stories from the front lines. Pierry continued talking as he and Engstrom strolled to the upscale Capital Grill a few blocks from the courthouse.

Engstrom checked his coat and glanced at the number on the claim ticket. A few days earlier at another restaurant, the claim number was 666 and Engstrom had kept it for good luck. He and Pierry, who was still talking on the phone, were soon seated, and Engstrom ordered rum and diet Cokes, insisting each come with a wedge of lime and a maraschino cherry. As he waited for an order of Atlantic-salmon appetizers, Engstrom reflected on the court case that had consumed so much of his energy over the past five months and had played a role in compelling Microsoft to kill Chrome.

He lamented that Microsoft's legal strategy had relied on a fallback, defensive position.

"Microsoft by and large reverted from its normal aggressive self," he said. "It withdrew from battle rather than engage an offensive. This could have been handled a lot better."

Although he agreed Microsoft was ruthless, cunning, and aggressive, he insisted the company was guiltless of illegally wielding monopoly power.

The waiter returned and Engstrom ordered a Macallan single-malt Scotch, neat. The twenty-five-year-old stuff.

"Ah, you must be celebrating," the waiter said, smiling.

The most stressful experience of Engstrom's life was now behind him. He could savor the fact he served his company with honor. The government said it had proved Engstrom had tried to get Apple to do things Microsoft's way, much the way Redmond had muscled Netscape. But Malone had landed only glancing blows on Engstrom. The Beastie Boy had won by a decision.

A *USA Today* story noted that Engstrom "offered a glimpse of the straightforward approach other company witnesses might have taken."

Another writer had said Engstrom "rode to the rescue." Still another noted that it was a shame Microsoft hadn't called a dozen Engstroms to the stand.

Ironically, the man who had caused Microsoft so much internal trouble through so much of the nineties proved to be the company's finest witness.

A devious grin crossed Engstrom's broad face as the Scotch worked its intended effect. Yes, Chrome's death still troubled him. But at least he had history's favorable mark of approval.

Engstrom reflected on the glowing press accounts.

"The fact my enemies at Microsoft will see this," he said, "makes me very happy."

INDEX

St. John, Alex (*cont.*):
theme parties and marketing stunts of, 83–84, 85–88, 105–7, 171–73
WildTangent company of, 261–63, 279–80
St. John, Amelia, 48
St. John, Kelley, 3, 7–11, 16, 19, 47–48, 112, 125
St. John, Rhomni, 11
Schaaff, Tim, 167, 168, 235, 236, 239, 258, 265
Schiller, Philip, 221, 235, 258
Scholz, Paul, 150–56, 157–60, 179, 189, 190–91, 196–97, 198, 209, 230–33, 250, 261–63, 274, 278
Schulman, Andrew, 34, 35
Schultz, David B., 87
Sculley, John, 64, 162, 180–81, 192–93, 224
Seattle Times, 265
Seekings, Kate, 94
Sega GameWorks, 1, 91, 97, 172–73
Segal, Rick, 41–42, 43, 44–45, 46–47, 48–52, 62, 63, 65, 69, 98
Sessions, Jeff, 256
Shaw, Greg, 219
Silicon Graphics Inc., 46, 129
Silverberg, Brad, 29, 35, 39–40, 66, 70–71, 77, 83, 95, 97–98, 130, 139, 175, 176, 204, 212
Snipp, David, 41
Spice (Caffeine), 140, 230
Spindler, Michael, 65
Spiner, Brent, 52
Sporkin, Stanley, 64, 79
Stac Inc., 64
Stevens, Ted, 128
stock options, 24–25
Stolar, Bernard, 91
Stonesifer, Patty, 83–84, 133
Stork, Carl, 73, 74, 75
streaming technology, 164–65, 166, 167, 168, 204
Sun Microsystems, 128, 138, 144, 162, 217, 286, 289
Surround Video, 43, 203
Symantec, 35

"Taking Fun Seriously" (Eisler and St. John), 53, 56
Talisman, 45, 100–101, 126, 127, 130, 136, 216, 257
Talk of the Nation, 183
Taniguchi, Bob, 25, 32
Taylor, Linda, 274
Tevanian, Avadis "Avie," Jr., 235, 266
Thomas, Craig, 128
3-D, 45, 56–57, 60, 73, 127, 133, 138, 139, 143
Chrome and, 110, 111–12, 120–21
Direct3D and, 60, 92–95, 96, 101, 124–25, 127, 129, 131, 132, 178
OpenGL and, *see* OpenGL
Talisman and, 45, 100–101, 126, 127, 130, 136, 216, 257
VRML and, 121, 138, 148, 194, 206–7
see also Chrome
throughput technology, 10
Tiemeier, Dustin, 155
tool bar, collapsible, 156, 157, 160
Torborg, Jay, 100–101, 103, 108, 126, 127, 130, 132, 134, 216, 257, 274
Torvalds, Linus, 202
Truher, Joel, 194

USA Today, 290

Van Flandern, Mike, 133
Veres, Jim, 130, 134
Video for Windows, 44, 63
VRML (virtual reality modeling language), 121, 138, 148, 194, 206–7

Waalkes, Adam, 32
Waggener Edstrom, 242
Wall Street Journal, 80, 217, 218, 258, 288
Warden, John, 229
Web, *see* World Wide Web
WildTangent Inc., 261–63, 279–80
Willans, Barb, 278
Williams, Stephen, 249
Windows, 13–14, 29, 32, 33, 38, 42, 95–96, 97, 109, 121–22, 145, 175–76, 195
Active Desktop, 117
games and, 44, 46, 49, 51, 52–53, 59–61, 73
hidden coding in, 34, 35, 36
Media Player, 100, 164, 165, 166, 167, 168, 178, 236, 237, 259, 274
OS/2 and, 28–29
32-bit extender for, 20–21
Windows 95, 17, 37, 42, 44, 45, 52, 53, 58, 60–61, 66–67, 69, 73, 77, 78–79, 82, 83, 97, 108, 135, 145, 175–76, 223, 242
Apple lawsuit and, 63–64, 65, 82
Internet Explorer bundled with, 99, 118–19, 122, 145, 168, 169–71, 173–75, 182, 184, 218, 223, 249, 264, 270
launching of, 80–81, 82–83, 249–50
OpenGL and, 124, 125
Windows 98, 97, 150, 159, 175–76, 197, 205, 217, 218, 220, 222, 224–25, 227, 228, 249–50

ABOUT THE AUTHOR

Michael Drummond has won numerous regional and national writing awards. He now covers telecommunications and Internet technology for the *San Diego Union-Tribune*. An outdoor and computer enthusiast, Drummond resides in San Diego with his wife, Alison; daughter, Harper Rose; and son, Eli.